新世纪翻译本科R&D系列教材

总主编 陈 刚 卢巧丹

A Coursebook on English ⇄ Chinese Legal Translation

法律英汉互译教程

滕 超 陈 刚 编著

ZHEJIANG UNIVERSITY PRESS
浙江大学出版社
·杭州·

图书在版编目（CIP）数据

法律英汉互译教程 / 滕超，陈刚编著. -- 杭州：
浙江大学出版社，2025.5. --（新世纪翻译本科 R&D 系列
教材 / 陈刚，卢巧丹总主编）. -- ISBN 978-7-308
-26226-2

Ⅰ. D9

中国国家版本馆 CIP 数据核字第 2025S1Q852 号

新世纪翻译本科 R&D 系列教材（总主编　陈　刚　卢巧丹）

法律英汉互译教程

A Coursebook on English ⇆ Chinese Legal Translation

滕　超　陈　刚　编著

丛书策划	包灵灵
责任编辑	张颖琪
责任校对	黄　墨
封面设计	周　灵
出版发行	浙江大学出版社
	（杭州天目山路 148 号　邮政编码 310007）
	（网址：http://www.zjupress.com）
排　　版	大千时代（杭州）文化传媒有限公司
印　　刷	杭州高腾印务有限公司
开　　本	787mm×1092mm　1/16
印　　张	14
字　　数	463 千
版 印 次	2025 年 5 月第 1 版　2025 年 5 月第 1 次印刷
书　　号	ISBN 978-7-308-26226-2
定　　价	48.00 元

学好翻译的时代要求

——"三化"与国家、社会需求

"新世纪翻译本科 R&D 系列教材"总主编序

学好翻译，须与时俱进。时代的要求乃是也应是高校培养翻译人才的主要要求。

何为时代要求？答案是"三化"+国家、社会需求。前者指"专业化""职业化""专门化"；后者即国家需求和社会需求，包含战略面向和战术面向两个维度。翻译人才培养和翻译队伍建设应上升到国家战略高度[①]，应服务于国家战略；同时，翻译人才更多的是战术人才，活跃于国家建设各个领域：一是面向近（中）期百工百业，着眼于行业及市场需求；二是面向中长期未来，在重视行业及市场需求的同时着眼于国家深度开创、发展，让人类命运共同体的中国哲理引领人类的发展。具体而言，时代要求应包括中华民族复兴需求、国家发展战略需求（如中国文化/思想/经济"走出去"、"一带一路"倡议落实）、国家外交需求（如公共外交、民间外交）、国家政策需求（如思政教育、语言/翻译服务）、行业需求（如文旅、外贸、电商、传媒）、涉外单位需求（如国际化医院、各级外办、高档酒店）、区域发展需求（如各种国际/区域一体化经济文化会展、博览会）、地方建设需求（如招商引资、共同开发）、学校及教育/培训机构需求（如师资、研究人员）等。与此同时，我们肯定也要考虑满足译者和译员个人及个体发展的需求。

总而言之，不论涉及何种类型的翻译人才，高校及其翻译院系应该始终将培养热爱翻译事业的人才放在第一位，并且落实到位。当然，与其坐而论道，不如起而行之；与其纸上谈兵，不如面对世界。

一、继往开来

今天的世界，对翻译学科专业而言，就是要勇于并善于面对时代挑战、AI 挑战、发展挑战、战略挑战、战术挑战、市场挑战、产业挑战、转型挑战、升级挑战、社会挑战，乃至全球化挑战。简而言之，翻译学科专业亟须改革、转型、发展、提升。

浙江大学翻译专业已经走过十几年的历史征程。回顾历史，翻译人才的专业建设理念及行动远早于体制建制。如今作为教育部一流本科专业建设点（2020），浙江大学翻译专业的教师团队正继往开来，编写优势本科专业（群）系列教材。本系列教材与"新世纪翻译学 R&D 系列著作"（陈刚总主编、主审，2004—2005 年策划、设计，2007 年首

---

① 详见："中译外"高层论坛：呼唤翻译人才建设国家战略. (2007-04-10)[2022-03-10]. https://www.translators.com.cn/archives/2007/04/1110.

推《高级商务口笔译：口译篇》《高级商务口笔译：笔译篇》）有一共同和共通的撰写理念，即 R&D（Research & Development）——基于并超越中国传统译论和西方译论，在全球化语境下进行口笔译实践、教学、研究，努力走在翻译专业的前列①，但这一撰写理念应该也必须有自己的层次及其要求。"新世纪翻译学 R&D 系列著作"（以下简称"系列著作"）主要服务于本科层次的学生（即 BA［翻译方向］生和后来的 BTI［翻译专业］生）与研究生层次的学生（即 MA 生和后来的 MTI 生）。而"新世纪翻译本科 R&D 系列教材"（以下简称"系列教材"）主要服务于本科层次的 BTI & BA 生。编写该系列教材要跟上时代的发展，坚持"六化"原则：本科化、专业化、学术化、职业化、专门化、思政化。而 BTI & BA 生要学好翻译，则要强调"时代要求"，即"三化"+国家、社会需求。（请扫描二维码继续扩展阅读）

二、"三化"阐释

对"三化"的阐释离不开时代背景，"三化"的要求就是时代的要求。2007 年出版的"系列著作"总序中提及翻译时代，其重要性如今愈显："Translate or die"（Paul Engle 语）或"不译则亡"。国际著名翻译学家尤金·奈达（Eugene Nida）特别指出，翻译工作既复杂（complex）又引人入胜（fascinating），"事实上，I. A. 理查兹（I. A. Richards）在 1953 年就断言，翻译很可能是世界史上最为复杂的一种活动"②。一个不争的事实是，中英互译是世界诸语言互译中最为复杂、最为困难的一种。翻译几乎与语言同时诞生，是一项历史悠久的实践活动（old practice），又是不断焕发勃勃生机的有 AI 赋能的新专业和职业（new profession and occupation with AI empowerment）。（请扫描二维码继续扩展阅读）

三、"需求"阐释

编写本系列教材，就是以需求为导向，为解决国家、地方、学科、专业等诸多需求做点实事——一句话，为行业育人，为社会育才。我们要紧跟时代步伐，在竞争中处于较为优势的地位，必须在国家新的建设发展时期，好好**培育**并不断**提升**自己的翻译专业。（请扫描二维码继续扩展阅读）

本系列教材的设计与编写将针对（本校）BTI 生的需求和特点，内容深入浅出，亦包含挑战性译题，反映编写团队老中青成员各自的多元工作经历、生活阅历、研究领域特色和最新研究成果。有关编写和编排体例将采用国家及出版社的最新标准，坚持立德树人，以人为本；坚持中国立场、国际表达；力求专业、严谨；讲究科学、规范；力戒教条、死板；努力推陈出新，同时尊重分册编写者的差异性（diversity）和鲜明个性（individuality）。综上，我们希望能够将教材编出新意，并体现专业性、实用性、思想性、时代性、知识性、学术性、趣味性、前沿性、创新性及独特性。

---

① 笔者事先不可能知道 2006 年教育部批准部分高校试办本科翻译专业（BTI）以及 2007 年开始设置翻译硕士专业学位。凭借口笔译实践"出身"的背景，笔者在 21 世纪初于浙江大学开创翻译（专业）的新天地。

② Nida, Eugene A. *Language, Culture, and Translating* [M]. Shanghai: Shanghai Foreign Language Education Press, 1993: 1.

　　鉴于处于学科/专业培育阶段的新编教材、教材建设（以及教学大纲、方法和手段、师资队伍建设、教学评估和管理）还有待深入探索、试错实践，本系列教材也有待在使用中不断提高、完善。我们真诚欢迎广大师生、专业人士、同业同行以及关心（浙江大学）翻译学科建设的所有人士不吝批评指正，帮助我们更上一层楼。

※　　　　　※　　　　　※

　　毋庸置疑，习近平总书记关于加强与改善国际传播工作，展示真实、立体、全面的中国的指示，国家多部委有关《翻译人才队伍建设规划（2021—2025）》的发文，以及习近平总书记针对外语院校及教师培养"三有"（有家国情怀，有全球视野，有专业本领）人才的回信，乃是我们编写"新世纪翻译本科 R&D 系列教材"的指导思想和行动准则，我们要将中国学术话语、大众话语、个人话语和国际话语等主动、自觉地用于编书实践之中。党的二十大报告指出，要"深化教育领域综合改革，加强教材建设和管理"，"统筹职业教育、高等教育、继续教育协同创新，推进职普融通、产教融合、科教融汇，优化职业教育类型定位"。①翻译学科/专业是服务于国家战略和社会需求的，翻译人才是国家战略人才。本系列教材的编写正是按照党的二十大报告的精神去努力的。翻译实践之职业特性鲜明，因此，融合高等教育和职业教育等要素也正是教材编写的重要方向——做到"职普融通、产教融合、科教融汇"，优化翻译专业的高教定位和职教定位。

　　"三化"不是树干，而是树根。"三化"是我们编好本系列教材的根基，也是学好翻译、教好翻译的大愿之行。根深才能叶茂。我们要有"三化"这一"深根"的理念和"叶茂"的理想，同时要有实现"三化"之方法，将其落到实处，以满足社会需求、人民需求、行业需求、国家需求、幸福生活的需求。

　　万丈高楼平地起。我们要重视本科，以本（科）为本；重视实践，以练为本；重视转换，以（文）本为本；重视通才，目标专才。

　　我们的教材和教师要引导、引领学生知行合一，我们的社会实践和社会服务要促使、培养学生译思并举，我们的"三化"观、"需求"观、成才观要使学生懂得天道酬勤，学道酬苦，业道酬精。

　　十五年前，我们的口号是：There is more to do in Translation Studies.

　　十五年后，我们的口号是：There is more to do in translation and communication.

总主编　谨识
2022 年初夏初稿
2024 年末定稿

新世纪翻译学 R&D 系列著作分册书目

---

① 习近平. 高举中国特色社会主义伟大旗帜　为全面建设社会主义现代化国家而团结奋斗——在中国共产党第二十次全国代表大会上的报告. 人民日报, 2022-10-26(01). http://paper.people.com.cn/rmrb/html/2022/10/26/nw.D110000 renmrb_20221026_3-01.htm.

工具书缩略语表（总主编序）

《辞海》——《辞海（缩印本）》第 6 版，上海辞书出版社，2010.

《规范》——《现代汉语规范词典》第 3 版，外语教学与研究出版社，2014.

《现汉》——《现代汉语词典》第 7 版，商务印书馆，2016.

CCED——*Collins COBUILD English Dictionary*, Collinsdictionary.com, HarperCollins Publishers Limited & Shanghai Foreign Language Education Press, 2000.

CamD——*Cambridge Dictionary* (online), Cambridge University Press.

LDCE——*Longman Dictionary of Contemporary English*, The Commercial Press & Longman, 1998.

MWALED——*Merriam-Webster's Advanced Learner's English Dictionary*, Encyclopedia of China Publishing House, 2010.

MWCD——*Merriam-Webster Collegiate Dictionary* (11th ed.), 21st Printing Quad Graphics Versailles, KY, 2018.

NOD——*New Oxford Dictionary*, Oxford University Press, 1998.

NOAD——*New Oxford American Dictionary* (online), Oxford University Press, 2010.

OALD——*Oxford Advanced Learner's English-Chinese Dictionary* (6th ed.), The Commercial Press & Oxford University Press, 2004.

OLD——*Oxford Learner's Dictionaries (American English)* (online), Oxford University Press.

RHWD——*Random House Webster's Dictionary of American English*, Random House, Inc.1997.

前 言

习近平总书记"一带一路"倡议的宏伟构想引起了全球的高度关注和强烈共鸣，使中国与世界各国在政治、经济、文化等领域的合作盛况空前。习近平总书记在二十大报告中强调，坚持全面依法治国，推进法治中国建设。同理，纷繁复杂的跨国交流只有在相关国家法律允许的范围内才能获得良性发展。这就要求我们深刻理解并严格遵守各国不同的法律制度。因此，法律翻译对构建人类命运共同体的重要性日益凸显。

正本溯源，法律翻译实践必须以法律语言学为基础。法律语言是一种技术性的机构语言，具有权威性和约束力，尤重准确无误。作为法律思想及法律信息的物化载体，法律语言折射的力量具有强制性，差之毫厘则谬以千里，动辄关乎个人生死荣辱、财产安全乃至国家主权。正是这种权力表象，使得法言法语更显威严神秘，令人顶礼膜拜，同时亦造就了法律语言倾向保守、抗拒变革的惯性。故英汉法律语言在词汇、语句及篇章三个层面都表现出不同于日常用语的严谨性，且这些典型结构是基于英、汉语言体系各自的固有特性发展演化而逐渐为法律专业人士所普遍接受的，通常在本语言体系中不可替换，却又无法移植到其他语言体系中。

至于法律语言的交际功能（communicative function），笔者以为应着眼于从法律语篇的文本类型及翻译目的展开分析，通过比较原文与译文目标读者群的差异，确定法律翻译属于强调信息传递准确性的应用翻译。当然，法律信息的准确传递不能脱离法律文化——法律翻译是不同法律文化之间的对话，唯有那些既精通语言又熟悉法律的译者，方能消除原文作者与译文读者之间因文化差异而形成的交流障碍。

有鉴于此，本教程的基础理论部分提纲挈领，依托英汉法律语言对比（第 1 章），阐明英汉法律翻译策略（第 2 章），帮助学生加深对英汉法律互译的理解。

法律翻译注重实践性，探索翻译理论的旨趣就在于为实践服务。笔者关注的焦点随后转向实务领域，从术语（法律概念）、句法（法律条文）及语篇（法律文件）三个层面详细分述规定性法律文件与非规定性法律文件的英汉互译问题，选用的实例均出自典型的成文法 [《统一商法典》（2005 年修正）（Uniform Commercial Code）、《中华人民共和国刑法》（2023 年修正）等]、综合性的跨国合同 [《施工合同条件》（Conditions of Contract for Construction）等]、结构完整的非规定性法律文件。

本教程的实例分析多围绕对照译文展开。其中《统一商法典》的对照译文来源于孙新强翻译的《美国〈统一商法典〉及其正式评述》[①]，《中华人民共和国刑法》等中国法

[①] 美国法学会，美国统一州法委员会. 美国《统一商法典》及其正式评述. 孙新强，译. 北京：中国人民大学出版社，2004.

律规范的对照译文则是原国务院法制办公室提供的,《施工合同条件》的对照译文由中国工程咨询协会编译。笔者针对上述公开出版、相对权威的译文,从法律和语言两个层面进行分析,并提出自己的意见,然后参考目的语平行文本(parallel text),推荐改进的译文,供读者斟酌。特别是在评述英译我国法律文件时,大量借鉴包括《统一商法典》、《美国模范刑法典》(Model Panel Code)、《跟单信用证统一惯例》(Uniform Customs and Practice for Documentary Credits ICC Publication No. 600 2007 Revision)、《跟单托收统一规则》(Uniform Rules for Collections ICC Publication No. 522 1995 Revision)等现行英美成文法及英文版国际商业规则的语言习惯,期望能使我国法律文件的英译本更为严谨、更接近法律英语的专业水准。

考虑到《中华人民共和国宪法》(2018 年修正)是国家根本大法,规定了我国的国体与政体、经济制度、公民基本权利与义务等重要内容,直接体现了中国特色社会主义核心价值观,本教程自第二编开始,补充了 6 篇"宪法翻译的启示"(术语、句法、语篇各2 篇),借鉴四卷本《习近平谈治国理政》(中英文版本)的权威阐释,对比分析了中共中央党史和文献研究院与北大法宝两个版本的宪法译文,从理论与实践相结合的高度,引领学生认识到法律翻译有助于我们面向全世界、有助于我国坚持中国特色社会主义法治道路。

本教程主要为综合性大学 BTI(翻译专业)生和英语专业 BA(翻译方向)生编写,对法律院校、外语院校的相关专业和学科方向的学生来说也是不错的教材。

《法律英汉互译教程》得以顺利出版,首先要感谢母校浙江大学暨本科生院的无私资助和外国语学院、浙江大学出版社的大力支持,同时要感谢复旦大学、上海外国语大学匿名外审专家的辛勤工作、宝贵意见和建议,感谢外院党政领导的政治和业务把关,感谢中英双语编辑张颖琪副编审的全程专业把关、技术支持、鼎力相助,感谢另一总主编卢巧丹同事的全力配合、协助。在本书的撰写过程中,笔者深受浙江大学陈刚教授的热情鼓励与悉心指导,谨此表示衷心感谢。鉴于笔者水平有限,疏漏之处在所难免,还望广大读者不吝赐教。

滕　超(执笔)

陈　刚、滕　超修订于 2025 年季春

目　录

第一编　基础理论

第二编　术语定义

第三编　法律句法编上：民事实质性条款（英译汉）

第四编　法律句法编下：刑事实质性条款（汉译英）

第五编　法律语篇

第一编

基础理论◆◆

第 1 章
英汉法律语言对比

◎**学习目标**◎

1. 比较英汉法律词汇特征及其对翻译的影响；
2. 比较英汉法律句法特征及其对翻译的影响；
3. 比较英汉法律篇章特征及其对翻译的影响。

> 法与法律制度是一种纯粹的语言形式，法的世界肇始于语言，法律是通过语词订立和公布的。
>
> ——休 谟

导 言

法律语言是法律思想与法律信息的物质化载体。作为一种技术性机构语言，它是法律专业人士工作的主要工具和人们了解法律的唯一途径。"无论我们是否喜欢，语言都是律师和法官的主要工具。法律语言之于我们正如手术刀和胰岛素之于医生。"[①]

法律语言承载的是一种强制性的力量，差之毫厘则谬以千里，动辄关乎个人生死荣辱、财产安全乃至国家主权。正是这种权力表象，使得法言法语更显威严神秘，令人顶礼膜拜，也因此赋予了法律语言最本质的两项特征——**权威性**与**约束力**。

然而，法律同时又是普遍性行为规则，必须能为社会公众所理解和遵循。2005 年 7 月 10 日，《中华人民共和国物权法（草案）》面向社会征求意见，其中立法语言的风格定位一直是重要话题。公众对该草案过于偏重法言法语、脱离日常生活实践的现象提出了疑问与责难。甚至这部法律于 2007 年 3 月 16 日正式颁布后，还面临"看得见的物权，看不懂的物权法"的舆论压力。

对此，法学界考虑到法律的技术性，认为立法文件中广泛存在脱离生活经验与日常语言的法言法语乃理所当然，非专业人士自然无法轻易理解；而语言学界则着眼大众，对立法机关语言驾驭能力的缺乏提出批评，认为应在立法成员中加入一定比例的语言学专家，以解决立法文本构造中的语言问题。与此相似，英美国家也掀起了简明法律语言

---

① Words are the principal tools of lawyer and judges, whether we like it or not. They are to us what the scalpel and insulin are to the doctor. (Chafee, 1942: 753)

风格的潮流，"在现代，几乎每一位法律写作者都视这些词汇为矫情及老式的词语，并以'深奥的法律用语'（legalese）来称呼这些词"（Dworsky, 2006: 7）。

从学科发展来说，法律语言学作为一门新兴的国际性边缘学科，是法学界和语言学界共同聚焦的交叉学科热点。1993 年在德国波恩成立的国际法律语言学家学会（International Association of Forensic Linguistics, 简称 IAFL）及其每两年举行一次的学术性会议成为法律语言学发展的国际性平台。法学界和语言学界对法律语言的探讨，从研究视角来说，有修辞学、逻辑学、心理学等；从研究重心来说，有立法语篇、法庭语篇等。时至今日，甚至出现了"法学的语言学转向"潮流。"法律与语言融合性交叉使法律语言学不再仅仅是法律事实的语言解释，而成为语言在法律问题中的直接实践。"[①]

这些视角纷呈、流派众多的学术理论不仅是各国法律语言应用的理论依据，更为跨国法律活动提供了充沛的参考资源。一旦法律活动跨越国界，法律翻译的重要性便立刻浮现。"凡有双语现象的地方，都有可能因为语言问题而引起法律问题……法律翻译是保证法律面前人人平等的一个工具。"（吴伟平, 2002: 141）

准确无误是法律语言的生命线（潘庆云, 2004: 145），综合把握源语言与目的语言特色乃法律翻译的起点。所以，本章将从词汇、句法、篇章三个层面，比较英汉法律语言的异同，研究其对法律翻译的影响。

1.1　英汉法律词汇特征及其差异

尽管形态是词汇研究的主要领域之一（汪榕培, 2002: 6），但具体到法律语境，法律词汇的形态与语言的法律功能变体并无密切联系。事实上，英语构词法中的派生法（derivation）、转类法（conversion）、合词法（composition）、拼缀法（blending）和逆成法（backformation）等，以及汉语构词法中的单纯、派生和复合等，都不是法律词汇所特有的。正如杜金榜所说："词语结构的研究可以作为法律词汇学研究的初步任务，在这一层次上与普通词汇学相去不远。"（2004: 77）因此，本节着重从词义、语法与风格层面分析英汉法律词汇的特征。

1.1.1　词义层面

怎样对法律语篇中的词汇进行分类？学界有不同的方法。法律语言学家戴维·梅林可夫（David Mellinkoff）将英语法律词汇划分成九种（参见 O'Barr, 1982: 16）：含有法律专业意义的普通词、来自古英语和中世纪英语的稀有词、拉丁词和短语、普通词汇中不包括的法语词、法律专业术语、专业行话、正式词语、多义词语和极端精确表达词语。孙懿华、周广然将汉语法律词汇概括为三类：法律专业术语、法律工作常用词语和民族共同语中的其他基本词与非基本词（1997: 58）。而潘庆云认为，"立法语言所用词语不外乎两类：法律词语和普通词语"（2004: 268），具体到法律文书中运用的词汇则包括法律

---

① 李振宇. 中国法律语言学研究的思索. http://www.flrchina.com/research/law/001/law037.htm.

术语、司法惯用语、文言词语和普通词语四类（302）。

仅就翻译而言，若从意义的角度出发，我们不妨将法律词汇简单划分为单义术语与多义术语。

1. 单义术语

所谓单义术语即指示单一概念的术语，其形式与内容完全对应，以产生严格定义。根据劳伦斯·霍恩（Laurence Horn）对意义的区分，此类术语传递的是"规约含义"（熊学亮，1997：3），特点在于：

（1）不随语境变化，因此无法取消（non-cancelability）；

（2）始终依附词汇，可与语句分离（detachability）；

（3）不必推导（non-calculability）。

故此类术语的语用意义较为固定，可有效地防止误解，是严谨的法律语言不可或缺的有机组成部分。英美法律中的单义术语多集中于古英语、拉丁语、法语和其他外来词部分，如"decreenisi"（离婚判决令）、"agoranomi"（希腊市政官）等；而我国法律中的"仲裁""滞纳金""行政争议""寻衅滋事罪"等亦是单义术语。

为了保证法律概念传递的准确性，规定性法律文件的起草者还常在相关法律文件中专门设置"定义条款"，统一解释术语及其适用范围，如【例1】。此类被定义的词汇在该特定语篇中亦可被视为单义术语。

【例1】

第二条　本法所称食品，是指《中华人民共和国食品安全法》规定的食品，包括各种供人食用或者饮用的食物。

本法所称食品浪费，是指对可安全食用或者饮用的食品未能按照其功能目的合理利用，包括废弃、因不合理利用导致食品数量减少或者质量下降等。

——《中华人民共和国反食品浪费法》（2021年）

2. 多义术语

当然，更多的法律术语是多义的，因为语言在使用时将产生与语境有关的附加意义（implicature）。熊学亮曾运用认知心理学的"识别相对性"来诠释语句的意义性与先设之间的关系（1997：5）。其研究颇具启发性。我们也可以借用格式塔心理学家埃德加·鲁宾（Edgar Rubin）的经典作品《鲁宾的面孔——花瓶的幻觉》来描述语境下的词义：

以黑色为背景（语境1），可以捕捉到一个白色的花瓶（概念1）；

以白色为背景（语境2），可以捕捉到两个黑色的头像（概念2）。

鉴于词汇意义的丰富性和法律内容的严谨性，源语言作者在法律起草（legal drafting）阶段，对如何选择恰当的词汇来诠释法律概念极为重视。"法律起草者选词犹如鉴酒师品酒。早在酝酿阶段，起草者已然澄清了客户将要在文件中接触的概念。"①

　　译者只有准确把握原法律术语所包含的概念，才能架起传递的桥梁，故至关重要的就是选择确切的词义：

　　（1）法律概念与一般概念之间；

　　（2）法律概念与法律概念之间。

【例2】

4.10　Site Data

(d) the Laws, procedures and labour <u>practices</u> of the country, and ...

—Conditions of Contract for Construction

【例3】②

Order 52　COMMITTAL

8. Discharge of person committed

(2) ... the Court may discharge the person committed and may give such directions for dealing with the thing taken by the <u>commissioners</u> as it thinks fit.

—O.52, r.8　Chapter 4A　THE RULES OF THE HIGH COURT

Section 3　Interpretation

(1) In this Ordinance, unless the context otherwise requires—

...

"affidavit for the <u>Commissioner</u>" means an affidavit in such form as may be prescribed by the Secretary for Financial Services and the Treasury, and verified by affidavit; ...

—Chapter 111　ESTATE DUTY ORDINANCE

Section 15　Commissioned works

(1) Where a work is made on the commission of a person and there is an agreement between the author and the <u>commissioner</u> of the work which expressly provides for the entitlement to the copyright, ...

—Chapter 528　COPYRIGHT ORDINANCE

【例4】

《中华人民共和国预防未成年人犯罪法》

《中华人民共和国未成年人保护法》

词汇	普通意义	法律语境1	法律语境2	法律语境3
practice	实践、练习等	惯例	/	/
commissioner	委员、高级公务员等	暂时扣押人	宣誓员	委托人
未成年人	/	juvenile	minor	/

---

① The legal drafter is very persnickety about words, savoring them like a connoisseur does a fine wine. At the thinking stage, the drafter has clarified the concepts that the client wants to deal with in the document. (Haggard, 2004: 23)

② 节选自电子版香港法例（Hong Kong e-Legislation)(https://www.elegislation.gov.hk/）。

实际上,【例3】【例4】两例反映的正是英汉法律互译中普遍存在的一个问题,即**术语不对称**——原文中的多义术语可能对应着传递不同法律概念的多个译文术语。考虑到法律翻译对准确性的高度追求,译者唯有不遗余力地探究英汉法律词汇在特定语境中传递的特定法律概念。对此,本书第2章将展开更为深入的讨论。

1.1.2 语法层面

关于法律词汇的语法特征,尤其需要译者关注的是代词、名词与动词、形容词与副词在英汉法律文本中的差异性表现。

1. 代 词

依据美国《统一和标准法案起草规则》确定的立法语言文字使用制度,法律文件应当"慎用代词,只有被指代的词不被误解并且是中性词时,或者是存在着一系列的名词如果不用代词则只能重复这些名词因而有明显的累赘毛病时,才可使用代词"(周旺生,2005)。实际上,在英语法律文本中,较为典型的是以"same""said""such"等词来指代前文相关内容,因为这三个词能在很大程度上明确被指代内容,减少模糊和歧义,但同时也会让语言变得臃肿。所以,现代法律文件特别是非规定性法律文件的起草,常在确保准确传递信息的前提下更倾向于追求表达的简洁性。

人称代词的使用也是法律英语中需要特别注意的。它要求法律起草者通过各种途径尽量在文本中实现性别平等,大体上可以借鉴的技巧包括人称复数化、代词中性化(如"one""you")、重复名词、被动语态或者"he or she"联用等。当然,为了行文简洁,方便理解,在规定性法律文件中插入一款解释性条文也是很常见的技巧。

【例5】

§1-106 **Use of Singular and Plural; Gender.**

In the Uniform Commercial Code, unless the statutory context otherwise requires: (1) words in the singular number include the plural, and those in the plural include the singular; and (2) words of any gender also refer to any other gender.

—U.C.C. ARTICLE 1 GENERAL PROVISIONS (2001)

相反,汉语法律文本中的"他"大都兼有女性含义,无须特别说明,如下例。

【例6】

第二十八条 对于被胁迫参加犯罪的,应当按照他的犯罪情节减轻处罚或者免除处罚。

第二十九条 教唆他人犯罪的,应当按照他在共同犯罪中所起的作用处罚。教唆不满十八周岁的人犯罪的,应当从重处罚。

——《中华人民共和国刑法》(2023年修正)

尽管如此,我国法律起草者同样倾向于重复使用名词,或者使用较为正式的中性化人称代词"其"。

【例7】

第十六条 涉及遗产继承、接受赠与等胎儿利益保护的,胎儿视为具有民事权利能力。但是,胎儿娩出时为死体的,其民事权利能力自始不存在。

——《中华人民共和国民法典》（2020 年）

2. 名词和动词

名词在法律英语中出现的频率远高于任何其他词性的词，因为用名词作主语或宾语的中心词时可附加较多的限定词。如【例 8】就含有 9 个短语，限定名词中心词"contract"。

【例 8】

Contract (1) on usual terms (2) at his own expense (3) for the carriage of the goods (4) to the agreed port of destination (5) by the usual route, (6) in a seagoing vessel (7) (not being a sailing vessel) of (8) the type normally used for the transport of goods of (9) the contract description.

英语法律文件中的名词多有如下两个特点：首先，"名词多用单数，复数应极少使用"（周旺生，2005），且规定性法律文件还大都专门设置条款，如【例 5】《统一商法典》（Uniform Commercial Code, U.C.C.）第 1-106 条第（1）项；其次是抽象名词居多。

此外，动词名词化是法律英语中随处可见的现象，因为名词化结构的非人格效果能产生一种不容置疑的权威性。而且，名词化结构组合方式多、词汇密度高、意义容量大，适宜表达精细复杂的概念。故英语名词短语可以代替汉语句子，避用人称主语，以免句式结构过于臃肿。从【例 9】摘自《美国法典》（U.S. Code）第 15 编（Title 15　Commerce and Trade）第 4 章（Chapter 4　China Trade）的目录中，不难发现画线部分皆为名词化结构。

【例 9】

Chapter 4　China Trade

§141　Short title

§142　Definitions

§143　Registrar; designation; station; supervision by Secretary of Commerce

§144　China trade corporations

§144a　Incorporation fee for perpetual existence

§145　Certificate of incorporation

§146　General powers of corporation

§146a　Jurisdiction of suits by or against China Trade Act corporation

§147　Stock; issuance at par value

§148　Payment of stock in real or personal property

§149　Bylaws

§150　Stockholders' meetings

§151　Directors

§152　Reports; records for public inspection

§153　Dividends

§154　Investigations by registrar; revocation of certificate of incorporation

§155　Authority of registrar in obtaining evidence

§156　Dissolution of corporation; trustees

§157　Regulations and fees; disposition of fees and penalties

§158　False or fraudulent statements prohibited; penalties

§159　Unauthorized use of legend; penalty

§160　Maintenance of agent for service

§161　Alteration, amendment, or repeal

§162　Creation of China corporations restricted

相反，汉语法律文件中使用更多的是动词，请看【例 10】《中华人民共和国刑法》（2023 年修正）第二编（分则）的目录，画线部分皆为动词。

【例 10】

第一章　危害国家安全罪

第二章　危害公共安全罪

第三章　破坏社会主义市场经济秩序罪

　　第一节　生产、销售伪劣商品罪

　　第二节　走私罪

　　第三节　妨害对公司、企业的管理秩序罪

　　第四节　破坏金融管理秩序罪

　　第五节　金融诈骗罪

　　第六节　危害税收征管罪

　　第七节　侵犯知识产权罪

　　第八节　扰乱市场秩序罪

第四章　侵犯公民人身权利、民主权利罪

第五章　侵犯财产罪

第六章　妨害社会管理秩序罪

　　第一节　扰乱公共秩序罪

　　第二节　妨害司法罪

　　第三节　妨害国（边）境管理罪

　　第四节　妨害文物管理罪

　　第五节　危害公共卫生罪

　　第六节　破坏环境资源保护罪

　　第七节　走私、贩卖、运输、制造毒品罪

　　第八节　组织、强迫、引诱、容留、介绍卖淫罪

　　第九节　制作、贩卖、传播淫秽物品罪

第七章　危害国防利益罪

第八章　贪污贿赂罪

第九章　渎职罪

第十章　军人违反职责罪

有鉴于此，我们在英汉法律互译过程中应当特别注意选取合适的词性，或通过其他

方式进行处理。

再者，汉语词汇的同一形态可以兼为动词和名词，极易引起语法歧义现象，译者应当格外警惕。例如《中华人民共和国民法典》（2020 年）第二百二十一条："当事人签订买卖房屋的协议或者签订其他不动产物权的协议，为保障将来实现物权，按照约定可以向登记机构申请预告登记。预告登记后，未经预告登记的权利人同意，处分该不动产的，不发生物权效力。"该条款中的"预告登记"在普通语言环境下无疑是"动宾结构"，而此处的法定内涵则表明其是"偏正结构"，故可译成"registration of a priority notice"，而非"notify registration in advance"。

3. 形容词和副词

由于法律英语文体的语言多为客观描述性或解释性，特别是规定性法律文件侧重信息功能，因此很少使用表示程度强弱、带有感情色彩的形容词和副词。但有些非规定性法律文件也不尽然，正如布赖恩·加纳（Bryan Garner）所指出的："法律不是一堆迂腐枯燥的戒律，法律是鲜活的，有血有肉的，你必须拥有一颗炙热的心，因为律师的最终目的就是还当事人以公正，在法律写作中，真诚地表达自己的感情对你大有裨益。"（Garner, 2005: 220）。请看以下两例。

【例 11】

What can more certainly arouse race hate, what more certainly create and perpetuate a feeling of distrust between these races, than state enactments which in fact proceed on the ground that colored citizens are so inferior and degraded that they cannot be allowed to sit in public coaches occupied by White citizens?（Garner, 2005: 220-221）

【例 12】

被告××总医院……导致武勇的病情在此期间急剧恶化，……。当时原告怀疑医院诊断有误，曾向被告明确提出：……。原告认为，被告……擅自在武勇病逝后 10 小时内解剖了尸体，……给原告造成了巨大的精神伤害。（刘国涛、范海玉，2005: 257）

上述画线词汇都带有一定的感情色彩。其中【例 11】明显体现了对黑人的同情，而【例 12】中原告则期望得到法院公正的裁判。

1.1.3　风格层面

"事实上，在大多数法律作品中，作者的个性是受到压抑的。"（Garner, 2005: 219）与普通语篇相比，法律文本，特别是规定性法律文本，在语言风格上要单一的多。就用词而言，法律词汇按其风格"可以划分为确定性词汇、不确定性词汇、概括性词汇、具体性词汇、精确性词汇、含糊性词汇、方向性词汇等"（杜金榜，2004: 82）。据此，我们就以下双重对立面展开分析。

1. 僵化保守与动态发展

法律词汇具有僵化保守的性质，因为保持法律的相对稳定性，反对朝令夕改，是法律创制的基本原则之一，也是保持法律权威性的要求。"如同在大自然的进程中一样，我们赋予了连续一致性以法律这个称谓。"（Cardozo, 1924: 40; 转引自博登海默, 1999: 236）

如 "grand serjeanty"（大侍君役土地保有）依据《元照英美法词典》可以解释为："这种土地保有形式现在尽管不再是一种骑士役土地保有（tenure by knight's services），但仍存在，1666 年的一部制定法将其转变成了一种自由和普通的农役保有（socage）形式，仅保留了那些荣誉性的劳役服务，后得到 1925 年的《财产法》（Law of Property Act）的继续确认。"（薛波，2003: 610）

我们还可以从法律词汇对正式文体的高度追求上来窥探法律语言的职业保守性。相对于汉语而言，正式用语与非正式用语在英语中的差别更为明显。为了使法律文书具有严肃、庄重而神秘的风格，在表达相同概念时，起草者往往更青睐正式程度较高的词汇和短语。英美法中保留了大量的拉丁语、法语、古英语词汇，既体现了法律语言的僵化保守，同时也突显了法律语言的庄严高贵。

至于我国，在旧中国时代属于大陆法系，在新中国时代则自成独立的社会主义法律体系。五四运动后，白话文取代文言文成为书面语的主要形式，但文言文并未就此完全消失。"法律文本的语体特点决定了法律文本语言中文言成分和用法最为突出"，"这是法律语体的'庄典'性特点与文言表达的特殊效果共同决定的"（张文，2020: 17, 27）。先秦时代的一些法律专业术语，如"罪""法""罚""刑法""刑罚""自首""诉状"等沿用至今仍然是现代常用法律词汇；而诸如"其""之""者""兹""念"等文言词语更可称作"司法惯用语"（潘庆云，2004: 307），虽嫌僵化保守，却也是为了行文庄严正式。请看以下例子。

【例 13】

第一百七十五条　单位犯<u>前款</u>罪的，对单位判处罚金，并对其直接负责的主管人员和其他直接责任人员，处三年以下有期徒刑或者拘役。（注：以"前款"代替"<u>以上条款</u>"）

——《中华人民共和国刑法》（2023 年修正）

【例 14】

第八条　一手除拇指外，其余任何三指挛缩畸形，不能对指和<u>握物</u>。（注：以"握物"代替"<u>拿东西</u>"）

——《人体重伤鉴定标准》

此外，汉语法律词汇的正式性还表现在语体色彩上，例如刑事法庭上使用"斗殴""残忍"就比"打架""惨不忍睹"更抽象、更客观、更能反映本质，因而成为规范的法律用语。

不过社会变化是绝对的，法律的变动性也是必然的。"尽管法律的规范性标准和一般性概括会防止法律变得过于不确定或不稳定，但是它的安排却要受制于人们根据社会生活的需要和公平与正义的要求所作出的定期性评价。"（博登海默，1999: 242）

因此，法律规范的稳定性和法律语言的保守性是相对的。即便是在特定历史时期，法律规范的本质虽应当维持不变，但应允许其具体内容有所变化。故法律语言作为法律规范的载体，必须是动态开放的。

就词汇包含的法律概念而言，许多新的社会现象已非原有的常规语言所能确切表达，因而生成了大量新词。这必然要在属于上层建筑领域的法律方面反映出来，伴随而来的也就是新兴法律术语的激增，如"cyberlaw""网络犯罪"等。此外，"旧词获得新义"也是一种值得译者注意的现象。

随着当今法治社会普及法律的呼声日甚一日，法律距离普通人越来越近，原先令普通民众觉得神秘莫测、晦涩难懂的法律语言势必难以顺应这种趋势。许多法学家和语言学家都已经关注到这个问题。"像律师一样写作意味着在文章种使用 aforesaid（前述的）、herein（在此）及其他类似的深奥词汇来替你的文章润色一下，但这些深奥的用语其实并没有特别或精要的法律意义。"（Dworsky, 2006: 7）

事实上，以美国为代表的法律英语更倾向于运用简明的常用语言（plain English）来表达法律思维，甚至掀起一场"plain English"运动，如用"show"替代"evince"，用"someone answer yes"替代"answer in the affirmative"。尽管该运动无果而终，但由此可见，法律语言在追求法言法语的同时，也不可过于阳春白雪，远离大众而显得曲高和寡。我们应当适当修正对法律语言专门化、单一性的片面理解，努力实现严肃性与平易性、精英化与大众化的水乳交融。

2. 精确与模糊、简洁与累赘并存

毫无疑问，精确性与简洁性是法律语言的两大风格要素，然而模糊性词汇与累赘用语现象在法律文本中仍是屡见不鲜。

●精确与模糊

自 20 世纪以来，律师对于法律语言精确性的追求较以往任何时候都更为强烈。"法律起草者最首要的任务是应当尽最大的可能、最精确地表述预期的意思。"（Stark, 1996: 8; 转引自陶博, 2004: 43）但"正如语言本身即是模糊的、变化的、相对确定的一样，即便法律语言崇尚精确、清晰，它都无法避免'灰色区域'的存在，法律解释的兴起大致肇因于此"（时延安, 2002: 75）。故成文法中的表述虽大都明晰确定，极少使用描绘性、情感性或协商性语言，却仍存在大量不确定的模糊规范，即法律条文本身并没有为司法裁决明确规定出一切细节，而是给法律使用者留出了自由裁量的空间。请看【例 15】。

【例 15】[①]

Section 17　Obtaining property by deception

(1) Any person who by <u>any</u> deception (whether or not such deception was the sole or main inducement) <u>dishonestly</u> obtains property belonging to another, with the intention of <u>permanently</u> depriving the other of it, shall be guilty of an offence and shall be liable on conviction upon indictment to imprisonment for <u>10 years</u>.

—Chapter 210　　THEFT ORDINANCE

【例 16】

第五十条　判处死刑缓期执行的，在死刑缓期执行期间，如果没有故意犯罪，二年期满以后，减为无期徒刑；如果确有<u>重大立功表现</u>，二年期满以后，减为<u>二十五年有期徒刑</u>；如果故意犯罪，<u>情节恶劣的</u>，报请最高人民法院核准后执行死刑；对于故意犯罪

---

① 节选自电子版香港法例（Hong Kong e-Legislation)(https://www.elegislation.gov.hk/)。

未执行死刑的，死刑缓期执行的期间重新计算，并报最高人民法院备案。

——《中华人民共和国刑法》（2023 年修正）

通过以上两例我们不难发现，即便同一法条之内，具体、精确的表述与概括甚至含糊的表述也时时交替出现：意义模糊的词汇"dishonestly"和"重大立功表现""情节恶劣"分别需要汇编判例、司法解释来明晰界限；而"any""permanently""10 years"和"二年期满""二十五年"等词汇则反映了法律规范的严格确定性。

●简洁与累赘

法律语言同时也有简洁的行文要求。实际上，前文提及的专业术语，特别是古英语、拉丁语和法语的使用，以及许多法律文件专用的缩略语都起到了使语言简洁的效果。

理查德·诺依曼（Richard Neumann）针对英美法律文件的用词简洁，提出了三点明确要求：（1）文本的简洁在于精心挑选名词和动词，许多修饰语因其词义已经融入名词和动词（有时融入更为简洁的修饰语）中而显得多余；（2）删除使用不当的词汇和短语；（3）任何词汇和短语都应斟酌再三是否可以用更少的文字表述相同的意思。[①]

汉语法律文件也追求简洁，包括运用言简意赅、富于音韵的成语或非成语的四字词语结构、精练利落的压缩语和简洁肃穆的文言词汇（潘庆云，2004: 304-308）。

然而，精确与简洁往往是一对矛盾，因为追求表述精确往往会不可避免地导致法律起草语言的累赘，或许实在不能奢望法律语言能真正做到"文约而事丰，言简而意赅"。相反，法律行文的冗长、累赘和烦琐是避免读者误解、弥补法律漏洞的有效语言手段。其中典型现象之一就是涉及性别的词汇。由于英语单数第三人称代词通常有性别限制，因此尽管行文稍嫌冗长，但为了意义的全面、精确，并列使用人称代词"he or she""his or her"或"him or her"是不可避免的。

再如英美规定性法律文件为了追求语意周全，确保有关条款在适用时能够外延至预想的某些事实，常常同时使用众多近义词（parallelism）。请看出自《美国法典》第 18 编（Title 18　Crimes and Criminal Procedure）第 I 分编（Part I　Crimes）第 1 章（Chapter 1 General Provisions）的【例 17】。

【例 17】

§8　Obligation or other security of the United States defined

The term "obligation or other security of the United States" includes all bonds, certificates of indebtedness, national bank currency, Federal Reserve notes, Federal Reserve bank notes, coupons, United States notes, treasury notes, gold certificates, silver certificates, fractional notes, certificates of deposit, bills, checks, or drafts for money, drawn by or upon authorized officers of the United States, stamps and other representatives of value, of whatever denomination, issued under any Act of Congress, and canceled United States stamps.

[①] The concise version focuses on well-chosen nouns and verbs, and many modifiers became unneeded because their meaning has been incorporated into nouns and verbs (and sometimes into more succinct modifiers); words and phrases were eliminated if they could not justify themselves; each word and phrase was weighed to see if the same thing could be said in fewer words. (Neumann, 2003: 209)

与之相类似，汉语规定性法律文件也大量使用联合词组。例如："严禁食品<u>生产</u>、<u>加工</u>、<u>包装</u>、<u>运输</u>、<u>储存</u>、<u>销售</u>过程中的污染。"

除上例所示通过细节描述实现精确表达的方式之外，法律英语中还存在三种特有的累赘用词现象。

（1）法律配对词（doublets）和三联词（triplets）以累赘的用词形式表达同一概念，如"acknowledge and confess""cease and desist""fixtures and fittings""null and void"等。鉴于汉语中并无同构的对应概念，可分别将之减译为"供认""停止""附属物"和"无效"。

（2）头韵（alliteration）造成语义赘言，如"aid and abet""safe and sound""rest, residue and remainder"等。由于修辞手法的介入，很难将此类搭配译成同样包含头韵特征的短语，只能采用相应的中文术语"同谋""安然无恙""剩余"。

（3）为了进一步阐明词义，或为了强调，或为了符合当时使用两种语言的习惯而借用外来语融入英语引起语意重复，如"deem and consider"（古英语，古法语）、"final and conclusive"（法语，拉丁语）、"in lieu, in place, instead, and in substitution of"（法语，法语，古英语，古法语或拉丁语）等。

1.2 英汉法律句法特征及其差异

句子是规定性法律条文表达完整意思的最小单位，句式类型与句法结构必须与相关条文的逻辑结构和意义特点相结合，才有利于实现特定的法律功能，如授权、禁止等。为此，法律条文还往往变异、创造出一些超越常规的句式句法，形成立法语言自己的表述常规，并反复出现在成文法语篇中。所以，相对于可读性而言，规定性法律条文的语句更加追求权威性、客观性、普遍适用性、逻辑严密性和准确性。这也是本节讨论的重心所在。

1.2.1 句式类型

根据功能的不同，句子可划分为陈述句、祈使句、疑问句和感叹句四类。规定性法律文件与非规定性法律文件（关于两类文件的区分，请参阅本书2.1中的相关论述）在句式类型的选择上存在差异。

规定性法律文件基于合法的制定程序而具有不容置疑的法律效力，权威性的严肃语言风格令其多选用陈述句，绝不使用疑问句和感叹句。完整的条文一般要求主题突出、指向明确，故陈述句显然是最佳的表现方式。而非规定性法律文件中的陈述句主要用于记述案情或相关法律事实、说明案件或相关证据情况等。但无论如何，法律文件中的陈述句都应当能够传达完整详尽的信息，因此要求句子成分相对完整，就所属对象进行准确的描述，如施事、受事、方式、时间、地点等因素。

此外，非规定性法律文件的句式选择不限于陈述句，有时撰写人对违法犯罪或侵权行为表示不满情绪时，偶尔也会在文书中用到感叹句，特别是法庭演说词，对祈使句、疑问句和感叹句更是青睐有加。如【例18】（节选自我国首起"安乐死"引发的刑事诉讼案件中，律师张赞宁为第一被告蒲连升所作的辩护词）。

【例18】

如上分析，患者夏素文的死并非由于"安乐死"所致，而是疾病本身所致。<u>虽然如此，被告人蒲连升对患者注射冬眠灵的行为是否违法呢？</u>本辩护人认为，这种行为与一般意义上的故意杀人行为有本质上的不同，它没有社会危害性，缺乏犯罪的基本特征，因此，此种行为无罪。（刘国涛、范海玉，2005: 345）

值得注意的是，也有学者认为在句式类型的选择上，汉语立法文本使用了大量的祈使句，例如："禁止重婚。禁止家庭成员间的虐待和遗弃。"（潘庆云，2004: 319）

但笔者以为此类句式并非祈使句，只不过在宣告类陈述句中，施事者在上下文明确的情况下常常省略，而祈使句尽管也没有主语，但"人们根据直觉就清楚地了解命令句的意义中暗示了省略掉的主语是第二人称的人称代词 you"（夸克等，1998: 1146）。而法律规范针对的不仅仅是读者，也包括立法者在内，这也是英语立法语句多采用"a person""everyone"或"whoever"等泛指适用该法的行为主体的原因。

1.2.2　句法结构

1. 语　态

在语态方面，法律文本内容的客观性决定了法律英语中被动语态比比皆是，这也是英美成文法能够大量使用完全主谓句的原因。比较而言，汉语立法文本却常见非主谓句（无主句），罕见被动语态。因此，英汉法律互译时应当特别注意英语完整句与汉语无主句的不同特征。如【例19】中的汉语条文采用的就是无主句，译成英语则可借被动语态转化为完全主谓句，但必须注意理顺英语句式的主谓逻辑关系，不应亦步亦趋地照搬汉语原文。

【例19】

第六十一条　对于犯罪分子决定刑罚的时候，应当根据犯罪的事实、犯罪的性质、情节和对于社会的危害程度，依照本法的有关规定判处。

——《中华人民共和国刑法》（2023 年修正）

【对照译文1】

Article 61　When <u>sentencing</u> a criminal, <u>a punishment</u> shall be meted out on the basis of the facts, nature and circumstances of the crime, the degree of harm done to society and the relevant provisions of this Law.

【对照译文2】

Article 61　When <u>deciding</u> the punishment of a criminal element, <u>the sentence</u> shall be imposed on the basis of the facts of the crime, the nature and circumstances of the crime, and the degree of harm to society, in accordance with the relevant stipulations of this law.

【推荐译文】

Section 61　<u>A criminal</u> shall be <u>sentenced</u> to a punishment on the basis of the facts, nature and circumstances of the crime, the degree of harm done to society as specifically provided in this Law.

【例 19】中的对照译文尽管通过被动语态生成了主语，却出现了所谓的"悬垂分词"现象，即分词割裂了与名词的关系，结果成为一个前置词（Garner, 2005: 52）。事实上，"决定刑罚"的必然是法院，而对照译文 1 中"sentencing"和对照译文 2 中"deciding"的逻辑主语却分别成了"a punishment"和"the sentence"。

法律写作方面的专家们总是提倡使用主动语态，因为主动语态通常比被动语态表达得更清楚、更有力，也更简洁。"在你能够清楚地确定是否要使用被动语态之前，你必须先分辨出主动语态与被动语态的差异。"（Dworsky, 2006: 13）

2. 时　态

在时态方面，汉语没有屈折变化，所以时间意义更多地依赖时间状语明示或通过相关语境暗示；而法律英语则富含各种屈折变化。

规定性法律文件具有普遍适用性，因此主要使用现在时态，阐述道理，确立规范或规定权利、义务等。"合同或成文法表述的都是经常性的语言。起草法律文件有个前提：假设处理的一切事务都发生于当前，而非昨天或明天。"[①]至于非规定性法律文件，在描述具体案件事实或相关主体背景时，则可相应采用将来时态或过去时态。

3. 平行结构

"立法语言语句的信息量大，其中一个原因是使用平行罗列结构的方法表达详尽的内容，……立法语言还常使用句内分条平行罗列的结构。"（杜金榜, 2004: 109）

请看节选自香港《破产条例》（Bankruptcy Ordinance）的【例 20】。该例第（1）款下的（a）和（b），（b）下的（i）和（ii），以及（ii）下的（A）和（B）平行罗列，显得层次分明、意义明确。

【例 20】[②]

Section 38　Priority of debts

(1) In the distribution of the property of a bankrupt there shall be paid in priority to all other debts-

(a) *(Repealed 47 of 1984 s. 5)*

(b) any-

(i) payment from the Protection of Wages on ...

(ii) wages and salary ...-

(A) beginning 4 months next before the date of the filing of the petition and ...

(B) beginning 4 months next before the last day of service within ...

—Chapter 6　BANKRUPTCY ORDINANCE

此类句式至少有三方面优势，即融合丰富的限定语，包含了完整、清晰和详尽的信息；保持单句的性质；减少句子数目，简化、明确立法内容。正因为如此，译文应当尽可能保留原文中的平行结构。

---

① A contract or statute is said to be constantly speaking. Drafted documents assume that whatever they are dealing with is currently happening, not that happened yesterday or is going to happen tomorrow. (Haggard, 2004: 351)

② 节选自电子版香港法例（Hong Kong e-Legislation)(https://www.elegislation.gov.hk/)。

1.2.3 长 句

在叙述过程中，法律英语的句子往往显示出扩展性，即输出信息时"先点睛后展开枝节"，是一种开门见山、先正后偏的逐渐外展形式；而法律汉语的句子则经常显示出向心性，是一种由轻到重、先偏后正的逐层包容形式（甘世安，2002: 188）。现以《中华人民共和国产品质量法》（2018 年修正）第三章第二十六条及其译文为例，通过下图进行说明。

这种扩展性与向心性的差别可用以解释英文法律语言多见长句的现象：扩展性使得英语语句呈现为框架式网状结构，因此法律英语出现长句的频率远高于汉语。请看【例 21】。

【例 21】①

【英文本】

Section 8　Acting appointments

If the office of Chief Judge of the High Court or any Justice of Appeal becomes vacant, by death or otherwise, the Governor may appoint another person, who is eligible to be appointed to be a judge of the High Court under section 9, to act in such office until the vacancy therein is filled.

—Chapter 4　HIGH COURT ORDINANCE

【中文本】

第八条　署理职位的委任

如高等法院首席法官或任何上诉法庭法官的职位因该法官死亡或其他原因而悬空，总督可委任另一名根据第 9 条有资格获委任为高等法院法官的人署理该职位，直至空缺获得填补为止。

类似【例 21】的长句之所以成为规定性法律语言中的突出现象，首先是因为实质性条款乃规定性法律文件的主要组成部分，包含法律主体（legal subject）、条件（condition）或情形（case description）、权利（right）或义务（obligation）等信息，表现在句子结构上，往往采用条件或让步状语从句。【例 21】正是法律英语中表述权利义务条款的典型句型，即"If X, then Y shall be Z"或"If X, then Y shall do Z"结构（此外，还常常使用由 whereas、provided that、where、when 等引导的状语分句）。而在汉语规定性法律文件

---

① 节选自电子版香港法例（Hong Kong e-Legislation)(https://www.elegislation.gov.hk/)。

中，最典型的假定条款句式则是"……的"结构。

其次，"语句主体是骨架，限定语才是立法语言的实质所在，删除限定语，立法条文便会有本质的改变"（杜金榜，2004: 109），故句子内部起修饰、限制作用的各种复杂成分也是长句的成因之一。【例21】中的"of""any""another"属于范畴限定，"by""under""in""until"是状语限定词，"who"则引导定语从句以限定"person"的身份，尽管整个句子因此显得冗长，但上述任何限定词都是实现法律语言准确性所不可或缺的。

由于汉语通过词序和虚词表示语法关系，若限定词过多，则词序难以安排妥帖，因此汉语法律文件的语句相对较短，显得明快有力。但长句可以把丰富的内容集中于同一单句或复句中，使语气更为连贯，条理更为明晰。故而"长""短"句式在法律汉语中也经常相互穿插、交替出现。

尽管长句大量存在于法律文件中，但法律写作专家们总是提倡使用短句，因为"使用短句可以促使作者尽量简化自己的意思表达，并使主体之间的关系尽可能地清晰"（科斯坦佐，2006: 86）。

1.2.4　语言功能

在微观层面上，规定性法律条文的句法功能可拆分为前提条件和行为模式两个要素。英语法律规范常表述为完全主谓句，其中条件部分多属两种情形，或为状语（如【例21】），或为主语（如以"any person who ...""whoever ..."等结构作主语）。有的没有任何标点，有的有逗号标明各种插入成分，如分词结构、非限制性定语从句等。

反观汉语规定性法律文件，无主句的情况比比皆是，以"……的"结构最为典型。从功能上讲，"……的"部分是适用特定规范的前提；而在句法上，则相当于条件或让步复句（例如"凡……者，都……""任何人都……"）。

在宏观层面上，法律语言旨在揭示并解决法律矛盾，法律语句的最终功能也在于此：通过陈述事实（陈述句）、提出要求（祈使句）、探求信息和细节（疑问句）等实现化解矛盾的目的。

首先，"与非法律语言相比，法律语言不表达特定行为的使用场合明显较少，……法律语言以动词为中心的句法结构分析显得尤为必要"（杜金榜，2004: 107-108）。例如，法律英语中一般不会出现"Excuse me.""How do you do?"之类并非特定行为的语句；普通汉语可在特定语境下使用"贪赃枉法""清正廉洁"等短语直接实现句子功能，表达观点、态度，但法律语句一般要求动词结合其他相关成分，如："他的行为属于贪赃枉法。""监察人员必须模范遵守宪法和法律，忠于职守、秉公执法，清正廉洁、保守秘密。"[《中华人民共和国监察法》（2018）第七章第五十六条]

其次，法律文件经常采用主题突出的句法结构，便于揭示问题，以确定症结、解决矛盾。如以下两例分别通过名词化"的"字结构及宾语前置的方式提炼主语，相应英语译文则可处理为被动语态和动词名词化结构。

【例22】
　　第五十二条　国家禁止出境的文物，不得转让、出租、质押给外国人。

——《中华人民共和国文物保护法》（2017 年修正）

【推荐译文】

Section 52 Antiquities prohibited by the state from exiting China may not be transferred, leased or pledged to foreigners.

【例 23】

第三章 专利的申请
第四章 专利申请的审查和批准
第五章 专利权的期限、终止和无效
第六章 专利实施的特别许可
第七章 专利权的保护

——《中华人民共和国专利法》（2020 年修正）

【推荐译文】

Article 3 Application for Patents
Article 4 Examination and Allowance of Patent Applications
Article 5 Term, Termination and Invalidation of Patents
Article 6 Compulsory License for the Exploitation of Patents
Article 7 Protection of Patent Rights

1.3 英汉法律篇章特征及其差异

篇章是一个多方面、多层次的语言现象。"篇章"概念的形成是以语用学理论为基础的。语用学研究的是交际行为的外部条件对语句结构和言语生成各个阶段的影响，而法律语篇最明显的语用特征就是语言的法律效力，因而法律篇章的特征是由法律语篇的不同类型及其相应的语篇功能决定的。

根据文本功能，法律文件可以划分为论述性法律文件（discursive writing）、涉诉性法律文件（litigation-related writing）和规定性法律文件（normative writing）。从译者的角度出发，法律文本的类型还可以进一步归纳为规定性法律文本和非规定性法律文本两大类（请参阅 2.1）。本节主要从格式规范与内容展开两个层面分析英汉法律篇章特征。

1.3.1 格式规范

无论是规定性法律文本（主要包括成文法与合同）还是非规定性法律文本（如起诉书、法律意见书、调查备忘、裁定书等），最突出的结构特征都在于高度程式化的格式。法的结构中的规范性内容和非规范性内容，需要经过排列、组合等一系列的科学安排才能成为法。而要把法的内容加以科学安排，就需要借助诸如序言、标题、括号、附件或附录这一系列要件。

1. 规定性法律文本

就成文法而言，"经过对比研究，我们发现英、汉立法语篇的结构大致相当，两类语篇都是由描写性成分过渡到规定性成分、由颁布命令和/或前言过渡到具体条文；其结构层次分明，都是采用从宏观到微观、从总论/总则到条文、从重要条文到次要条文的语篇结构"（张新红，2000: 285）。立法机关通过并发布实施的各项法律法规，必须遵照一定的立法方针、根据一定的立法技术，并且采用格式比较固定的语篇模式把立法结果记录下来，其目的在于：

（1）更加准确地传达立法者的意图和法律法规的具体内容，以便司法者和执法者在用法的过程中能够正确理解和使用法律；

（2）保持法律规范的庄严性及其内容的严谨合理和准确规范，使法律规范的内涵得到最充分的体现；

（3）为所涉及的法律条文、专业术语和概括性词语设定具体的阐释语境，减少曲解或误解法律条文和概括性词语的可能性，瓦解那些想钻法律漏洞者的企图；

（4）符合专业用法者的阅读习惯和阅读期待，在理解和使用法律的过程中尽可能减少犯错误的机会。

合同的篇章结构也是有章可循的，如一份完整的英文合同通常可以分为五大部分：

（1）Title（标题）：开宗明义地显示合同的性质；

（2）Preamble（前言）：用最简单的说明，大略介绍合同订立的背景；

（3）Habendum（正文）：包括依各种合同性质的不同而约定的具体条款以及各种类型合同都会出现的一般条款；

（4）Schedule（附录）：对前述合同正文条款做必要的补充（不是所有合同都有该部分）；

（5）Attestation（结尾词）：当事人签名前的一段文字。

2. 非规定性法律文本

非规定性法律文本在形式上多数也有比较固定的结构。如汉语法律文书的体式包括信函式、致送式、宣告式、表格式和笔录式。宁致远（2006: 13）将其基本结构分解如下：

（1）首部 ⎰ 制作机关（单位）、文种名称、编号
　　　　⎱ 当事人基本情况
　　　　　 案由、审理经过等

（2）主体 ⎰ 案情事实
　（正文）⎱ 处理（请求）理由
　　　　　 处理（请求）意见

（3）尾部 ⎰ 交代有关事项
　　　　⎱ 签署、日期、用印
　　　　　 附注说明

其中，主体（正文）部分的处理（请求）意见在诉状中，按格式规定应置于案情事实之前，即：

```
        ┌ 处理（请求）意见（诉讼请求）
主体    ┤ 案情事实
        └ 处理（请求）理由
```

考虑到法律文件在篇章上的严格设定，译者在注重传递文本信息的同时，也不可忽略篇章的技术性框架。一方面，我们"应当遵循'客随主便'的原则，翻译时尽可能保留原文的结构表述，保留原文的整体格式"（李克兴、张新红，2006: 266）；另一方面，"在翻译某些意见式文书的开头及总结时，我们认为不一定要完全翻译，应当顾及中文和英文表达习惯以及文化背景的差异"（387）。

尽管如此，译者对法律文本结构形式的调整，必须保持在适度的范围内，例如翻译信函式或致送式的法律文书可以采用归化的翻译手法，像信头、称呼、落款等方面不妨遵循英美国家的格式，但涉及具体内容则不可轻易改变原文。【例 24】是我国辩护词的典型开头方式。

【例 24】

辩护词

尊敬的审判长、审判员：

　　××律师事务所接受本案被告人××的委托，并指派××律师为其辩护人，依法出庭。辩护人通过会见被告人、勘察现场、走访相关人员和查阅本案卷宗对本案案情有了全面的了解。在法庭调查的基础上，结合我国现行有效的法律规定，发表辩护意见如下：

　　……

有学者认为，此部分无须全部对译，应当根据英美国家律师的撰写习惯，翻译时将其简化，突出重点，弱化律师的自我描述，并将叙述性语气转换成祈使语气，因而如果将该文书致送外国法院，英译本应表述为："Please refer to the following submissions on behalf of the Plaintiff based upon a substantial amount of investigations into the facts and records of this case."（387）

毫无疑问，借鉴平行文本对译者而言无疑是有益的。但若是将该文书致送外国法院，这么操作似有不妥：

第一，在外国法院参加法庭辩论的只能是该国律师，因此辩护词应当由该国律师撰写；

第二，律师撰写的辩护词是以其专业知识为基础受委托完成的，而译者却不具备足够的专业技能，对原文进行任何删减都必须慎之又慎。

1.3.2　内容展开

在内容展开上，规定性法律文件主要以分列的条文组成，形式单一，远不如非规定性法律语篇丰富多彩，别具一格，值得译者特别关注。

1. 表达方式

语言表达方式尽管有记叙、描写、抒情、议论、说明等，但法律文书作为一种实用公文，使用频率最高的只有记叙、议论和说明三种。例如现场勘查笔录以说明为主；辩护词、代理词则以议论为主。对大多数法律文书而言，一般性的规律是：采用记叙方式来表达犯罪事实和纠纷事实，采用议论方式阐述理由，采用说明方式介绍当事人基本情况及处理意见。

2. 层次组织

法律文书结构的层次组织特征主要针对正文部分，因为正文才是法律文书的核心。中外法律专家似乎均对三段式框架格外青睐。如："正文主要包括事实及证据、理由和处理结果等三部分内容，即为一个提出问题、分析问题和解决问题的全过程。"（刘国涛、范海玉，2005：58）"法律论证也应该是这种三段论结构，省略其中一切无助于理解问题本身的细节。"（Garner，2005：233）

【例 25】（Garner，2005：229）

The Iraq Sanctions Regulations prohibit the importation of goods in which the Government of Iraq has any interest－present, future or contingent.（第一部分简练陈述相关法规，作为大前提）In February 2001, Pallasko Oil Traders imported oil that was once the property of Iraq, but that had changed hands in February 1992, when Iraq's interest in the oil terminated. Yet the U.S. Customs service seized Pallasko's imported oil.（第二部分明确、具体地陈述案件事实，构成小前提）Was the seizure authorized?（第三部分以问题形式作为结论）

汉语法律文书的正文部分也经常作三部分安排。例如中华人民共和国最高人民法院发布的刑事判决书，主体部分的结构通常如下：

> 被告人×××
> 经复核查明：……
> 上述事实有被告人证据证实，被告人亦供认，足以认定。　　　　　　　} → **事实**
>
> 本院认为，……　　　　　　　　　　　　　　　　　　　　　　　→ **理由**
>
> 裁定如下：……　　　　　　　　　　　　　　　　　　　　　　　→ **处理**

这种三段式体例还可用我国古文的内在逻辑结构来解释，即"起（当事人基本资料）、承（案情事实）、转（处理理由）、合（判决裁定）"。为了适应法律语言的特殊风格，并实现其法律功能，法律篇章的"开头（起）""主体（承和转）""结尾（合）"三部分的安排照应上都有其特殊方式。最为普遍的开头和结尾方式分别是提纲挈领、点明主旨式和言止意尽、端庄有力式。而在主体的承转部分，还特别注意篇章中的语义粘连，法律文书多用顺承、断承与引承，反承、逆承等连接方式则较为罕见（潘庆云，2004：330）。

3. 章法选择

从章法选择来看，起草者可以多种方式进行记叙、说明、议论，做到内容与形式的完美统一。

（1）记叙。叙述事实尽管不追求华丽的辞藻和积极的修辞手法，但事件的记叙顺序和方法却是多样的，文学作品中普遍采用的顺叙、倒叙、插叙、补叙、分叙等叙事手法都可以灵活借用。进一步细分，撰写者还可以在司法实践中根据案情材料的特点、性质采用自然顺序法、突出主罪（重罪）法、突出主犯法、综合归纳法、纵横交错法等手段。

（2）议论。"理由论证是法律文书的灵魂，是体现文书主旨的核心内容，必须依法论述，说理有据。"（宁致远，2006：28）法律文书中的论证部分应该精辟有效，可以采取以法为据、阐明事理的分析法，由散及聚、归纳定论的综合法，针对案情、旁征博引的引证法，驳斥错误、树立观点的驳论法，等等。

（3）说明。说明适用于各类法律文书，主要用于介绍客观存在的事物或某种主张规定等。在法律文书中，说明的对象主要是具体事物，如事项、物体、人物、景象等。根据说明方式，起草者可以采取介绍性、诠释性、宣示性、附注性等手法。说明性的文字务必简明准确、条理清晰。

例如上文提到的刑事判决书，尽管主体部分由事实、理由、结果组成，在结构上表现为并列关系，但其中的事实部分，又可以时间顺序、空间顺序、罪责性质顺序等方式展开，而理由部分则可进一步划分为事实论证和法律论证两个相互并列的小层次，即从事实与法律两方面论证判决结果的正确性。

结束语

归根结底，英汉法律语言的异同是由英汉两大语言符号系统的内在本质决定的，译者难以规避，只能深入理解，这也是我们研究英汉法律互译的出发点。

◎思考题◎

如何理解中英法律术语体系的不对称及其对法律翻译的影响？

第 2 章
英汉法律翻译策略

◎学习目标◎
1. 掌握法律文件的功能分类；
2. 分析法律文件的文本类型；
3. 理解法律文件的翻译目的；
4. 认识目的语平行文本在法律翻译中的借鉴作用。

导　言

　　但凡讨论翻译策略的选择，都无法撇开文本类型。译者研究文本类型学，无非是希望理论能够指导翻译实践，因此，唯有以翻译为导向（translation-oriented），基于语言的交际功能对文本进行分类，方能使我们有针对性地确定翻译策略（Reiss, 2004: 24-25）。

　　就此而言，卡塔琳娜·赖斯（Katharina Reiss）的学说无疑最有价值。她依据德国心理学家卡尔·布勒（Karl Bühler）的语言功能模型（*organon* model of language）将文本分为三大类型，并在此基础上提出了以文本为导向的翻译策略（text-oriented translation strategy），即以内容为重的文本（content-focused text），其功能是客观重现（objective representation）；以形式为重的文本（form-focused text），其功能是主观表达（subjective expression）；以诉情为重的文本（appeal-focused text），其功能是富有说服力的感召（persuasive appeal）（25）。

　　不可否认，以文本为导向的翻译策略针对的是赖斯所谓的正常的翻译（normal translation）。若是我们期望译文实现某种不同于原文的特殊功能（special function），那么以目的为导向的翻译策略（goal-oriented strategy）显然更胜一筹。

　　众所周知，法律文件不同于文学作品，属于典型的应用语言，无论是原文的撰写，还是翻译活动，目的性都极为明确。因此，本章将通过比较原法律文件与其译文文本功能之异同，论述优化英汉法律互译的策略。

2.1　法律文件的功能分类与文本类型

　　法律文件不仅包括宪法、法律、法规、规章等普遍适用的规范性法律文件，还包括仅对特定当事人具有约束力的诉讼文书、律师文书、合同等非规范性法律文件（沈宗灵，2001: 315）。形式包罗万象，起草者也并非仅限于法官、律师等专业人士。

但就法律翻译而言，本书研究的主要是法律职业者运用法言法语制作或参与制作的各种具有法律效力的文件。

2.1.1 法律文件的功能分类

南卡罗来纳大学法学院教授托马斯·R. 哈格德（Thomas R. Haggard）将这些看似杂乱无章的法律文件归结为三大类：论述性法律文件、涉诉性法律文件和规定性法律文件（Haggard, 2004: 10-13）。

论述性法律文件主要是指律师文书，以法律意见书、代理词、辩护词、调解信等为主，写作目的在于通过分析相关事实和法律，进行预测或者劝说（Neumann, 2003: 54-55），因而文本主体常以议论形式（the form of argument）展开。

与论述性法律文件相近的是涉诉性法律文件，包括起诉书、答辩书、判决书、裁定书等诉讼文书，撰写者通常为诉讼参加人，除律师外，还有法官、检察官等。此类文书最大的作用是能够触发特定的诉讼程序。

至于规定性法律文件不仅指成文法，还有合同，内容涉及法律关系的设立、变更或终止，并规定了相关主体享有的权利和承担的义务。

2.1.2 法律文件的文本类型

法律文件多表现为特殊语言文本（special language text），因而赖斯认为其信息功能（information function）凸显（Reiss, 2004: 27）。但也有学者认为，法律文件的主要文本功能应为呼吁、规范，而非提供信息。在笔者看来，这些观点似乎都有以偏概全之嫌。

1. 规定性法律文件的文本类型

《中国大百科全书·法学》（电子版）将"法"定义为"国家按照统治阶级的利益和意志制定或认可，并由国家强制力保证其实施的行为规范的总和"①。由此可见，规范作用是法律的本质特征之一，它可细分为指引、评价、教育、预测和强制等五种功能（沈宗灵，2001: 81-82）。

但"法律"与"成文法文本（判例法无所谓文本）"是两个不同的概念，二者功能不可混为一谈。译者讨论成文法的文本功能，指的是根据布勒模型确定的语言功能。而法律之所以具有规范作用却是其效力的体现。所谓法律效力，一般而言，"来自制定它的合法程序和国家强制力"（315），因此很多国家的宪法或宪法性法律文件都规定了法律的有效性应当以符合立法体制、遵守立法程序及其他一些基本原则为条件，并由国家强制力保证实施。如世界上第一部成文宪法——《美国宪法》（Constitution of the United States）中就有很多条款涉及联邦立法的基本原则，其中第 1 章第 1 条（Section 1　Legislative

---

① 摘自《中国大百科全书·法学》（电子版）"法"字条目。此处所谓的"法"指的是广义的法律，包括一切正式法律渊源。

powers; in whom vested）便规定了国家最高立法机关（legislature）——参议院和众议院的立法权限：

> All legislative powers herein granted shall be vested in a congress of the United States, which shall consist of a Senate and House of Representatives.

而《中华人民共和国宪法》（2018 年修正）第五十八、六十二、六十四、六十七、八十、八十九、九十、一百、一百十六条及《中华人民共和国立法法》（2023 年修正）等法律规范也对我国立法权限的划分和立法程序的设置做了详细规定。

可见，成文法的文本仅仅是法律内容的文字记录和语言载体，其本身并不具有规范功能。若该文本不是合法主体制定的，或是未经法定程序通过，或是内容违宪，有悖于社会公序良俗……那么它就毫无规范作用可言。反之，只要程序合法，判例法作为概念系统也能如文本系统构成的成文法一样发挥规范作用。

而且从言语行为的角度分析，成文法除标题和导言外，其他条款主要是宣告性（declarative）的："法律①就是一种规定，一种陈述何谓法律的规定；也是关于公民的权利、义务及其限制的一种宣言。与其说法律是一种直接的号召，号召公民行使其权利、履行其义务以及遵守法律的约束，倒不如说法律是一种关于权利、义务和限制内容的定义。"（陶博，2004: 74）

所以，笔者认为，成文法的主要文本功能在于通过语言向读者提供有关权利、义务及其限制的准确信息。至于特殊立法语言的运用，其目的当然是增加权威性，以便更好地督促人们自觉遵守法律，但相对于内容功能而言，这种诉情功能无疑是相对次要的。

与成文法相似的是另一类规定性法律文件——合同，但这类文件是适用法律的结果，而非法律本身，因此不具有普遍约束力。显然，合同的规范作用源于其合法性：违法合同无法律效力；而合同文本的语言功能则以内容为重，旨在准确记录特定当事人的权利与义务。

2. 非规定性法律文件的文本类型

非规定性法律文件包括论述性法律文件和涉诉性法律文件两大类，也有学者将之合称为法律文书。它们都是根据事实和法律，为了解决实际法律问题而制作的，因而主旨的实效性对其至关重要——"只有把主旨建立在解决具体案件的有效性上，才能充分发挥法律文书的作用"（刘国涛、范海玉, 2005: 27）。由此可见，非规定性法律文件的文本功能以诉情为重。

赖斯认为，以诉情为重的文本，其语言功能并非只是传递信息；作者站在特定的立场上组织安排材料，为的是实现某个明确的目的（Reiss, 2004: 38）。具体到非规定性法律文件，其文本表达方式总是视议论为灵魂，而议论的要求是以事实为根据，以法律为准绳，且针对性极强（刘国涛、范海玉, 2005: 50）。请看下列侵害计算机软件著作权纠纷二审民事裁定书②。

---

① 此处从言语行为的角度考察法律，因而实质上指的就是法律文本。
② 摘自中国裁判文书网，https://wenshu.court.gov.cn/。

浙江省高级人民法院

民事裁定书

（2024）浙民终 464 号

上诉人（原审被告）：湖州智某公司。

上诉人（原审被告）：盛某。

被上诉人（原审原告）：浙江禾某公司。

上诉人湖州智某公司、盛某因与被上诉人浙江禾某公司侵害计算机软件著作权纠纷一案，不服浙江省杭州市中级人民法院（2023）浙 01 知民初 400 号民事判决，向本院提起上诉。本院依法组成合议庭对本案进行了审理。

本院审理过程中查明，上诉人湖州智某公司、盛某未在法院指定的期限内预交上诉案件受理费，也未提出司法救助申请。依照《中华人民共和国民事诉讼法》第一百五十七条第一款第十一项，《最高人民法院关于适用〈中华人民共和国民事诉讼法〉的解释》第三百一十八条规定，裁定如下：

本案按上诉人湖州智某公司、盛某自动撤回上诉处理。一审判决自本裁定书送达之日起发生法律效力。

本裁定为终审裁定。

审判长 何 琼

审判员 路 遥

审判员 刘建中

二〇二四年四月七日

书记员 姜 镭

该裁定书正文共分四段，其中第一段准确记叙了案件事实：上诉人不服浙江省杭州市中级人民法院（2023）浙 01 知民初 400 号民事判决，向本院提起上诉；最后两段则详细说明了法院的处理结果：本案按上诉人自动撤回上诉处理，以及该裁定的生效时间和法律效力。文本的重心却是第二段，合议庭根据依法认定的事实强有力地论述裁定的理由及适用的法律规范，从而有效地实现了撰写目的——就争议案件做出结论性的公正评价。

裁定书属于涉诉性法律文件，用于解决程序问题或者用于断定涉及实体问题而不决定实体问题的事项（刘家兴，2001: 197）。但这不属于裁定书的文本功能，其效力基础是法院依法行使的诉讼管辖权。

实际上，一切涉诉性法律文件在推进诉讼程序方面的作用都取决于文书的合法效力，而非译者所要研究的文本功能。因此，对译者来说，论述性法律文件与涉诉性法律文件之间的划分并无实质意义，只是后者更加强调法定格式。当然，文本的法定格式不同于语言形式（linguistic form），应当归入技术性格式（technical formalities）的范畴（Reiss, 2004: 29）。

2.2　法律文件的翻译目的

目的论（*Skopostheorie*）认为，翻译作为目的性行为（purposeful activity），决定其过程的根本原则在于该行为的总体目的（*skopos*），即译本（target text）的功能（Nord，2001：27-28）。换言之，翻译策略的选择最终取决于译文的文本功能。特别是高度专业化的文本，品评翻译的优劣更应当注重译本功能的分析（39）。因此，我们对法律翻译的讨论，必须围绕目的展开。

2.2.1　规定性法律文件的翻译目的

随着现代社会国际交往的不断增加，成文法的翻译日趋重要。但我们必须注意：原成文法与其译文的法律效力绝不可相提并论。

如上一节所述，法律的效力主要源于合法的制定程序。原成文法是立法者依照法定程序制定的，因此文本承载的信息具有法定的普遍约束力；而译本却是译者工作的成果。译者并非立法者，译本也就不能被视为"统治阶级利益和意志"的文字记录和语言载体。

一言以蔽之，成文法的翻译不同于为国立法，译文不具有任何法律效力。这就是国务院法制权威部门在翻译重要法律法规时均附上以下文字的原因：

All information published in this website is authentic in Chinese. English is provided for reference only.

本网站发布的所有信息均以中文内容为准，英文仅供参考。

而合同作为另一类规定性法律文件，其译文对于相关当事人同样没有约束力。例如国际咨询工程师联合会（International Federation of Consulting Engineers，法文缩写 FIDIC）授权中国工程咨询协会组织专家翻译最新英文版合同条件时，就在授权书中明确要求：

b) make a statement on the inside cover of the translation that the translator takes full responsibility for the accuracy of the translation and that in case of dispute, the original version in English shall dispute.

b）在译文的扉页上注明译者对译文的准确度承担全部责任，如果发生争端，以英文原版为准。

——摘自《施工合同条件》第 III 页

因而 FIDIC 合同的中译本扉页上都写有"译者对译文的准确度承担全部责任，正式使用发生争端时，以英文原版为准"。

再者，跨国合同的当事人通常都会在协议中订立有关合同语言的条款，引用 FIDIC 合同条件的协议也不例外。如《施工合同条件》（Conditions of Contract for Construction）第 1.4 条（Law and Language）第 2 款就规定：

If there are versions of any part of the Contract which are written in more than one language, the version which is in the ruling language stated in the Appendix to Tender shall prevail.

合同任何部分的文本采用两种以上文字订立的，应当以投标书附录中写明的主导文字订立的文本为准。

综上所述，如果说原规定性法律文件采用的是以内容为重兼有诉情功能的文本类型，那么译文的文本功能更强调忠实传递原法律文件所包含的信息。至于原文借以增加权威性的法言法语则应通过同化的手段转换成译入语法律文化中的相应表达方式，但前提是绝不可以损害内容重现的准确性。

2.2.2 非规定性法律文件的翻译目的

法律文书语言最突出的特点就是准确性（刘国涛、范海玉，2005: 37）。故笔者以为这类文件的翻译，应当致力于实现译文与原文在内容层面上的动态对等性（dynamic equivalence）。关于这个问题，下文就涉诉性法律文件与论述性法律文件分别进行讨论。

1. 涉诉性法律文件的翻译目的

分析涉诉性法律文件的翻译目的，必须基于两项国际公认的司法原则。

第一项司法原则就是主权国家的司法机关在处理涉外案件时，应当使用本国通用的语言、文字。这既是维护国家主权的需要，也是独立行使司法权的体现（刘家兴，2001: 327）。如《中华人民共和国民事诉讼法》（2023 年修正）就规定：

第二百七十三条 人民法院审理涉外民事案件，应当使用中华人民共和国通用的语言、文字。当事人要求提供翻译的，可以提供，费用由当事人承担。

虽然《中华人民共和国行政诉讼法》（2017 年修正）与《中华人民共和国刑事诉讼法》（2018 年修正）中没有类似条款，但是《最高人民法院关于适用〈中华人民共和国刑事诉讼法〉的解释》（法释〔2021〕1 号）作了补充规定：

第四百八十四条 人民法院审判涉外刑事案件，使用中华人民共和国通用的语言、文字，应当为外国籍当事人提供翻译。翻译人员应当在翻译文件上签名。

人民法院的诉讼文书为中文本。外国籍当事人不通晓中文的，应当附有外文译本，译本**不加盖人民法院印章，以中文本为准**。

外国籍当事人通晓中国语言、文字，拒绝他人翻译，或者不需要诉讼文书外文译本的，应当由其本人出具书面声明。拒绝出具书面声明的，应当记录在案；必要时，应当录音录像。

所谓使用中华人民共和国通用的语言、文字，具体而言就是人民法院在审理涉外案件时应当使用汉语言文字，唯有少数民族聚居或者多民族共同居住的地区例外。至于不晓我国语言文字的外国人则可聘请翻译。但译文全无法律效力，即便是在刑事诉讼中，由人民法院提供的外文译本也"不加盖人民法院印章，以中文本为准"。

不过，由于译文与原文针对的读者都是诉讼当事人，因此通过论述理由、适用法律，公正评价当事人行为的文本功能依旧。只是司法人员代表国家依法行使职权，其撰写的文书具有法律效力，不容译者凭主观意愿随便篡改内容。所以，译本的功能只能是以内容为重，忠实传递原文信息。

第二项司法原则是，外国人、无国籍人和外国组织在本国进行诉讼，只能委托本国律师作为诉讼代理人或辩护人。这也是国家主权的体现，因为"律师制度是一国司法制度的组成部分"，"只能适用于本国，而不能延伸于外国"（327）。故《中华人民共和国民事诉讼法》（2023 年修正）第二百七十四条与《中华人民共和国行政诉讼法》（2017 年修正）第一百条均作了相应规定，而《最高人民法院关于适用〈中华人民共和国刑事诉讼法〉的解释》（法释〔2021〕1 号）中的条款最为详尽：

第四百八十五条　外国籍被告人委托律师辩护，或者外国籍附带民事诉讼原告人、自诉人委托律师代理诉讼的，应当委托具有中华人民共和国律师资格并依法取得执业证书的律师。

既然接受外国当事人委托的是我国律师，其撰写的诉讼文书必定使用汉语言文字，故无须翻译即可提交司法人员。这类诉讼文书的译本仅供外国当事人了解其内容，非但不具有原文件的法律效力，连据理力争、试图说服司法人员听取其意见的诉情功能也消失殆尽。

当然，这两项国际原则同样也适用于英美国家，因而我们完全有理由认为，涉诉性法律文件的译本功能旨在准确重现原文内容。

2. 论述性法律文件的翻译目的

论述性法律文件的功能与涉诉性法律文件相似，均以诉情为重，信息的提供也以议论的需要为转移。这一点我们在上一节中已经分析过。接下去，我们要研究的是译本的功能。

根据读者的不同，论述性法律文件也就是律师文书，大致可分三类：第一类针对的是司法、行政人员，如代理词、辩护词等，目的在于说服司法、行政人员采纳其意见；第二类针对的是委托人，如法律意见书等，目的在于报告其办理委托事务的相关情况，并就委托人行为的法律后果做出预测；第三类针对的是与委托人发生争议的对方当事人，如调解信等，目的在于迫使对方采取符合委托人利益的措施。

其中第一类文书与律师撰写的涉诉性法律文件情况相似——译文针对的读者不同于原文，翻译只是为了使外国当事人了解原文的内容。

而翻译第二类律师文书，针对的读者主要是外国委托人，这与原文并无差别。问题在于译者虽然可能通晓法律知识，但毕竟不是持有执业证书的律师，无法胜任提供法律意见这样专业的工作。故此类翻译行为也应忠实于原文的内容。

至于第三类律师文书，其译文读者既可能是外国委托人，这就有别于原文，翻译旨在使外国委托人了解原文的内容；也可能是与委托人发生争议的外国人或组织，即译文与原文针对的是同一读者，但语言功能大相径庭。

律师与委托人之间的代理关系受法律规范调整，律师在代理权限内的所作所为，由委托人承担相应的法律责任。因此，律师代表委托人向对方当事人发出律师信，该信件的内容对委托人具有当然的约束力。如果律师在撰写法律文书时因用词不慎导致委托人的利益受到损害，就必须赔偿其遭受的一切损失。若译者基于原法律文本的功能以诉情为重，为使译本也能够发挥此功能而增删内容，一旦影响到委托人的利益，那么应当由谁负责呢？显然，译者并无足够的专业技能承担相应的法律责任。所以，笔者认为，该类律师文书的翻译仍应忠实于原文的内容。

由此可见,论述性法律文书的种类虽然繁多,但译文都应当以准确传递原文信息为重。

值得译者特别注意的是,非规定性法律文件的主体多以议论的方式实现撰写者的特定目的,故深入分析原文围绕具体诉情功能展开的谋篇布局、遣词造句,对译者准确理解并忠实重现原文信息无疑是至关重要的。

结束语

基于上两节的分析,笔者完全认同玛丽·斯内尔-霍恩比（Mary Snell-Hornby）的观点,法律文件的翻译应当归入注重文本信息功能的特殊语言翻译（special language translation）（Snell-Hornby, 2001: 32）。为了使读者更好地接受原文提供的信息,译文语言形式须尽可能遵从目的语（target-language）习惯表达方式（Reiss, 2004: 30-31）。

有鉴于此,尽管任何翻译活动都必须以原文为基础,但目的语中近似文本（parallel text）的研究对于关注目的语语言形式的法律翻译工作者具有特殊意义,因为参阅这类文本有助于我们把握同类信息在不同语言中的独特表现形式（Snell-Hornby, 2001: 86）。

笔者试通过比较以下两个文本,说明近似文本对译文语言表现形式的借鉴作用,并以此作为本章的结尾。

〈文本一〉《中华人民共和国专利法》（2000 年修正）第二十二条第二款:

新颖性,是指在<u>申请日</u>[1]以前没有同样的发明或者实用新型<u>在国内外出版物上公开发表过</u>[2]、<u>在国内公开使用过或者以其他方式为公众所知</u>[3],也没有同样的发明或者实用新型<u>由他人向</u>国务院专利行政部门<u>提出过申请并且记载在</u>申请日以后<u>公布</u>的专利申请文件中[4]。

〈文本二〉《美国法典》第 35 编（Title 35　Patents）第 102 条（§102 Conditions for patentability; novelty and loss of right to patent）（2002 年修正）:

A person shall be entitled to a patent unless—

(a) the invention was **known or used by others in this country**[3], or patented or **described in a printed publication in this or a foreign country**[2], before the invention thereof by the applicant for patent, or

(b) the invention was patented or described in a printed publication in this or a foreign country or in public use or on sale in this country, more than one year prior to **the date of the application for patent**[1] in the United States, or

...

(e) the invention was **described in**

(1) an application for patent, **published** under section 122(b), **by another filed** in the United States before the invention by the applicant for patent[4] or

...

〈文本一〉节选自《中华人民共和国专利法》（2000 年修正）第二章（授予专利权的条件）;而〈文本二〉则出自《美国法典》第 35 编第 II 部分（Part II　Patentability of

Inventions and Grant of Patents）。

　　一方面，由于历史的原因，中国专利法的制定较西方各国晚，且在制定过程中考察了很多国家的立法，其中就包括美国；另一方面，中美两国均为《保护工业产权巴黎公约》（Paris Convention for the Protection of Industrial Property）、《专利合作条约》（Patent Cooperation Treaty）以及《与贸易有关的知识产权协定》（The Agreement on Trade-Related Aspects of Intellectual Property）等国际公约的缔约国。因此，在知识产权领域，两国的国内法不乏相通之处，美国专利法文本可以作为英译我国专利法时的参考。

　　笔者所引原文虽短，仍分为两段。前者包含两个条件：一是没有同样的发明或者实用新型在国内外出版物上公开发表过，二是没有同样的发明或者实用新型在国内公开使用过或者以其他方式为公众所知。后者规定的则是"没有同样的发明或者实用新型由他人向国务院专利行政部门提出过申请并且记载在申请日以后公布的专利申请文件中"。

　　仔细比较两个文本，我们不难发现以下四点相似甚至相同之处：

〈文本一〉	〈文本二〉
申请日	the date of application for patent
在国内外出版物上公开发表过	described in a printed publication in this or a foreign country
在国内公开使用过或者以其他方式为公众所知	known or used by others in this country
由他人向国务院专利行政部门提出过申请并且记载在申请日以后公布的专利申请文件中	described in (1) an application for patent, published under section 122 (b), by another filed in the United States before the invention by the applicant for patent

　　更值得译者注意的是，所引美国专利法的句法结构以被动语态为主，以便突出该法条的主题——"the invention"，且多用过去时态强调条件成就的时间要素。再对照中华人民共和国中央人民政府英文网站提供的译文：

　　Novelty means that, before the date of filing, no identical invention or utility model has been publicly disclosed in publications in the country or abroad or has been publicly used or made known to the public by any other means in the country, nor has any other person filed previously with the Patent Administration Department Under the State Council an application which described the identical invention or utility model and was published after the said date of filing.

虽然译文语言流畅，但在处理原文第二节时改变了句子的主位（theme）：以泛指的"any other person"取代"没有同样的发明或者实用新型"。这使得译文非但没有凸显主题，还破坏了原文的平行结构。

　　主题突出的句法安排是为了体现法律对症下药的特点（杜金榜, 2004: 104）；平行罗列的句式可以将"详尽的信息融入一个单句"，"使立法内容相对简化、明确"（109）。这也是英汉法律语言共同的特征。因此，笔者以为可将译文修改成：

　　"Novelty" means that, before the date of application for patent, no identical invention or utility model was publicly described in a publication in this or a feign country or publicly used or made known to the public by any other means in this country, <u>and no identical invention or</u> <u>utility model was described in patent application documents published after the said date of</u> <u>application by another filed with the patent administration department under the State Council</u>.

需要补充说明的是，全国人民代表大会常务委员会于 2020 年 10 月 17 日通过了《中华人民共和国专利法》的第四次修正，将该条款变更如下：

新颖性，是指该发明或者实用新型不属于<u>现有技术</u>；也没有任何单位或者个人就同样的发明或者实用新型在<u>申请日</u>以前向<u>国务院</u>专利行政部门<u>提出过申请，并记载在</u>申请日以后<u>公布</u>的专利申请文件<u>或者公告</u>的专利文件中。

而《美国法典》第 35 编第 102 条也在 2011 年进行了修正，该条第 2 项现表述如下：

(a) Novelty; <u>Prior Art</u>.—A person shall be entitled to a patent unless—

(1) ...; or

(2) the claimed invention was **<u>described in</u>** a patent **<u>issued</u>** under section 151, or in an application for patent **<u>published</u>** or deemed published under section 122(b), in which the patent or application, as the case may be, names another inventor and was effectively **<u>filed before the</u>** **<u>effective filing date of</u>** the claimed invention.

平行文本的借鉴作用依然不可小觑：

"Novelty" means that the claimed invention or utility model is not **<u>a prior art</u>**, and no identical invention or utility model was described in patent application documents **<u>published</u>** or patent documents **<u>issued</u>** after the said date of application, in which the application or the patent, as the case may be, was filed by any other organization or individual with the patent administration department under the State Council **<u>before the filing date of</u>** the claimed invention or utility model.

尽管我们在此讨论的只是一个极为短小的成文法片段，但是已经不难从中窥探出研究近似文本的价值所在，难怪斯内尔-霍恩比将之视为"翻译模本（model translation）"（Snell-Hornby, 2001: 86）。

◎思考题◎

如何在跨越法律文化的翻译过程中，在确保充分性（adequacy）的前提下，尽可能提升译文的可接受性（acceptability）？

第二编

术语定义◆◆

第 3 章
英汉法律术语互译

◎学习目标◎

1. 比较英汉法律渊源的差异；

2. 掌握辨析法律概念的方法；

3. 传译在目的法律文化中存在对等概念的术语；

4. 传译在目的法律文化中没有对等概念的术语。

导 言

如果说翻译是跨文化的交流，那么法律翻译无疑是不同法律文化之间的对话。作为文化中介（cultural mediator），译者的首要任务是消除原文作者与译文读者之间因文化差异而形成的交流障碍（Hatim & Mason, 2001: 223）。总体上，法律翻译属于专门领域（specialized field）的应用翻译，因而未经专业培训（specialized training）的普通翻译工作者很难胜任。译者必须既精通语言，又熟悉法律，方能游刃有余。当然，技术层面的文化（technical culture）可以通过科学分析，逐步掌握（Katan, 2004: 31）。

具体到英汉法律术语的互译，我们关注的焦点是英美国家与中国大陆在法律文化方面的巨大差异。尽管比较法律传统的研究及国际法的发展使得不同国家的法律制度正趋向于融合，特别是在国际贸易（international trade）领域，然而二者之间的差别仍是显而易见的。这是因为"一系列社会的、经济的、心理的、历史的和文化的因素以及一系列价值判断，都在影响着和决定着立法和司法"（博登海默, 1999: 199）。为了建立与社会主义市场经济相适应的现代法治，中国大陆的立法主要借鉴了欧陆民法法系国家和地区的法律模式。可是法律移植不能脱离本土资源，最终目的还是"建立有中国特色的社会主义法"，这绝非法的全盘"西方化"（沈宗灵, 2001: 108）。

而英美国家和地区（包括绝大多数前英国殖民地）的法律文化则起源于诺曼底公爵威廉征服英格兰后推行的普通法制度。该制度的基石是独特的不成文宪法以及口口相传并最终记录下来的由才华横溢、备受尊重的法官们做出的判决（Glendon, Gordon & Carozza, 2004: 150）。这与欧洲大陆以罗马法传统（Roman tradition）为基础的民法制度截然不同。它们是当今西方世界最具影响力的两大法系。

深刻理解不同法律传统的特点，对于提高法律翻译质量的意义是不言而喻的。本章将通过比较英美国家与中国大陆在法律传统的重要组成部分——法律渊源（source of law）方面的差异，着重研究英汉法律术语（legal term）的互译。这也是法律文化交流的起点，因为术语即表达概念的语言形式（linguistic expression），而抽象的概念不仅是人类基于事物的特征和/或其关系将之范畴化的工具（Bussmann, 2000: 332），还是人类借以认识并理解周围世界的认知单位（cognitive unit）（Baker, 2004: 259-260）。

3.1　依托法律渊源辨析法律概念

传译法律术语就是用目的语的语言形式来传递原法律术语所包含的概念①。由于法律概念（legal concept）是理性思考法律问题必不可少的工具——法律规则和法律原则大多以之为核心展开（博登海默, 1999: 485），因此辨析概念的严格定义（definition）是准确理解原法律文件的基础。

3.1.1　法律渊源——法律概念最具权威性的出处

我们如何才能获取特定法律概念的准确定义呢？显然，法律渊源具有最终的权威性（ultimate authority）。所谓法律渊源，指的是法律的形式渊源，即法的创制方式和表现形式（沈宗灵, 2001: 269），它也是法官解决具体争议应当适用的法律规范的出处。因此，为了正确理解法律概念的定义，我们有必要考察英美国家与中国大陆在法律渊源方面的差异。

普通法传统中最引人瞩目的莫过于判例制度，即遵循先例（stare decisis）原则：法院判决，尤其是终审法院的判决，成为英美法律最主要的正式渊源。虽然这些国家也颁布了大量成文法，但奠定普通法制度基础的仍是先例（precedent）（Glendon, Gordon & Carozza, 2004: 262），且成文法（statute law）的适用同样离不开诠释立法文本的司法意见（Cohen & Olson, 2004: 139），尽管其效力高于包括判例法（case law）在内的其他法律渊源。

反观中国大陆自近代变法以来，立法参照欧陆民法法系的模式——"立法机关制订的法律乃是法官适用法律的主要依据"（王利明, 2002: 6）。鉴于成文法具有概括性、抽象性和滞后性的特点，有权机关对成文法做出的正式解释也被赋予法律上的约束力。此外，权威法律学说（legal doctrine）虽不属于正式法律渊源，然而根据大陆法系的传统，立法者和法官制定、解释或适用法律都无法摆脱学说的指导，难怪成文法亦被视为学者制定的法律（scholar-made law）（Glendon, Gordon & Carozza, 2004: 90）。

法律渊源的差异决定了法官在适法过程中阐释法律概念的不同标准。"制定法②概念必须表明其出自制定法文本，由此才能证明制定法概念的正当性"，而"普通

---

① 实质上，术语与概念的关系即形式与内容的关系。

② 制定法即成文法。

法①概念也必须表明自己出自合理的公众政策，以此才能证明普通法概念的正当性"（波斯纳，2002: 314）。尽管波斯纳针对的仅仅是美国的成文法与判例法，但推而广之，这同样有助于译者把握一切成文法与判例法概念之间的差别。

3.1.2　运用认知语言学理论诠释法律概念

值得我们注意的是，翻译亦可视为语言的解释性使用（interpretive use）（Gutt, 2004: 127）。根据关联理论（relevance theory），译文与原文之间的关系应为解释性相似（interpretive resemblance）。这就意味着译者必须首先理解原法律文件，特别是其中所包含的法律概念。不过，译者理解法律概念的过程与法官为适用法律而对法律概念进行解释，二者虽在一定程度上有着相通之处，却又不能完全等而视之。

1. 基于典型理论确定法律概念的类典型

博登海默在谈到法律概念时写道："一个概念的中心含义也许是清楚的和明确的，但当我们离开该中心时它就趋于变得模糊不清了，而这正是一个概念的性质所在。"（1999: 487）

其实，这一现象也引起了认知语言学家的注意。他们在研究概念的形成时提出了典型理论（prototype theory）。该理论认为，普通语言使用者要实现正常交流，通常仅需了解该概念的类典型，也就是特定范畴的典型特征的集合（Bussmann, 2000: 389）；至于其指示意义（denotation）的界限模糊而不确定，只能交由该领域的专家来决定。即便如此，客观的判断仍非易事（Lyons, 2000: 96）。

就以英美刑事法律概念"principal"为例，《布莱克法律辞典》（*Black's Law Dictionary*）将其定义为：

Someone who commits or participates in a crime.—Also termed *criminal principal*. Cf. ACCESSORY (2); ACCOMPLICE (2). (Garner, 2019: 1443）

接着又阐明了两个相关概念：

principal in the first degree. The perpetrator of a crime.—Also termed *first-degree principal*.
principal in the second degree. Someone who helped the perpetrator at the time of the crime.—Also termed *accessory at the fact; second-degree principal*.（1444）

再参照"accessory"项下的概念：

accessory before the fact. An accessory who assists or encourages another to commit a crime but who is not present when the offense is actually committed ... See ACCOMPLICE.

及其所注引文：

---

① 根据《布莱克法律词典》的定义，"common law"包含四层意思：1. The body of law derived from judicial decisions, rather than from statutes or constitutions; CASELAW. 2. The body of law based on the English legal system, as distinct from a civil-law system; the general Anglo-American system of legal concepts, together with the techniques of applying them, that form the basis of the law in jurisdictions where the system applies. 3. General law common to the country as a whole, as opposed to special law that has only local application. 4. The body of law deriving from law courts as opposed to those sitting in equity. 由此可见，波斯纳所谓的普通法即判例法。为免歧义，本章以术语"判例法"指示上述第一层含义，而术语"普通法"则用于指示上述第二层含义。

"In most jurisdictions, the common-law distinctions between principals and accessories have largely been abolished, although the pertinent statutes vary in form and substance. Conceptually, the common-law pattern remains the same: The person who aids, abets, commands, counsels, or otherwise encourages another to commit a crime is still regarded as **a party to the underlying crime** as at common law, even though the labels principal in the first degree, principal in the second place, and accessory before the fact are no longer used, and even though it usually does not matter whether the aider and abettor is or is not present at the scene of the crime."
1 Charles E. Torcia, *Wharton's Criminal Law* §35, at 202-203 (15th ed. 1993).（18）
实际上，不少英美国家的成文法已经开始使用"party to a crime/an offense①"，如《加拿大刑法典》[Canada Criminal Code (R.S., 1985, c. C-46)]。

由此可见，普通法概念"principal"与"accessory"之间的划分日趋模糊。《牛津法律大辞典》（*The Oxford Companion to Law*）中的"principals and accessories"词条下也有类似说明：

In treasons (q.v.) participants of all four categories② may be indicted as principals; in felonies (q.v.) the quadruple distinction was drawn, and in misdemeanours (q.v.) participants of the first three categories might be charged as principals and participants of the fourth category were not chargeable at all. By reason of the abolition in 1967 of the distinction between felony and misdemeanour the rule as to misdemeanours now applies to all crimes other than treasons.（Walker, 1980: 989）

综上所述，我们不难发现"principal"的定义就是该概念的类典型，核心外延（focal extension）就是"principal in the first degree"，而"principal in the second degree/accessory at the fact"；"accessory before the fact"则为指示意义的争议领域，并随着司法区域（jurisdiction）的不同而有所变化。

作为专业人士，法官在适用法律解决具体争议时考虑的不只是法律概念的典型特征，还必须判断特定案件事实是否为该概念的外延（extension）所涵盖。而译者的任务则是交流，把握法律概念的类典型即可满足需要。

源自成文法的概念有时查阅立法文本便可锁定其类典型，但成文法一般不系统表述概念的定义（波斯纳，2002: 313），因此，译者必须根据中国大陆与英美国家的不同法律渊源分别处理：中国法律概念的理解必须基于法定解释并参照权威学说；而英美法律概念则取决于终审法院的裁判，这使得附录司法意见的注释版英美法典（annotated code）成为最常用的检索资料（Cohen & Olson, 2004: 139）。此外，我们还必须特别留意：英美成文法中的概念往往隐含着普通法传统。如前文提及的"principal"便源于判例法，后来才被引入某些英美国家的刑法典另行定义。

---

① 在英联邦国家，"crime"多用于普通法，"offense"多用于制定法；而美国英语中这两个法律概念的差别较为模糊（Garner, 2003: 614）。
② 即 principal in the first degree, principal in the second degree, accessories before the fact 和 accessories after the fact。

相反，判例法概念仅见于英美国家，它们虽由司法裁判（judicial decision）确立，却"又并非这些司法意见本身，也不用这些意见中的特定语言来表述"（波斯纳，2002：302）。那么译者是否也得像英美法官那样检索浩瀚的判例汇编呢？事实上，这既不可能，也无此必要。我们完全可以借助权威的普通法词典，特别是《布莱克法律辞典》。它还是英美国家法学院学生理解法律语言的首选工具书（Cohen & Olson, 2004：10）。

2. 借助认知框架及语义域分析法律概念的类典型

正确理解原法律概念的类典型，是准确传译法律术语的前提。而认知语义学中有关"域"（domain）及"框架"（frame）的理论为我们的分析提供了便利，特别是有助于我们把握英美法律术语包含的概念，因为英语词汇往往具有多重意义，向来以含混难解著称（Haggard, 2004：237）。

约翰·B.泰勒（John B. Taylor）在其著作《语言的范畴化：语言学理论中的类典型》（*Linguistic Categorization: Prototypes in Linguistic Theory*）中提出，词汇意义的理解不能脱离与之相关的各个认知结构共同构成的背景（Taylor, 2001：84）。所谓"域"指的就是与理解词汇意义有关的认知结构，"框架"则是这些认知结构共同构成的背景。

我们不妨仍以"principal"为例。《布莱克法律辞典》中有关该术语的释义如下：

1. Someone who authorizes another to act on his or her behalf as an agent.

2. Someone who commits or participates in a crime.

3. Someone who has primary responsibility on an obligation, as opposed to a surety or indorser.

4. The corpus of an estate or trust.

5. The amount of a debt, investment, or other fund, not including interest, earnings, or profits.（Garner, 2019：1443-1444）

要把握刑法概念"principal"的类典型，就必须将它置于刑事法律的框架下、"犯罪"的语义域中加以理解。同理，只有在民事法律的框架下，我们才能借助语义域"代理"理解"principal"在代理关系中的类典型，或是借助语义域"债务"理解"principal"在债务关系中的类典型。至于最后两项概念指的显然不是法律关系上的主体。

当然，理解多义法律术语在特定语境中所包含的确切概念不能脱离上下文，因为"词汇"是在"语篇"过程中被选择并获得意义的。孤立地分析单个术语很可能南辕北辙，《布莱克法律辞典》在解释"principal"时特意强调：

"… in criminal law the word 'principal' suggests the very converse of the idea which it represents in mercantile law. In the former, as we have seen, an accessory proposes an act, and the 'principal' carries it out. But in the law of contract, and in that of tort, the 'principal' only authorizes an act, and the 'agent' carries it out. Where the same transaction is both a tort and a crime, this double use of the word may cause confusion. For example, if, by an innkeeper's directions, his chamber-maid steals jewels out of a guest's portmanteau, the maid is the 'principal' in a *crime*, wherein her master is an accessory before the fact; whilst she is also the agent in a *tort*, wherein her master is the 'principal'." J. W. Cecil Turner, *Kenny's Outlines of*

Criminal Law 89 (16th ed. 1952).（Garner, 2019: 1443-1444）

事实上，语境的作用就在于它能够唤起译者脑海中相应的认知框架及语义域，从而促进译者对法律术语的理解。请看下面这个例子：

An <u>agent</u> who purports to <u>contract</u> <u>on behalf of</u> another makes an implied <u>warranty</u> of authority to the other party. The <u>warranty</u> is that he has the power to bind his *principal*. The <u>warranty</u> operates against even an innocent <u>agent</u> who <u>in good faith</u> thinks he is authorized but who subsequently discovers that he did not have the power to bind his *principal*.（Hynes, 2004: 157）

如何理解此处的"principal"？笔者以为上下文至关重要。由于这段文字通篇讲述的都是"warranty（担保）"，且提到了"contract（合同）"与"in good faith（善意）"，这使得熟悉法律知识的译者自然而然地会在民法的框架下解读文本。此外，该段文字围绕"agent"与"principal"之间的相互关系展开，其中"on behalf of"一语至关重要，不由使我们想起了"agency"。根据《布莱克法律辞典》的定义，"agency"所含概念之一为"代理"：

A relationship that arises when one person (a principal) manifests assent to another (an agent) that the agent will act <u>on the principal's behalf</u>, subject to the principal's control, and the agent manifests assent or otherwise consents to do so.（Garner, 2019: 76-77）

至此，译者完全可以肯定该处"principal"必须在"代理"的语义域中加以理解，并应当诠释为前文"principal"词条下的第一项定义："Someone who authorizes another to act on his or her behalf as an agent."

除了帮助我们理解多义法律术语在特定上下文中的含义外，认知框架及语义域理论还有利于译者比较不同法律文化孕育的近似概念。关于这个问题，我们将于下一节详细展开。

3.2　跨越法律文化传译法律术语

法律概念是人类活动的产物。英美国家与中国大陆基于不同的法律文化，构筑了各自的法律体系，二者的概念系统远不是一一对应的，这就要求译者深入辨析原文化与目的文化中近似法律概念的类典型。

笔者以为，不同法律文化孕育的法律概念，在比较类典型隐含的认知结构后，可将之解析成两大类分别处理。

3.2.1　原法律术语在目的法律文化中存在概念对等的术语

如果目的法律渊源中存在与原法律术语所含概念的类典型对等的术语，那自然是最理想的情形。但我们应当始终牢记：只有揭开法律术语的表层，才能认识法律概念的实质。如中国大陆的侵权法术语"混合过错"，其概念是指"侵权行为所造成的损害结果的发生或扩大，不仅加害人有过错，而且受害人也有过错"（王利明、杨立新，1996: 203）。这似乎与英美侵权法术语"contributory negligence"相近。然而根据《布莱克法律辞典》

的定义，后者意为：

A plaintiff's own negligence that played a part in causing the plaintiff's injury and that is significant enough (in a few jurisdictions) to bar the plaintiff from recovering damages. （Garner, 2019: 1245）

《中华人民共和国民法典》（2020 年）第一千一百七十三条却明确规定：

被侵权人对同一损害的发生或者扩大有过错的，可以减轻侵权人的责任。

可见二者的法律后果大相径庭，不可混为一谈。实际上对于"混合过错"，我国司法实践中"通常将双方当事人的过错程度具体确定为一定的比例，从而确定出责任范围"（王利明、杨立新, 1996: 213），因而与之概念对等的是另一普通法术语，即"comparative negligence"：

A plaintiff's own negligence that proportionally reduces the damages recoverable from a defendant. —Also termed *comparative fault*; *nonabsolute contributory negligence*. See COMPARATIVE-NEGLIGENCE DOCTRINE.（Garner, 2019: 1245）

毫无疑问，准确传译法律术语要求译者细致地分析近似概念的类典型，否则我们很可能失之毫厘，差之千里。英美刑事法律术语"principal"常常被误译成"主犯"，这就是明证。

"主犯"是中国大陆刑法中的术语，按照《中华人民共和国刑法》（2023 年修正）第二十六条的规定：

组织、领导犯罪集团进行犯罪活动的或者在共同犯罪中起主要作用的，是主犯。

该条款出自刑法典第一编（总则）第二章（犯罪）第三节（共同犯罪）。显然，理解"主犯"的概念不能脱离语义域"共同犯罪"。换言之，只有共同犯罪才有主犯，单独犯罪则无所谓主从之分。

而英美刑法术语"principal"的定义"Someone who commits or participates in a crime."却表明此概念绝不限于共同犯罪，这一点很多英美国家的刑法典均可引为旁证。如《美国法典》第 18 编（Title 18　CRIMES AND CRIMINAL PROCEDURE）第 1 部分（Part I　Crimes）第 1 章（Chapter 1　General Provisions）第 2 条（§2　Principals）就对"principal"规定：

(a) Whoever commits an offense against the United States or aids, abets, counsels, commands, induces or procures its commission, is punishable as a principal.

(b) Whoever willfully causes an act to be done which if directly performed by him or another would be an offense against the United States, is punishable as a principal.

《加拿大刑法典》甚至都没有使用这个术语，只是在第 1 部分第 2 章第 21 条第 1 款定义了刑法术语"parties to an offense"：

Everyone is a party to an offence who

(a) actually commits it;

(b) does or omits to do anything for the purpose of aiding any person to commit it; or

(c) abets any person in committing it.

正如我们在 3.1 中所提及的：源于判例法的概念"principal"与成文法中的"party to a crime/an offense"并无本质差别。

轻率地将"principal"和"主犯"视为概念对等的术语，无疑失之偏颇。实际上，与之相应的法律术语在我国刑法典中虽未作规定，但刑法理论常有涉及，即"正犯"。扩张正犯论认为，"凡对实现犯罪构成要件之结果，赋予任何因果条件之关系者，皆为正犯，不分其为亲自实施，或利用教唆、帮助他人实行"；而限制正犯论则认为，"行为人自行实施犯罪行为而实现构成要件者为正犯"（陈兴良，2001: 520-521）。争论的焦点是利用教唆、帮助他人实行犯罪的人是否为"正犯"概念的外延所涵盖，这属于指示意义上的模糊领域，与英美刑法中"principal"是否包括"accessory before the fact"的争议性质相近。考虑到二者类典型的对等性，将"principal"译成"正犯"无疑是恰当的。

3.2.2　原法律术语在目的法律文化中没有概念对等的术语

深谙法律文化的译者都知道不同法律传统孕育的法律概念鲜有完全对等的（杜金榜，2004: 88），然而相关概念却是普遍存在。这就需要我们综合运用法律知识和语言技能，构造新的法律术语，尽可能准确地传递原法律概念的类典型。

如前文提到的刑法术语"主犯"就是中国大陆所特有，与"从犯"相对立。按照我国现行刑法第二十六条及第九十七条的规定，"主犯"包括以下三类：

1. 犯罪集团中的组织犯；
2. 聚众犯罪中的组织犯；
3. 共同犯罪中起主要作用的实行犯。（刘家琛，2002: 123-124）

换言之，并非所有主犯都是实行犯，而实行犯也不都是主犯。由于普通法中并无对等概念，译者只能另辟蹊径。在目的法律文化中检索相关概念，特别是与其语义域对等的概念，往往可以给我们很多启示。就"主犯"而言，英美法律术语"joint offense"与其语义域"共同犯罪"不无相通之处。根据《布莱克法律辞典》的定义，此概念意为：

An offense (such as conspiracy) committed by the participation of two or more persons. —Also termed *joint crime*.（Garner, 2019: 1301）

近似于我国刑法第二十五条的规定：

共同犯罪是指二人以上共同故意犯罪。

又鉴于英美法律术语"party to a crime/an offense"常用来泛指一切犯罪参与人（薛波，2003: 1030），我们完全有理由将"主犯"译成"primary party to a joint crime/offense"，"从犯"则可相应译成"secondary party to a joint crime/offense"。

当然对于译者来说，准确传递原法律概念的类典型只是一个方面。译文术语的选择不仅应当有效地反映其传递的概念，且术语的外在形式应当能为目的文化所普遍接受（Baker, 2004: 261）。因此，译者在用词方面至少应当注意以下两点。

1. 切忌望文生义，依据法律概念的类典型确定译文用词

法律概念是"一系列元素经过长时间的积累沉淀，经过演变、淘汰，最后凝缩而成"（杜金榜，2004: 87）的，在翻译过程中我们应当尽力避免仅凭原法律术语的外在形式望文生义。如将"avoid the contract"中的"avoid"想当然地译成"避免"或"逃避"，只会使读者更加迷惑。其实，此处所谓"avoid"即"void"，可译为"使无效，撤销"。

在处理目的文化中没有对等概念的法律术语时，这一点显得尤为重要。译者必须仔细斟酌该术语所含概念的类典型，方可避免混淆。如英美行政法律术语"primary jurisdiction doctrine"，《布莱克法律辞典》将其定义为：

A judicial doctrine whereby a court tends to favor allowing an agency <u>an initial opportunity</u> to decide an issue in a case in which the court and the agency have concurrent jurisdiction. （Garner, 2019: 1442）

我国行政法中虽无对等概念，但与之相关的术语却是不少。只要仔细分析原文所含法律概念的类典型，便能给译者以启示。

根据"primary jurisdiction doctrine"的定义"... to favor allowing an agency ... to decide an issue ..."，我们不难确定此术语中的"jurisdiction"指"agency jurisdiction"。事实上，"行政管辖权"在我国也是常用术语，且二者所含概念的类典型对等。因此，真正需要译者留意的是"primary"一词，草率地将其处理成"首要的"或"基本的"等等，显然差强人意，无法准确传递原法律概念中的要素——"an initial opportunity"，不如将之译成"行政管辖权优先原则"更能反映此概念的实质。

2. 慎用一般语言，借鉴法言法语传递法律概念的类典型

法律语言不同于一般语言，具有相当的权威性和约束力，从而自成完整的体系。新创法律术语的使用必须接受"原有法律语言体系的制约"（杜金榜，2004: 81）。只有尽量运用法言法语，才能使所译法律术语真正融入目的法律文化。轻易使用一般语言，如弃置英美法律术语"administrative agent"，却将"行政机关"译成"administrative organ"等等，很难为英美法律文化所接受。

就此而言，我国特有法律术语"行政复议"的翻译便是一个范例。按照《中华人民共和国行政复议法》（2023年修订）第二条的规定，所谓"行政复议"，是指"公民、法人或者其他组织认为行政机关的行政行为侵犯其合法权益，向行政复议机关提出行政复议申请，行政复议机关办理行政复议案件"的制度。尽管英美国家也各自建立了解决行政争议的救济制度，但其名称、规则及程序迥然不同。既然没有对等概念，译者就应当优先考虑表达近似概念的法言法语。

熟悉普通法文化的译者，必然会联想到英美国家的议会法术语"reconsideration"。"reconsider"意为"To discuss or take up (a matter) again."（Garner, 2004: 1300），《元照英美法词典》将"reconsideration"译成"重新审议"（薛波，2003: 1158）无疑是合理的。而"行政复议"这一术语的构成根据法律学者的解释，"复"即重新或再次，"议"即审议并决定；前冠"行政"，表明由行政机关对行政争议进行复核、审查（应松年、刘莘，1999: 1）。据此，我们完全可以构造全新的术语"administrative reconsideration"，以此传递原法律概念的类典型，不仅浅显易懂，而且符合目的法律语言的使用习惯。

匹配不同文化中孤立的意义单位只是翻译过程的前奏，因为译者接触的概念总是出现在上下文中，只有根据语境才能为之选择适当的语言表达形式（Baker, 2004: 251）。相关问题，我们将在后续内容中进一步详细讨论。

结束语

传译法律术语是所有法律文件翻译的基础。如何因地制宜、恰如其分地理解法律概念，消除原法律文化与目的法律文化之间的巨大差异，对于充当文化中介的译者来说无疑是严峻的挑战。因此，我们要从事法律翻译，至少应当从两方面时刻完善自己：既要努力提高英汉双语能力，又要不断积累法律专业知识。

此外，"工欲善其事，必先利其器"。作为工具书，权威的法律词典绝不可少，如《布莱克法律辞典》《牛津法律词典》《元照英美法词典》等都应常备。我们还可以充分利用网络资源，获取新鲜的法律知识。经常性地浏览下列法律网页会使我们受益匪浅：

https://thelawdictionary.org/；

https://www.findlaw.com/；

https://www.ilrg.com/forms；

https://www.lawinfo.com/。

本书讨论的英汉法律互译实践，不涉及计算机辅助翻译技术。毋庸置疑，利用计算机辅助翻译软件如塔多斯（SDL Trados Studio）、翻译记忆库（TM）技术，可以高效地创建、编辑和审校翻译文本，从而在很大程度上提升团队合作翻译项目的完成速度。尽管如此，笔者以为，翻译专业本科阶段的学生，首先需要培养的是自身的实操能力。过早地接触计算机辅助翻译技术，或将误导学生贪恋捷径，忽视基础阶段应当努力掌握的双语能力与译者素养，而后者才是信息化时代翻译家独有的核心价值。

只有在这一切都准备就绪后，我们才可以真正开始法律文件的翻译工作！

【重要说明】

本书第4—10章着重分析规定性法律文件中定义条款与实质性条款的句式及其翻译技巧。尽管现代国家的法律制度纷繁复杂，但就句式而言，区别最大的无疑就是民事法律条款与刑事法律条款。

我们选择民事法律条款作为英汉法律翻译的研究对象，这是考虑到英语在国际商事活动中的通用性。笔者引用了大量实例，其中多数来源于《统一商法典》与《施工合同条件》。

《统一商法典》是英美国家历史上最杰出的一部成文法典（美国法学会、美国统一州法委员会，2004: 1）。该法典是由民间组织美国全国统一州法委员会（National Conference of Commissioners on Uniform State Laws）与美国法学会（American Law Institute）联合编撰的，因而在被各州采纳以前并无任何法律效力可言。但鉴于该法典的编纂别具特色，既有效地解决了普通法系判例庞杂与缺乏系统性的问题，也在某种程度上克服了大陆法系法典僵化与滞后的弊病，所以截至1968年，除路易斯安那州外，其余49个州及哥伦比亚特区和维尔京群岛都通过了《统一商法典》（18）。

　　而《施工合同条件》是国际咨询工程师联合会（Federation Internationale des Ingenieurs Conseils）制定的。该联合会也是一个非官方机构，成立于 1913 年，其编制的适用于国际承包市场的高水平工程合同条件享誉全球（张水波、何伯森, 2003: iv）。显然，这类大型复杂的涉外合同才是译者关注合同实质性条款翻译的重心所在。

　　我们在论述英美规定性法律文件的汉译过程中，将深入比较英汉民事法律条款的句式特征，因此，本书对我国法律英译的探讨，依托句式迥异于民事条款的《中华人民共和国刑法》2023 年最新修正版。

　　笔者对我国刑法典的分析包括总则部分的定义条款（第四章第 2 节）和分则部分的实质性条款（第八至十章）。关注的焦点是总则条款包含的大量法律术语以及分则中反复出现的固定句式结构，翻译时须前后相互印证，以便保持一致性的文本风格。

◆第二编翻译实践练习（上）

　　专业领域的翻译，尤其是专业领域的汉译英，需要从了解、熟悉、模仿有代表性的、权威性的文本开始。本编翻译实践练习（上）特提供"宪法翻译的启示 1：法律术语篇"，供读者参考；此外，第 4、10、12 章后另分别提供"宪法翻译的启示 2—6"。请扫二维码阅读。

●宪法翻译的启示 1：法律术语篇

第4章
英汉定义条款互译

◎学习目标◎

1. 英美民事法律术语定义的目的及其分类；

2. 英美民事法律术语定义的方式及其翻译；

3. 我国刑事法律术语独立条款定义的翻译；

4. 我国刑事法律术语内嵌条款定义的翻译。

4.1 英译汉：以民事法律定义条款为例

英美成文法及大型合同的总则部分（General Provisions）通常都包含独立的定义条款，将文件涉及的关键性术语按字母排序并确定其含义，从而方便读者查阅（Haggard，2004: 401）。

以《施工合同条件》为例。该合同范本通用条件的第一条（General Provisions）第一款就是定义（§1.1 Definitions），总计 6 项，分别为"§1.1.1 The Contract""§1.1.2 Parties and Persons""§1.1.3 Dates, Tests, Periods and Completion""§1.1.4 Money and Payments""§1.1.5 Works and Goods"和"§1.1.6 Other Definitions"，共汇集了 58 个术语。

当然，法律文件前部集中定义的都是普遍适用于整个文件的术语。若是需要定义的术语只出现在法律文件的某个章节，那么显然该章节才是安置定义条款的合适位置（Haggard，2004: 401）。如《统一商法典》，除第 1 编（General Provisions）第 2 章（General Definitions and Principles of Interpretation）第 1 条（§1-201 General Definitions）集中定义了 43 个贯穿法典始终的术语外，其余 8 编也各就仅适用于本编的术语制定了专门的定义条款，且此条款多位于各编的第 1 章。

根据言语行为理论，定义部分内容无疑具有宣布性的效力；换言之，它们赋予特定词汇新的含义（陶博，2004: 78），从而成为专门术语。笔者以为，翻译定义条款，就必须基于其自身的特点。

4.1.1 术语定义的目的及其分类

规定性法律文件中设置定义条款，其作用主要有二：一是为了统一术语的含义；二是为了避免烦累的重复（79）。据此，我们可以将定义分为两大类。

1. 标签定义（labeling definition）或简称定义（nickname definition）

此类定义如同缩写（如《施工合同条件》§1.1.2.10）或者近似缩写［如《统一商法典》§3-104(b)］，固有此名。其功能主要在于避免烦累的重复。就翻译而言，它们相对易于处理。

【例1】

1.1.2.10 "FIDIC" means the Federation Internationale des Ingenieurs-Conseils, the international federation of consulting engineers.

—Conditions of Contract for Construction

【推荐译文】

1.1.2.10 "菲迪克"（FIDIC）是指国际咨询工程师联合会。

【例2】

§3-104(b) "Instrument" means a negotiable instrument.

—U.C.C. ARTICLE 3　NEGOTIABLE INSTRUMENTS (2002)

【推荐译文】

§3-104(b) "票据"是指流通票据。

2. 约定定义（stipulative definition）

此类定义修改了词汇所具有的通用意思，以便满足法律文件制定者传递特定概念的需要。约定定义远比标签定义复杂，是法律翻译研究的重点。因此，本节将主要以《统一商法典》§1-201(b)与《施工合同条件》§1.1为例研究民事法律文件中约定定义条款的翻译。

约定定义的功能主要在于统一术语的含义，并可大致细分为四种：（1）完全定义；（2）部分定义；（3）混合定义；（4）范例型定义。

（1）完全定义（full definition）

这类定义条款规定的是术语完整的、唯一的含义①，多以"mean(s)"为谓语。这也是各类定义中最常见的一种：《统一商法典》§1-201(b)就包含27个完全定义，而《施工合同条件》§1.1中的完全定义更有51个之多。

【例3】

§1-201(b)(32) "Remedy" means any remedial right to which an aggrieved party is entitled with or without resort to a tribunal.

—U.C.C. ARTICLE 1　GENERAL PROVISIONS (2001)

【推荐译文】

§1-201(b)(32) "救济"是指受害人享有的任何补救权利，无论该权利的行使是否需要诉诸法庭。

（2）部分定义（partial definition）

这类定义条款以术语隐含的词汇意思（lexical meaning）为出发点，通过包含（include）或排除（exclude）某些具体指示对象（specific referent），明确该术语的界定

---

① A full definition provides the complete and exclusive meaning of the term. (Haggard, 2004: 390)

范围①。《统一商法典》§1-201(b)中有 10 个术语采用了部分定义。

【例4】

§1-201(b)(34)　"Right" includes remedy.

—U.C.C. ARTICLE 1　GENERAL PROVISIONS (2001)

【推荐译文】

§1-201(b)(34)　"权利"包括救济。

（3）混合定义（combing full and partial definition）

这类定义条款将完全定义与部分定义合二为一：完全定义为部分定义奠定基础；而部分定义则进一步明晰完全定义的模糊领域（Haggard, 2004: 396）。混合定义的数量虽然不多——《统一商法典》§1-201(b)所涉术语仅有 6 个混合定义，《施工合同条件》§1.1 中也只有 7 个术语采用混合定义，但如此定义的术语大都比较重要，且其指示对象相对模糊，值得译者特别留意。

【例5】

§1-201(b)(24) "Money" means a medium of exchange currently authorized or adopted by a domestic or foreign government. The term includes a monetary unit of account established by an intergovernmental organization or by agreement between two or more countries.

—U.C.C. ARTICLE 1　GENERAL PROVISIONS (2001)

【推荐译文】

§1-201(b)(24)　"货币"是指本国或外国政府当前法定或认可的交换媒介。该术语包括政府间国际组织确定的或者两个或两个以上国家协议确定的货币记账单位。

（4）范例型定义（example definition）

这类定义条款由完全定义与范例构成，就形式而言，近似混合定义。但混合定义条款列举指示对象，其目的是明确完全定义的边缘领域；而范例却必须满足完全定义的要求，方可视为被定义术语的指示对象（397）。不过，此类型定义是由于其他各类定义均不能满足要求，法律文件制定者万不得已才退而求其次的结果。正因为如此，范例型定义在法律文件中出现得不多，《统一商法典》§1-201(b)和《施工合同条件》§1.1 中都没有设置这类定义。欲进一步了解，读者不妨参阅本节【例15】《施工合同条件》第 19.1 条（Definition of *Force Majeure*）。

4.1.2　术语定义的方式及其翻译

根据哈格德的理论（398-400），术语的定义方式（methodology）如下：

（1）使用更为熟悉的词汇（use more familiar terms）；

（2）使用更为精确的词汇（use more precise terms）；

（3）明确组成部分（identify components）；

---

① A partial definition takes the lexical meaning of a word as the point of departure and clarifies its boundaries, by inclusion or exclusion of specific. (Haggard, 2004: 393)

（4）明确具体指示对象（identify specific referents）；

（5）表明与较大概念单位之间的关系（indicate relationship to a larger unit）。

不同的定义方式要求译者特别关注的侧重点亦有所不同，下文将逐一分析。

1. 使用更为熟悉的词汇

使用读者更为熟悉的词汇来描写术语的典型特征是比较常见的定义方式之一，特别有助于普通读者理解专业术语。

译者处理此类定义时必须注意：通常人们耳熟能详的词汇，总是具有多重含义。我们应当基于法律专业知识，借助上下文，审慎确定其译文。

【例6】

§1-201(b)(6)　"Bill of lading" means a document evidencing the receipt of goods for shipment issued by a person engaged in the business of transporting or forwarding goods.

—U.C.C. ARTICLE 1　GENERAL PROVISIONS (2001)

【值得商榷的译文】

§1-201(b)(6)　"提单"指由从事运输或者递送业务的人签发的、证明收到待运货物的单据。

实际上，《中华人民共和国海商法》（1992年）中也有定义"提单"的条款。

第七十一条　提单，是指用以证明海上货物运输合同和货物已经由承运人接收或者装船，以及承运人保证据以交付货物的单证。

当然，《统一商法典》规定的"提单"，其指示范围远大于我国海商法中的"提单"，不仅涉及海上运输，还涉及其他类型的运输。但有一点是熟悉运输法律规范者所共知的：提单是货物运输法律关系中特有的物权凭证。更何况，"bill of lading"的定义两次提到了"goods"："the receipt of goods"和"transporting or forwarding goods"。

由此可见，"forwarding"的理解必须与货运相联系。《布莱克法律辞典》中有一词条"freight forwarder"：

Maritime law. A person or company whose business is to receive and ship goods for others. • A freight forwarder may be an agent of the cargo's owner or of the carrier, or may be an independent contractor acting as a principal and assuming the carrier's responsibility for delivering the cargo.（Garner, 2019: 810）

而《元照英美法词典》则将"Forwarder Act"译成《货运代理法》（薛波，2003: 575）。因此，"forwarding"应当译成"货运代理"才更为准确。再参照我国法律平行定义条款的行文，笔者认为以下译文值得推荐。

【推荐译文】

§1-201(b)(6)　"提单"是指用以证明收到待运货物的单证，由从事货物运输或货运代理业务的人签发。

2. 使用更为精确的词语

有的专业术语本身语焉不详，下定义时为了澄清其含义，需要使用更具科学性的精确词语。

【例 7】

1.1.3.1 "Base Date" means the date 28 days prior to the latest date for submission of the Tender.

—Conditions of Contract for Construction

【推荐译文】

1.1.3.1 "基准日期"是指递交投标书的截止日期前 28 日的日期。

翻译此类定义的关键在于"精确",尤其是条款中的科学语言,更是不能有丝毫的偏差或删减,否则便无法贯彻法律文件制定者的意图。

由于此种方式定义的术语多为技术性概念,与法律本身的关系相对疏远,笔者不再深入探讨。

3. 明确组成部分

通过定义明确术语的组成部分,使读者能够更为透彻地把握其所包含的概念,也是法律文件惯用的定义方法。

对于此类定义,译者必须仔细地辨别、比较术语所涉各组成部分的含义:有些成分在法律文件中没有专门的定义,我们只需考虑其词汇意思即可;而另一些成分则由法律文件制定者赋予了特定的含义。要确定它们的准确含义,唯有交叉参照(cross-reference)所涉术语的定义。

【例 8】

1.1.1.1 "Contract" means the Contract Agreement, the Letter of Acceptance, the Letter of Tender, these Conditions, the Specification, the Drawings, the Schedules, and the further documents (if any) which are listed in the Contract Agreement or in the Letter of Acceptance.

—Conditions of Contract for Construction

实际上,该合同范本的通用条件不仅定义了"contract",还有如下相关条款:

§1.1.1.2 "Contract Agreement" means the contract agreement (if any) referred to in Sub-Clause 1.6 [*Contract Agreement*]

§1.1.1.3 "Letter of Acceptance" means the letter of formal acceptance, signed by the Employer, of the Letter of Tender, including any annexed memoranda comprising agreements between and signed by both Parties.

§1.1.1.4 "Letter of Tender" means the document entitled letter of tender, which was completed by the Contractor and includes the signed offer to the Employer for the Works.

§1.1.1.5 "Specification" means the document entitled specification, as included in the Contract, and any additions and modifications to the specification in accordance with the Contract. Such document specifies the Works.

§1.1.1.6 "Drawings" means the drawings of the Works, as included in the Contract, and any additional and modified drawings issued by (or on behalf of) the Employer in accordance with the Contract.

§1.1.1.7 "Schedules" means the document(s) entitled schedules, completed by the

Contractor and submitted with the Letter of Tender, <u>as included in the Contract</u>. Such document may include the Bill of Quantities, data, lists, and Schedules of rates and/or prices.

这些条款分别定义了"Contract"的主要组成成分："Contract Agreement""Letter of Acceptance""Letter of Tender""Specification""Drawings""Schedules"，以便确定其指示对象。尤其是最后三个术语的定义中特别强调"as included in the Contract"，其目的就是厘清各术语之间的上下位关系。译者只要明晰了这些术语的概念，就能够正确地理解并翻译"contract"的定义。

【推荐译文】

1.1.1.1 "合同"是指合同协议书、中标函、投标函、本通用条件、规范要求、图纸、资料表以及合同协议书或中标函中所列的其他文件（如果有）。

4. 明确具体指示对象

各种定义方式中使用最为频繁的也许就是明确术语的具体指示对象，常见于各类约定定义，特别是部分定义条款。

部分定义条款以词汇的自然意思为基础（尽管此类词汇意思并未明示在其定义中），其主要目的是确定位于该术语边缘的具体指示对象是否涵盖在内（Davies, 2005: 180）。

【例 9】

§1-201(b)(14)　"Defendant" includes a person in the position of defendant in a counterclaim, cross-claim, or third party claim.

—U.C.C. ARTICLE 1　GENERAL PROVISIONS (2001)

【推荐译文】

§1-201(b)(14)　"被告"包括反诉、交叉诉讼或第三人诉讼中处于被告地位的人。

该定义虽未提及"Defendant"的通常含义："A person sued in a civil proceeding or accused in a criminal proceeding."（Garner, 2019: 528）但却是不言而喻地包含在此术语的指示范畴之内。

相比之下，尽管全部定义条款也有采用此种方式的，却是意在明确将该术语的含义局限于所列指示对象。

【例 10】

§1-201(b)(17)　"Fault" means a default, breach, or wrongful act or omission.

—U.C.C. ARTICLE 1　GENERAL PROVISIONS (2001)

【推荐译文】

§1-201(b)(17)　"过错"是指不履行合同义务，违约，或者不当行为或不作为。

因此，在处理列举指示对象的定义条款时，必须区分"include(s)"与"mean(s)"的差别。这关系到读者在理解概念时是否应当将该术语的词汇意思包含在内。

翻译此种方式定义的条款，我们应当先确定所列指示对象的含义。既然这些指示对象同属一个概念范畴，相互之间必然具有某种联系，而把握这种联系正是准确翻译此类条款必不可少的。

【例 11】

§1-201(b)(33)　"Representative" means a person empowered to act for another, including an agent, an officer of a corporation or association, and a trustee, executor, or administrator of an estate.

—U.C.C. ARTICLE 1　GENERAL PROVISIONS (2001)

该条款采用混合定义，可解析为两段：前者属于全部定义，意思明确，可译为"经授权代表他人作为的人"；而后者为部分定义，除"agent"一词容易理解外，其他几个指示对象都需谨慎处理。曾有人将之误译为"公司或联合体的职员、受托人、财团的执行人、管理人"，实则大谬不然。

从语言学的角度仔细分析"a trustee, executor, or administrator of an estate"的句法结构，我们不难发现，"trustee""executor""administrator"由同一不定冠词充当限定词，构成一组平行术语，而"an estate"也是它们共同的修饰语，将之拆开理解，译成"受托人、财团的执行人、管理人"显然不妥。译者应当从整体着眼，将四个术语所包含的概念联系起来研究，找出它们在法律领域中的共通点。依据《布莱克法律辞典》的定义：

Executor: A person named by a testator to carry out the provision in the testator's will.（Garner, 2019: 716）

Administrator: A person appointed by the court to manage the assets and liabilities of an intestate decedent.（56）

Estate: The property that one leaves after death; the collective assets and liabilities of a dead person.（690）

至于"trustee"，《布莱克法律辞典》中亦收录了"estate trust"这一条目：

A trust that is established to qualify a deceased spouse's property for the marital deduction.（1820）

由此可见，"representative"定义中的"estate"实际上指的是"遗产"，而"trustee""executor""administrator"也应作相应理解。故笔者推荐以下译文。

【推荐译文】

§1-201(b)(33)　"代表人"是指经授权代表他人作为的人，包括代理人、法人或非法人组织的官员，及遗产受托人、执行人或管理人。

5. 表明与较大概念单位之间的关系

法律文件制定者为了明确术语的含义，常常利用关系从句，将之与更大的概念单位联系起来。

【例 12】

1.1.6.2　"Country" means the country in which the Site (or most of it) is located, where the Permanent Works are to be executed.

—Conditions of Contract for Construction

该定义条款包含两个关系从句。显然，要正确理解其含义必须厘清它们之间的联系。毫无疑问，前者［"in which the Site (or most of it) is located"］修饰的先行词是"the country"；而后者却略嫌模糊：到底是"the country"还是"the Site (or most of it)"？笔者以为，其先行词应当是"the Site (or most of it)"，理由如下：

若"where the Permanent Works are to be executed"修饰的亦是"the country"，那么它与前一从句之间应当是并列关系。然而，原文制定者却没有使用并列连词"and"。

比较《施工合同条件》第1.1.6.7项定义：

1.1.6.7 "Site" means the places where the Permanent Works are to be executed and to which Plant and Materials are to be delivered, and any other places as may be specified in the Contract as forming part of the Site.

可见，该合同条件中所谓的"Site"包括以下三类场所：

(a) the places where the Permanent Works are to be executed；

(b) the places to which Plant and Materials are to be delivered；

(c) any other places as may be specified in the Contract as forming part of the Site。

而【例12】中提及的"the Site (or most of it)"，实际上指的只是（a）类场所——二者遣词造句一丝不差。

因此，笔者认为以下译文值得推荐。

【推荐译文】

1.1.6.2 "工程所在国"是指实施**永久工程**的现场（或大部分现场）所在的国家。

鉴于关系从句的特殊性，处理此类定义条款，译者应当特别注意以下两个方面。

（1）应当仔细斟酌源语与目的语的言语习惯。

【例13】

1.1.1.9 "Appendix to Tender" means the completed pages entitled appendix to tender which are appended to and from part of the Letter of Tender.

—Conditions of Contract for Construction

该条款运用关系从句"which are appended to and from part of the Letter of Tender"修饰"the completed pages entitled appendix to tender"。

尽管这个限制性关系从句与过去分词"completed""entitled appendix to tender"同为"pages"的修饰语，但若将三者尽行处理成前置定语，那么译文中"的"字必然过多，虽可解读，却有些拗口。

【值得商榷的译文】

1.1.1.9 "投标书附录"是指附在**投标函**后作为其一部分的名为投标书附录的填写完整的文页。

相反，若是译者根据两种语言的不同特点，将"which are appended to and from part of the Letter of Tender"另起一句，非但不会误导读者，还会使得译文更加符合目的语的行文习惯。

【推荐译文】

1.1.1.9 "投标书附录"是指名为投标书附录的填写完整的文页，这些文页附在**投标函**后构成该**投标函**的一部分。

当然，译者如此断句的前提是，既不能模糊，更不能扭曲原文的含义。

（2）必须时刻牢记法律文体与普通文体的差别：其遣词造句以明确、严谨、无疑议为要。

【例14】

§1-201(b)(16)　"Document of title" includes bill of lading, dock warrant, dock receipt, warehouse receipt or order for the delivery of goods, and also any other document which in the regular course of business or financing is treated as adequately evidencing that the person in possession of it is entitled to receive, hold, and dispose of the document and the goods it covers. ...

——U.C.C. ARTICLE 1　GENERAL PROVISIONS (2001)

该条款虽属于部分定义，却包含有一个兜底款项："any other document which in the regular course of business or financing is treated as adequately evidencing that the person in possession of it is entitled to receive, hold, and dispose of the document and the goods it covers"。这个指示对象的理解和翻译对于该定义条款而言至关重要。

此短语包含的关系从句本身结构复杂，甚至还内嵌一个宾语从句"that the person in possession of it is entitled to receive, hold, and dispose of the document and the goods it covers"，将之译成前置定语，相对比较困难，不如断为两句。

【值得商榷的译文】

§1-201(b)(16)　"所有权凭证"包括提单、码头提货单、码头收据、仓单或提货单，还包括任何其他单据，此种单据在正常交易或融资过程中被视为可充分证明其占有人有权接收、持有及处置该单证及其所代表的货物。……

然而同样值得注意的是，此关系从句属于限制性定语。换言之，关系从句中描述的单证特征是任何所有权凭证必须具备的。遗憾的是我们却无法从前译中觉察到此种修饰关系，甚至可能将其误解成：一旦任何其他单据被认定为所有权凭证，就可以"在正常交易或融资过程中视为可充分证明其占有人有权接收、持有及处置该单证及其所代表的货物"。如此理解，因果关系岂不完全倒置了？所以，笔者认为，准确的译文应当能够揭示原文内在的逻辑关系。

【推荐译文】

§1-201(b)(16)　"所有权凭证"包括提单、码头提货单、码头收据、仓单或提货单，还包括任何其他单证，**只要**这种单证在正常交易或融资过程中被视为足以证明持单人有权接收、占有和处置该单证及其所代表的货物。……

4.1.3　疑难定义条款的翻译

考虑到规定性法律文件的内容包罗万象，其中定义的术语必然涉及社会、政治、经济、科技等各个方面。为了阐明这些术语所包含的概念，制定者常常将上述五种方法综合起来加以运用。因而，有的术语条款极其复杂，译者必须谨慎处理。

杰克·戴维斯（Jack Davies）在其著作《立法法与程序》（*Legislative Law and Process*）

（Davies, 2005: 180-181）中分析规定性法律文件的起草问题时，谈到了设置定义条款的规则，其中不乏富有启发性的箴言。笔者以为，这些注意事项同样值得译者深思，特别是自然含义规则（natural meanings）与避免滥用规则（avoid excessive use）。

所谓自然含义规则，是指术语的定义不能完全脱离其词典含义（180）；而避免滥用规则，是指术语的定义不应完全等同其词典含义，否则就无须专门为此制定条款（181）。二者相辅相成，明示译者在处理疑难定义条款时，不妨对照该术语的词汇意思。

【例 15】

19.1 In this clause, "*Force Majeure*" means an exceptional event or circumstance:

(a) which is beyond a Party's control,

(b) which such Party could not reasonably have provided against before entering into the Contract,

(c) which, having arisen, such Party could not reasonably have avoided or overcome, and

(d) which is not substantially attributable to the other Party.

Force Majeure may include, but is not limited to, exceptional events or circumstances of the kind listed below, so long as conditions (a) to (d) above are satisfied:

(i) war, hostilities (whether war be declared or not), invasion, act of foreign enemies,

(ii) rebellion, terrorism, revolution, insurrection, military or usurped power, or civil war,

(iii) riot, commotion, disorder, strike or lockout by persons other than the Contractor's Personnel and other employees of the Contractor and Subcontractors,

(iv) munitions of war, explosive materials, ionising radiation or contamination by radio-activity, except as may be attributable to the Contractor's use of such munitions, explosives, radiation or radio-activity, and

(v) natural catastrophes such as earthquake, hurricane, typhoon or volcanic activity.

—Conditions of Contract for Construction

该条款的批注（head-note）为"Definition of *Force Majeure*"。制定者为了明确其概念，主要采用了两种定义方式：前段用以表明该术语与较大概念单位之间的关系，属完全定义；而后段则列举了五类典型例子，属范例型定义。由于该条第 2 款规定："*Force Majeure* may include, but is not limited to, exceptional events or circumstances of the kind listed below, <u>so long as conditions (a) to (d) above are satisfied</u>"，因此如何理解前一款，对于此定义的翻译举足轻重。

仔细分析该款定义，我们注意到四个相互平行的关系从句，由"and"连接在一起。摆在译者面前的问题是："*Force Majeure*"所指的"an exceptional event or circumstance"必须同时满足四项条件，还是符合其中任一项即可？

从语言学的角度看，"and"虽被用于连接（conjunction），却有歧义：不仅可以理解为"共同（jointly）"，还可以理解为"分别（severally）"（陶博，2004: 264）。如前文提及的《施工合同条件》第 1.1.6.7 项："'Site' means the places where the Permanent Works are to be executed <u>and</u> to which Plant and Materials are to be delivered, and any other places as may be specified in the Contract as forming part of the Site." 其中连接两个关系从句的 "and"，就只能解释成"分别"，而不能认为必须同时具备此两个条件的场所才属于现场。这一点【例12】可作为佐证。

既然语言分析不能解决问题，我们只有求助于该法律术语的词汇意思。所谓 "*Force Majeure*" 即我国法律中所谓的"不可抗力"。《中华人民共和国民法典》（2020年）第一百八十条第二款规定："不可抗力是不能预见、不能避免且不能克服的客观情况。"

而《布莱克法律辞典》则将之定义为：

An event or effect that can be neither anticipated nor controlled; esp., an unexpected event that prevents someone from doing or completing something that he or she had agreed or officially planned to do. • The term includes both acts of nature (e.g., floods and hurricanes) and acts of people (e.g., riots, strikes, and wars).（Garner, 2019: 788）

根据《元照英美法词典》的解释，合同中设置不可抗力条款的目的是"在合同当事人因非其所能控制的且以正当注意仍无法避免的原因而致其不能履行合同时，对该当事人提供保护"（薛波，2003: 565）。

综上所述，我们不难得出结论：【例15】中所指的"an exceptional event or circumstance"，如果仅满足前款规定的四项条件之一，并不构成 "*Force Majeure*"。因而，此处的 "and"应当理解为"共同"。

> 【推荐译文】
>
> **19.1** 在本条中，**"不可抗力"**是指满足下列条件的特殊事件或情况：
>
> （a）一方当事人无法控制；
>
> （b）上述当事人在签订合同前，无法合理预防；
>
> （c）发生后，上述当事人无法合理避免或克服；且
>
> （d）实质上不能归因于对方当事人。
>
> ……

4.1.4　定义条款译文之检验

鉴于定义条款涉及的术语在规定性法律文件中所处的重要地位，在继续文件其他条款的翻译前，必须先验证定义条款的译文是否正确，这是最为明智的决定。

那么如何验证呢？笔者以为哈格德提出的将术语的定义代入使用该术语的实质性条款（Haggard, 2004: 403）的方法颇有可取之处。

众所周知，被定义的术语在该文件中的含义必须始终与其定义保持一致，此即戴维斯所谓的定义约束规则（bound by definitions）（Davies, 2005: 180）。因而运用代入法，我们便可确定对术语定义的理解是否出现了本质性的偏差。

【例16】

§1-201(b)(12) "Contract", as distinguished from "agreement", means the total legal obligation that results from the parties' agreement as determined by the Uniform Commercial Code as supplemented by any other applicable laws.

—U.C.C. ARTICLE 1 GENERAL PROVISIONS (2001)

【推荐译文】

§1-201(b)(12) "合同"不同于"协议",是指根据当事人之间的协议产生的全部法律义务,该协议由《统一商法典》确定并由所有其他准据法补充。

检验此条款的译文,就是要将"合同"的定义代入法律文件中使用该术语的具体条款。我们不妨以该法典第 1-304 条为例。

§1-304 Obligation of Good Faith.

Every contract or duty within the Uniform Commercial Code imposes an obligation of good faith in its performance and enforcement.

—U.C.C. ARTICLE 1 GENERAL PROVISIONS (2001)

该条款将"contract"与"duty"两个术语并置为主语,其所含概念必然同属一类范畴。细察【例 16】,我们不难发现,"contract"实质上被理解为"[...] legal obligation",所以译文中才会使用"合同"是指"[……]法律义务"的措辞。

将此定义原文代入第 1-304 条:"Every [...] legal obligation or duty within [the Uniform Commercial Code] imposes an obligation of good faith in its performance and enforcement."那么,"legal obligation"与"duty"可以相提并论吗?由于"duty"在该法典中并无专门定义,我们不妨参阅《布莱克法律辞典》的解释:

A legal obligation that is owed or due to another and that needs to be satisfied; that which one is bound to do, and for which somebody else has a corresponding right.(Garner, 2019: 637)

可见"contract"与"duty"均属"legal obligation"。就此而言,推荐译文对该定义条款的理解并无不妥。

4.1.5 固定表达形式的翻译

规定性法律文件中的固定表达形式最常见的有两种:一是术语本身的表达形式;二是适用范围的表达形式。

1. 术语本身的表达形式

民事定义条款中术语的表达形式主要有两种:

(1)术语带引号的表达形式,常见于美国和英国等国家的法律,如本章【例 1】—【例 16】;有时还会冠以"the term",如【例 19】。

(2)黑体加斜体的表达形式,常见于加拿大、中华人民共和国香港特别行政区的法例。

【例 17】

2(1) In this Act,

article means real and personal property of every description including

(a) money,

(b) deeds and instruments relating to or evidencing the title or right to property or an interest, immediate, contingent or otherwise, in a corporation or in any assets of a corporation,

(c) deeds and instruments giving a right to recover or receive property,

(d) tickets or like evidence of right to be in attendance at a particular place at a particular time or times or of a right to transportation, and

(e) energy, however generated; (article)

—Competition Act (R.S.C., 1985, c. C-34)

【例 18】

2. Interpretation

In this Ordinance, unless the context otherwise requires—

antiquity means—

(a) a relic; and

(b) a place, building, site or structure erected, formed or built by human agency before the year 1800 and the ruins or remains of any such place, building, site or structure, whether or not the same has been modified, added to or restored after the year 1799;

...

—Antiquities and Monuments Ordinance

考虑到汉语法律文件的书写习惯，译文中的术语可采用加引号的表达形式，如本节提供的推荐译文所示；也可以效仿我国法律文件，不使用任何特殊表达形式。

2. 适用范围的表达形式

术语的定义，特别是约定定义，通常只适用于某部法律或该法律的某个章节甚至是某个条款，因而表述时必须明确其适用范围。

定义条款适用范围的表达主要有以下三种形式，而汉语法律文件中与之相对应的表达只有两种："在本法/条/款中……"或者"本法/条/款所称……"：

（1）"in this Act/Ordinance/clause/article ..."，如【例 15】【例 17】和【例 18】。

（2）"As used in ..."

【例 19】

As used in this title:

The term "department" means one of the executive departments enumerated in section 1 of Title 5, unless the context shows that such term was intended to describe the executive, legislative, or judicial branches of the government.

The term "agency" includes any department, independent establishment, commission, administration, authority, board or bureau of the United States or any corporation in which the United States has a proprietary interest, unless the context shows that such term was intended to be used in a more limited sense.

—18 U.S. Code §6—Department and agency defined

（3）"for the purpose of ..."

【例 20】

Affiliation

(2) For the purposes of this Act,

(a) one entity is affiliated with another entity if one of them is the subsidiary of the other or both are subsidiaries of the same entity or each of them is controlled by the same entity or individual;

(b) if two entities are affiliated with the same entity at the same time, they are deemed to be affiliated with each other; and

(c) an individual is affiliated with an entity if the individual controls the entity.

—Competition Act (R.S.C., 1985, c. C-34)

4.2　汉译英：以刑事法律定义条款为例

我国刑事法律术语的定义条款主要出现在刑法总则部分。所谓刑法总则，是关于刑法的基本原则和适用范围，以及犯罪和刑罚一般原理的规范体系（陈兴良，2001: 10）。就我国刑法典而言，其总则（General Provisions）共有五章：第一章涉及刑法的基本原则和适用范围；第二章规定犯罪；第三、四章规定刑罚；而第五章则囊括了其他难以分类的杂项内容。

综观这部分刑法条款不难发现，它们与绝大多数民事法律定义条款的表达形式大相径庭。相关规范大致可分为两类。

4.2.1　独立条款定义

所谓独立条款定义，即在刑事法律文本中以独立条款的形式界定专门术语。通常，独立定义条款表现为包含"的"字结构的"是"字句（刘红婴，2007: 143）。其中，"的"字结构在我国规定性法律文件中总是用于囊括规范的假定因素（132）。而此类刑法条款多数将被定义的法律术语置于句末，如【例21】。

【例21】

第十四条　明知自己的行为会发生危害社会的结果，并且希望或者放任这种结果发生，因而构成犯罪<u>的</u>，<u>是故意犯罪</u>。

【对照译文】

Article 14　<u>An intentional crime refers to an act</u> committed by a person who clearly knows that his act will entail harmful consequences to society but who wishes or allows such consequences to occur, thus constituting a crime.

该例所引条款定义的是"故意犯罪"。根据原文句型展开的方式，笔者以为应套用"A conduct is a ... crime if ..."的句式来表述此类规范。这符合英美成文法的语言习惯，如《美国模范刑法典》（Model Panel Code）第1.04条第（3）款：

(3) <u>A crime is a misdemeanor if</u> it is so designated in this Code or in a statute other than this Code enacted subsequent thereto.

其最大的优势还在于可恰如其分地反映出原文"……的"所隐含的条件关系，并使全部三个相关法条以排比方式罗列，从而更能体现规定性法律文件一致性的语言风格。

第十五条　……的，是过失犯罪。

【推荐译文】

Section 15　A conduct is a negligent crime if ...

第十六条　……的，不是犯罪。

【推荐译文】

Section 16　A conduct is not a crime if ...

故笔者推荐以下译文：

【推荐译文】

Section 14　A conduct is an intentional crime if it is committed by a person who knows that his conduct to constitute a crime will cause harmful consequences to society and wishes or allows such consequences to occur.

译者应作类似处理的尚有"犯罪预备""犯罪未遂""犯罪中止"及"主犯""从犯"等多组概念。不过，将被定义术语置于句末的条款主要为我国刑法典所特有。除此之外，当然还有些刑法条款将被定义的法律术语置于句首，如【例22】。

【例22】

第二十五条　共同犯罪是指二人以上共同故意犯罪。

【对照译文】

Article 25　A joint crime refers to an intentional crime committed by two or more persons jointly.

本例定义"共同犯罪"的句式与【例21】略有不同：被定义的术语出现在句首而不是句末。因此，笔者认为其翻译亦需作相应变化。尽管对照译文也以"A joint crime"起首展开，但"refers to"却并非英语规定性法律文件中的常用词汇，译者应当代之以"means"。

【推荐译文】

Section 25　A joint crime means an intentional crime jointly committed by two or more persons.

4.2.2　内嵌条款定义

所谓内嵌条款定义，即在法律文本中将专门术语的界定（特别是涉及行为或其主体的概念）及实质性规定表述为同一条款，如【例23】。

【例23】

第二十条　为了使国家、公共利益、本人或者他人的人身、财产和其他权利免受正在进行的不法侵害，而采取的制止不法侵害的行为，对不法侵害人造成损害的，属于正当防卫，不负刑事责任。

【对照译文】

Article 20　An act that a person commits to stop an unlawful infringement in order to prevent the interests of the State and the public, or his own or other person's rights of the person, property or other rights from being infringed upon by the on-going infringement, thus harming the perpetrator, is justifiable defense, and he shall not bear criminal responsibility.

　　该例所引条款将"正当防卫"的定义，即"为了使国家、公共利益、本人或者他人的人身、财产和其他权利免受正在进行的不法侵害，而采取的制止不法侵害的行为，对不法侵害人造成损害的"，以条件的形式内嵌于其刑事责任的表述之中。但对照译文却将其处理成并列句，其中前一分句的主语过于冗长而表语则极为简短，且与后一分句的逻辑关系相对暧昧，显然不可取。笔者以为，其英语译文应当采用条件状语从句，并将概括此类行为的法律术语"正当防卫"以非限制性定语从句的方式表现出来。

　　【推荐译文】

Section 20　A person shall not be criminally responsible for his conduct if it is committed and thus harms an infringer to stop his unlawful infringement for the purpose of protecting the interests of the State or the public, or his own or another's person, property or other rights against such infringement on the present occasion, which is a justifiable defense.

　　即便条款定义的术语并非指行为而是其主体，译文亦可采用类似句式，只需略作调整。请看【例 24】。

　　【例 24】

　　第六十五条　被判处有期徒刑以上刑罚的犯罪分子，刑罚执行完毕或者赦免以后，在五年以内再犯应当判处有期徒刑以上刑罚之罪的，是累犯，应当从重处罚……

　　【对照译文】

Article 65　If a criminal commits another crime punishable by fixed-term imprisonment or heavier penalty within five years after serving his sentence of not less than fixed-term imprisonment or receiving a pardon, he is a recidivist and shall be given a heavier punishment ...

　　本例原文在表述刑事处罚原则的同时，以条件形式内嵌行为主体"累犯"的定义。笔者以为，对照译文将"被判处有期徒刑以上刑罚的犯罪分子，刑罚执行完毕或者赦免以后，在五年以内再犯应当判处有期徒刑以上刑罚之罪的"处理成条件状语从句固然不错，然使之位于句首，不如后置从句，更可与其他内嵌定义条款保持结构上的一致性。有鉴于此，法律术语"累犯"的表现也应代之以介宾短语。具体句式的展开还可以参考《布莱克法律辞典》中有关"recidivist"的释义：

A criminal who, having been punished for illegal activities, resumes those activities after the punishment has been completed.（Garner, 2019: 1523）

　　【推荐译文】

Section 65　An offender shall be sentenced to a heavier punishment as a recidivist if he, having been sentenced to a punishment not less extensive than imprisonment, resumes a crime, on which a sentence not less extensive than imprisonment shall be imposed, within five years after his previous punishment has been completed or pardoned ...

◆第二编翻译实践练习（下）

●英译汉

1. 《美国法典》第 7 编第 1a 条定义（7 U.S. Code §1a—Definitions）第 1 款

As used in this chapter:

(1) ALTERNATIVE TRADING SYSTEM　The term "alternative trading system" means an organization, association, or group of persons that—

(A) is registered as a broker or dealer pursuant to section 15(b) of the Securities Exchange Act of 1934 [15 U.S.C. 78o(b)] (except paragraph (11) thereof);

(B) performs the functions commonly performed by an exchange (as defined in section 3(a)(1) of the Securities Exchange Act of 1934 [15 U.S.C. 78c(a)(1)]);

(C) does not—

(i) set rules governing the conduct of subscribers other than the conduct of such subscribers' trading on the alternative trading system; or

(ii) discipline subscribers other than by exclusion from trading; and

(D) is exempt from the definition of the term "exchange" under such section 3(a)(1) [15 U.S.C. 78c(a)(1)] by rule or regulation of the Securities and Exchange Commission on terms that require compliance with regulations of its trading functions.

2. 《美国法典》第 18 编第 3 条事后从犯（18 U.S. Code §3—Accessory after the fact）

Whoever, knowing that an offense against the United States has been committed, receives, relieves, comforts or assists the offender in order to hinder or prevent his apprehension, trial or punishment, is an accessory after the fact.

3. 《美国法典》第 18 编第 6 条部门和机关的定义（18 U.S. Code §6—Department and agency defined）

As used in this title:

The term "department" means one of the executive departments enumerated in section 1 of Title 5, unless the context shows that such term was intended to describe the executive, legislative, or judicial branches of the government.

The term "agency" includes any department, independent establishment, commission, administration, authority, board or bureau of the United States or any corporation in which the United States has a proprietary interest, unless the context shows that such term was intended to be used in a more limited sense.

4. 《英国公司法（2006）》第 1 编总则：公司和公司法（Companies Act 2006—Part 1　General introductory provisions: *Companies and Companies Acts*）

1　Companies

(1) In the Companies Acts, unless the context otherwise requires—

"company" means a company formed and registered under this Act, that is—

(a) a company so formed and registered after the commencement of this Part, or

(b) a company that immediately before the commencement of this Part—

(i) was formed and registered under the Companies Act 1985 (c. 6) or the Companies (Northern Ireland) Order 1986 [S.I. 1986/1032 (N.I. 6)], or

(ii) was an existing company for the purposes of that Act or that Order, (which is to be treated on commencement as if formed and registered under this Act).

(2) Certain provisions of the Companies Acts apply to—

(a) companies registered, but not formed, under this Act (see Chapter 1 of Part 33), and

(b) bodies incorporated in the United Kingdom but not registered under this Act (see Chapter 2 of that Part).

(3) For provisions applying to companies incorporated outside the United Kingdom, see Part 34 (overseas companies).

5. 《加拿大刑法典》释义部分定义第 2 条（Criminal Code R.S.C., 1985, c. C-46—Interpretation: Definitions 2）

bank-note includes any negotiable instrument

(a) issued by or on behalf of a person carrying on the business of banking in or out of Canada, and

(b) issued under the authority of Parliament or under the lawful authority of the government of a state other than Canada,

Intended to be used as money or as the equivalent of money, immediately on issue or at some time subsequent thereto, and includes bank bills and bank post bills;

6. 《加拿大刑法典》释义部分定义第 2 条（Criminal Code R.S.C., 1985, c. C-46—Interpretation: Definitions 2）

day means the period between six o'clock in the forenoon and nine o'clock in the afternoon of the same day;

7. 《加拿大刑法典》释义部分定义第 2 条（Criminal Code R.S.C., 1985, c. C-46—Interpretation: Definitions 2）

dwelling-house means the whole or any part of a building or structure that is kept or occupied as a permanent or temporary residence, and includes

(a) a building within the curtilage of a dwelling-house that is connected to it by a doorway or by a covered and enclosed passage-way, and

(b) a unit that is designed to be mobile and to be used as a permanent or temporary residence and that is being used as such a residence;

8. 《香港法例》第 1 章《释义及通则条例》第 3 条词语和词句的释义（Chapter 1　Interpretation and General Clauses Ordinance—3 Interpretation of words and expressions）

act（作为），when used with reference to an offence or civil wrong, includes a series of acts, an illegal omission and a series of illegal omissions;

9. 《香港法例》第 1 章《释义及通则条例》第 3 条词语和词句的释义（Chapter 1　Interpretation and General Clauses Ordinance—3 Interpretation of words and expressions）

adult（成人，成年人）means a person who has attained the age of 18 years; (*Amended 32 of 1990 s. 6*)

infant（幼年人）and *minor*（未成年人）mean a person who has not attained the age of 18 years; (*Amended 32 of 1990 s. 6*)

10. 《香港法例》第 1 章《释义及通则条例》第 3 条词语和词句的释义（Chapter 1　Interpretation and General

Clauses Ordinance—3 Interpretation of words and expressions）

property（财产）includes—

(a) money, goods, choses in action and land; and

(b) obligations, easements and every description of estate, interest and profit, present or future, vested or contingent, arising out of or incident to property as defined in paragraph (a) of this definition;

11. 《香港法例》第 1 章《释义及通则条例》第 3 条词语和词句的释义（Chapter 1　Interpretation and General Clauses Ordinance—3 Interpretation of words and expressions）

Offices set up by the Central People's Government in the Hong Kong Special Administrative Region（中央人民政府在香港特别行政区设立的机构）means—

(a) the Liaison Office of the Central People's Government in the Hong Kong Special Administrative Region;

(b) the Office of the Commissioner of the Ministry of Foreign Affairs of the People's Republic of China in the Hong Kong Special Administrative Region; and

(c) the Hong Kong Garrison of the Chinese People's Liberation Army; (Added 2 of 2009 s. 2)

12. 《香港法例》第 53 章《古物和纪念物条例》第 2 条释义（Chapter 53　Antiquities and Monuments Ordinance—2 Interpretation）

In this Ordinance, unless the context otherwise requires—

antiquity（古物）means—

(a) a relic; and

(b) a place, building, site or structure erected, formed or built by human agency before the year 1800 and the ruins or remains of any such place, building, site or structure, whether or not the same has been modified, added to or restored after the year 1799;

●汉译英

1. **第二条**　本法所称食品，是指《中华人民共和国食品安全法》规定的食品，包括各种供人食用或者饮用的食物。

　　本法所称食品浪费，是指对可安全食用或者饮用的食品未能按照其功能目的合理利用，包括废弃、因不合理利用导致食品数量减少或者质量下降等。

《中华人民共和国反食品浪费法》（2021 年）

2. **第二条**　本法所称乡村，是指城市建成区以外具有自然、社会、经济特征和生产、生活、生态、文化等多重功能的地域综合体，包括乡镇和村庄等。

《中华人民共和国乡村振兴促进法》（2021 年）

3. **第十七条**　十八周岁以上的自然人为成年人。不满十八周岁的自然人为未成年人。

《中华人民共和国民法典》（2020 年）

4. **第七十六条**　以取得利润并分配给股东等出资人为目的成立的法人，为营利法人。

　　营利法人包括有限责任公司、股份有限公司和其他企业法人等。

《中华人民共和国民法典》（2020 年）

5. **第八十七条** 为公益目的或者其他非营利目的成立，不向出资人、设立人或者会员分配所取得利润的法人，为非营利法人。

非营利法人包括事业单位、社会团体、基金会、社会服务机构等。

《中华人民共和国民法典》（2020 年）

6. **第九十六条** 本节规定的机关法人、农村集体经济组织法人、城镇农村的合作经济组织法人、基层群众性自治组织法人，为特别法人。

《中华人民共和国民法典》（2020 年）

7. **第一百零二条** 非法人组织是不具有法人资格，但是能够依法以自己的名义从事民事活动的组织。

非法人组织包括个人独资企业、合伙企业、不具有法人资格的专业服务机构等。

《中华人民共和国民法典》（2020 年）

8. **第一百三十三条** 民事法律行为是民事主体通过意思表示设立、变更、终止民事法律关系的行为。

《中华人民共和国民法典》（2020 年）

9. **第三百九十四条** 为担保债务的履行，债务人或者第三人不转移财产的占有，将该财产抵押给债权人的，债务人不履行到期债务或者发生当事人约定的实现抵押权的情形，债权人有权就该财产优先受偿。

前款规定的债务人或者第三人为抵押人，债权人为抵押权人，提供担保的财产为抵押财产。

《中华人民共和国民法典》（2020 年）

10. **第九十一条** 本法所称公共财产，是指下列财产：

（一）国有财产；

（二）劳动群众集体所有的财产；

（三）用于扶贫和其他公益事业的社会捐助或者专项基金的财产。

在国家机关、国有公司、企业、集体企业和人民团体管理、使用或者运输中的私人财产，以公共财产论。

《中华人民共和国刑法》（2023 年修正）

11. **第十五条** 应当预见自己的行为可能发生危害社会的结果，因为疏忽大意而没有预见，或者已经预见而轻信能够避免，以致发生这种结果的，是过失犯罪。

《中华人民共和国刑法》（2023 年修正）

12. **第十六条** 行为在客观上虽然造成了损害结果，但是不是出于故意或者过失，而是由于不能抗拒或者不能预见的原因所引起的，不是犯罪。

《中华人民共和国刑法》（2023 年修正）

●宪法翻译的启示 2：定义条款篇

第三编

法律句法编上：

民事实质性条款（英译汉）◆◆

第 5 章
实质性条款的行为模式

概述：权利与义务

在实质性条款中，行为模式这一结构要素表述的是当事人的权利（right）与义务（duty），因此也是法律规范的重心所在。所谓**权利**是指法律规范承认的主体行为的<u>正当性</u>（张恒山，2006: 339），即当事人可以这样行为；而**义务**则指主体按照法律规范的指示作为或不作为的<u>应当性</u>（308），即当事人应当这样行为或者不得这样行为。在英美国家的规定性法律文件中，这种"正当性"与"应当性"通常借助情态动词"may""can""shall"和"must"来体现。译者在处理这些情态助动词时，必须注意其译文的用词应当尽可能保持一致，这也是规定性法律文件一致性风格的要求。

5.1 授予权利（It is authorized that ...）：may (can)

实质性条款授予权利部分内容规定的是当事人可以这样行为，在英美规定性法律文件中常用情态助动词 may 来表述其制定者授予权利的意图。

【例 1】

§2-302 Unconscionable Contract or Clause.

(1) If the court as a matter of law finds the <u>contract</u> or any clause of the contract to have been unconscionable at the time it was made the court *may* refuse to enforce the contract, or it *may* enforce the remainder of the contract without the unconscionable clause, or it *may* so limit the application of any unconscionable clause as to avoid any unconscionable result.

—U.C.C. ARTICLE 2　SALES (2002)

上例节选自《统一商法典——买卖》第 302 条第（1）款。有关该法条的正式评述指出，"本条意在允许法庭直接判断合同或者其某项具体条款是否显失公平"，并就此做出法律上的裁决（美国法学会、美国统一州法委员会，2004: 73）。尽管传统法学理论总是将这类条款视为遵守或者违反具体行为模式引发的法律后果，然而这同样可以理解为允许司法机关在特定条件下行使特定权力。因此，法典制定者选择"may"来实现其意图：列举三种行为方式，授权法院自由裁量。对于"may"的此类用法，我国规定性法律文件中与之相对应的能愿动词是"可以"（孙懿华，2006: 124）。如《中华人民共和国民法典》（2020 年）第二十四条前两款就是用"可以"来表示授权的：

不能辨认或者不能完全辨认自己行为的成年人，其利害关系人或者有关组织，<u>可以</u>向人民法院申请认定该成年人为无民事行为能力人或者限制民事行为能力人。

被人民法院认定为无民事行为能力人或者限制民事行为能力人的，经本人、利害关系人或者有关组织申请，人民法院<u>可以</u>根据其智力、精神健康恢复的状况，认定该成年人恢复为限制民事行为能力人或者完全民事行为能力人。

因此，笔者对【例 1】推荐如下译文。

【推荐译文】

第 2-302 条　显失公平的合同或合同条款

（1）法院依法认定合同或合同的任何条款在该合同订立时就显失公平的，<u>可以</u>拒绝强制执行该合同，或者强制执行该合同显失公平条款以外的其他部分，或者为避免显失公平的结果而限制适用显失公平的合同条款。

当然，权利这一概念有狭义和广义之分：狭义的权利"指人们可以要求他人这样行为或不行为"；而广义的权利还包括特权（privilege），即人们可以不受他人干涉而这样行为或不行为（Walker, 2003: 970）。有的英美法学家认为，在起草规定性法律文件时，"may"只能用于表示特权，而不应用于表示狭义的权利（Haggard, 2004: 419-421）。但细察现行的英美法律与合同文本，我们不难注意到"may"也时常表述狭义的权利。下例通过"may"授予"the buyer（买方）"的权利——可以请求"the seller（卖方）"给付赔偿金，就是狭义的权利。

【例 2】

§2-714　Buyer's Damages for Breach in Regard to Accepted Goods.

(1) Where the buyer has accepted goods and given notification (subsection (3) of Section 2-607) he _may_ recover as damages for any non-conformity of tender the loss resulting in the ordinary course of events from the seller's breach as determined in any manner which is reasonable.

—U.C.C. ARTICLE 2　SALES (2002)

【推荐译文】

第 2-714 条　买方就已接受货物享有的违约赔偿金

（1）买方已经接受货物并通知卖方的[第 2-607 条第（3）款]，<u>可以</u>请求卖方给付不适当履行赔偿金，补偿正常情况下因卖方违约产生的、以任何合理方式确定的损失。

值得特别注意的是，实质性条款中的"may"不全是用于表示"许可（permission）"。依据《布莱克法律辞典》的解释，"may"的法律含义大致如下：

1. To be permitted to　　　　　　　（许可）
2. To be a possibility　　　　　　　（可能）
3. Loosely, is required to; shall; must　（义务）（Garner, 2019: 1172-1173）

如何才能辨别某个具体的"may"是否表示授权呢？笔者以为，只有借助实例分析授权性"may"的表述方式及非授权性"may"的独特性，才能总结出其使用规律。

5.1.1　授权性"may"的表述方式

不言而喻，权利针对的是当事人及其行为，因而，用"may"表示"许可（possibility）"，必须指明被授权"可以这样行为"的主体，或至少应当通过上下文向读者暗示被授权者的身份。根据英语句型的特点，笔者以为，授权性"may"的表述方式大致可分为以下四类。

1. 明示权利主体的主动句式

【例3】

§2-305　Open Price Term.

(3) When a price left to be fixed otherwise than by agreement of the parties fails to be fixed through fault of one party the other *may* at his option treat the contract as cancelled or himself fix a reasonable price.

　　　　　　　　　　　　　　　　—U.C.C. ARTICLE 2　SALES (2002)

【例4】

§2-328　Sale by Auction.

(2) ... Where a bid is made while the hammer is falling in acceptance of a prior bid the auctioneer *may* in his discretion reopen the bidding or declare the goods sold under the bid on which the hammer was falling.

　　　　　　　　　　　　　　　　—U.C.C. ARTICLE 2　SALES (2002)

如【例3】【例4】所示，以权利主体为主语，通过主动句式直接宣告该主体享有的权利，是授权性规范最常见的表述方式。若"may"后面同时使用了类似"at his option"或"in his discretion"这样的短语，那么其自由裁量的含义更是确定无疑。

【推荐译文】

第2-305条　价格待定条款

（3）价格留待由双方当事人协议以外的其他方式确定，却因一方当事人的过错未能确定的，另一方当事人可以自由选择视合同已经撤销或者自行确定一个合理的价格。

【推荐译文】

第2-328条　拍卖

（2）……在拍卖人落槌接受前一竞价时提出竞价的，拍卖人可以自由决定重新开放竞价或者宣布货物已经按照落槌时接受的竞价售出。

2. 明示权利主体的被动句式

【例5】

§2-309 Absence of Specific Time Provisions; Notice of Termination.

(2) Where the contract provides for successive performances but is indefinite in duration <u>it</u> is valid for a reasonable time but unless otherwise agreed <u>*may*</u> be terminated at any time by <u>either party</u>.

—U.C.C. ARTICLE 2   SALES (2002)

有的授权性规范虽然采用被动句式，却又借助"by"引导的介宾结构指明权利主体，如【例5】。翻译这类条文，我们必须注意：中文实质性条款在表示授权时几乎很少使用被动句式。为了更好地体现原文的意图，笔者以为，应当尽可能将之译成主动句式。

【推荐译文】

第2-309条 缺少具体的时间条款；通知终止合同

（2）合同规定连续履行，但没有确定履行期限的，该合同在合理期间内有效，但除双方当事人另有约定外，<u>任何一方当事人</u>都<u>可以</u>随时终止合同。

3. 暗示权利主体的主动句式

【例6】

§2-303 Allocation or Division of Risks.

Where this Article allocates a risk or a burden as between the parties "unless otherwise agreed", <u>the agreement</u> *may* not only shift the allocation but may also divide the risk or burden.

—U.C.C. ARTICLE 2   SALES (2002)

尽管【例6】采用的是主动句式，但其主语并非权利主体，而是无生命的"the agreement（协议）"。笔者以为，该条款中的"the agreement"与前文的"unless otherwise agreed"应当联系起来考察：虽然充当主语的是"the agreement"，然而达成协议的却是当事人。实际上，该条款意在授权当事人以协议方式变更交易风险的划分。因而，此句中的"may"也应译作"可以"。

【推荐译文】

第2-303条 风险的分配或划分

本编在当事人之间分配风险或负担时规定"但当事人另有约定的除外"的，<u>当事人之间的协议</u>不仅<u>可以</u>改变该分配方式，还<u>可以</u>划分上述风险或负担。

4. 暗示权利主体的被动句式

【例7】

§2-202 Final Written Expression: Parol or Extrinsic Evidence.

<u>Terms</u> ... *may* be explained or supplemented: ...

—U.C.C. ARTICLE 2   SALES (2002)

【推荐译文】

第2-309条 最终书面表述：言辞或外部证据

……条款<u>可以</u>由下列事项予以解释或者补充：……

【例 7】这类没有指明权利主体的被动句式用于表述授权性规范，被授权的对象通常就隐含在上下文中。如本款授权的就是有权解释或者补充合同条款的当事人及法院。

由此可见，实质性条款授予权利的方式不外乎两种：或者直接授予当事人某项权利，即允许当事人做出某种行为（第 1、2 类表述方式）；或者间接授予当事人某项权利，即允许某种情况的发生，但该情况的发生同样源于当事人的行为（第 3、4 类表述方式）。因而，译者可以通过判断具体条款是否涉及当事人的行为来推定其中的 may 是否可能表示"许可"。

5.1.2 非授权性"may"的独特性

除授权外，情态助动词"may"还常表示"可能（possibility）"。不过，该用法极少出现于成文法，在合同文本中却是屡见不鲜（陶博，2004: 135）。

【例 8】

3.3 Instructions of the Engineer

The Engineer *may* issue to the Contractor (at any time) instructions and additional or modified Drawings which *may* be necessary for the execution of the Works and the remedying of any defects, all in accordance with the Contract. ...

—Conditions of Contract for Construction

本例节选自合同范本《施工合同条件》，其中第一处"may"用于授权"the Engineer（工程师）"在需要的时候向"the Contractor（承包商）"发出指示及相关图纸。与第二处"may"相比，我们不难发现，后者的逻辑主语并非人，而是关系代词"which"，用于指代无生命的先行词"Drawings"。仔细分析该句的结构及上下文后，笔者以为它表示的只是一种可能的情况，且该情况的出现与当事人的行为没有直接关系；将句中的"may"理解为授权，很难令人信服。因此，将之译成"可能"是合理的。

【推荐译文】

3.3 工程师的指示

工程师可以（在任何时候）根据合同的约定向承包商发出指示及实施工程和修补缺陷可能需要的附加图纸或修正图纸。……

据笔者研究，在限制性关系从句中使用情态助动词"may"，绝大多数情况下都是为了表示可能性。因为权利是实质性条款规定的主要内容之一，文件制定者不应将之置于条文中相对次要的修饰地位，以免误导读者的注意力。当然也有例外。

【例 9】

17.1 Indemnities

The Engineer shall indemnify and hold harmless the Contractor, the Contractor's Personnel, and their respective agents, against and from all claims, damages, losses and expenses (including legal fees and expenses) in respect of (1) ..., and (2) the matters for which liability *may* be excluded from insurance cover, as described in sub-paragraphs (d) (i), (ii) and (iii) of Sub-Clause 18.3 [Insurance against Injury to Persons and Damage to Property].

【推荐译文】

17.1　免责

对于有关下列行为的一切索赔、损害、损失和开支（包括法律费用和开支），**雇主应当免除承包商、承包商人员及其各自代理人的责任**：（1）……；以及（2）**第18.3条[人身伤害险和财产损失险]**（d）项（i）（ii）和（iii）目中规定<u>可以</u>排除在保险责任范围外的各类事项。

此例中的"may"就是用于表示授权，但制定者如此行文显然是有原因的。参阅《施工合同条件》第18.3款的规定：

18.3　Insurance against Injury to Persons and Damages to Property

...

Unless otherwise stated in the Particular Conditions, the insurance specified in this Sub-Clause:

(a) ...

...

(d) *may* however exclude liability to the extent that it arises from:

...

我们不难发现，【例9】中第2目规定的意图在于引用第18.3款的内容作为"the matters"的限定成分。因此，后者才是真正的授权条款，而前者仅为重述罢了。

相反，如果"may"出现在主句中，译者就只能凭借自身的语言能力和法律知识，根据上下文仔细辨别其内涵，审慎处理其译文了。请看下例。

【例10】

3.2　Delegation by the Engineer

The Engineer *may* from time to time assign duties and delegate authority to assistants, and *may* also revoke such assignment or delegation. These assistants *may* include a resident engineer, and/or independent inspectors appointed to inspect and/or test items of Plant and/or Materials. ...

—Conditions of Contract for Construction

【例10】中共有三处使用"may"：前两处显然表示授权——许可权利主体"the Engineer（工程师）"实施"assign""delegate""revoke"等行为；而最后一处则不那么明确，尽管其主语"these assistants（助手）"指的也是人，但动词"include"却并非该人的行为。那么此处"may"到底是用于表明工程师指定助手的可能范围呢？还是用于授权工程师在有限范围内指定助手呢？笔者以为，本项第一句既然规定工程师可以向助手指派任务、托付权力，那么其助手将要承担的职责显然极为重大，不是任何人都可以胜任的。该款第二项还特别规定：

3.2　Delegation by the Engineer

Assistants shall be suitably qualified persons, who are competent to carry out these duties and exercise this authority, and who are fluent in the language for communications defined in Sub-Clause 1.4 [Law and Language].

因此，本项后段意在限制工程师可以指定为其助手的人员范围。

【推荐译文】

3.2　工程师托付

工程师<u>可以</u>随时向其助手指派任务和托付权力，也<u>可以</u>撤销上述指派和托付。上述助手<u>可以</u>包括驻地工程师，和/或被任命为检验和/或试验各项**工程设备**和/或**材料**的独立检查员。……

此外，英美法院也有通过判例将成文法中个别由"may"表示的行为模式理解为强制性义务的情况，其目的在于更好地实现立法者的意图（Garner, 2004: 1000）。某些英联邦的评论甚至认为，法院是在纠正制定法中的错误——立法者在法律文本中应当使用"shall"的地方使用了"may"（陶博, 2004: 130）。

其实，这种情况在我国的立法实践中也曾发生过。如《中华人民共和国婚姻法》（已被纳入《中华人民共和国民法典》）第二十二条：

子女可以随父姓，可以随母姓。

该条款中的"可以"貌似授予父母给子女取名的权利，实际情形却并非如此简单。为了阐明其真实立法意图，全国人民代表大会常务委员会曾于 2014 年 11 月专门做出了关于《中华人民共和国婚姻法》第二十二条的解释："公民原则上应当随父姓或者母姓。"最新颁布实施的《中华人民共和国民法典》（2020 年）第一千零一十五条则直接将之变更为：

自然人<u>应当</u>随父姓或者母姓，但是有下列情形之一的，<u>可以</u>在父姓和母姓之外选取姓氏：……

当然，译者不同于法官，无权擅自判断立法者的真实意图，以免误导读者。除非有确切而又权威的判例作为佐证，否则译者不应随便将"may"等同于"shall"。再者，法律文本强调用词的一致性，其目的是尽可能避免混淆（李克兴、张新红, 2006: 157）。若一部成文法使用"shall"表示义务性行为模式，那么其中的"may"表示同样意思的可能性就很小了。

除"may"以外，偶尔规定性法律文件也会使用"can"表示授权。如《统一商法典——买卖》第 305 条第 1 款。

【例 11】

§2-305　Open Price Term.

(1) The parties if they so intend _can_ conclude a contract for sale even though the price is not settled. ...

——U.C.C. ARTICLE 2　SALES (2002)

就本质而言，该例中的"can"与常用立法语言"may"无甚差别，也表示授权，同样应当译成"可以"。

【推荐译文】

第 2-305 条　价格待定条款

（1）双方当事人愿意的，即使价格未定，也<u>可以</u>订立买卖合同。……

尽管"can"用于规定性法律文件不易引起歧义，然而它终究并非标准的法律语言，因此较为罕见。

5.2 施加义务（It is obliged that ...）

5.2.1 应当这样行为：shall (must)

依据《布莱克法律辞典》的解释，情态助动词"shall"的用法虽然不少，但就起草法律文件的严格标准而言，其含义通常是唯一的：

Has a duty to; more broadly, is required to. ... • This is the mandatory sense that drafters typically intend and that courts typically uphold.（Garner, 2019: 1653）

换言之，"shall"在规定性法律文件中主要用于施加必为性义务，即强制当事人应当这样行为，如【例12】。

【例12】

§2-317 Cumulation and Conflict of Warranties Express or Implied.

Warranties whether express or implied _shall_ be construed as consistent with each other and as cumulative, but if such construction is unreasonable the intention of the parties _shall_ determine which warranty is dominant. In ascertaining that intention the following rules apply: ...

—U.C.C. ARTICLE 2 SALES (2002)

【推荐译文】

第2-317条 明示或默示担保的累加与冲突

无论明示担保还是默示担保，其解释都<u>应当</u>相互一致、彼此累加。但上述解释不合理的，<u>应当</u>根据当事人的意思确定何项担保优先。在查明该意思的过程中，适用下列规定：

……

有些英美法学家认为，合同文本不同于法律文本，使用"will"来表述当事人的必为性义务更为恰当，理由是订立合同的双方当事人处于平等的地位，故任何一方都无权命令另一方作为或者不作为（Haggard, 2004: 413）。据此撰写的合同，其中的"shall"不再具有情态意义，而是单纯地表示将来，译者应当注意区分。

当然，笔者以为，当事人制定合同文本，旨在正式宣布双方协议的内容，任何人都无权单方面变更或者撤销其约定，因而使用命令式的"shall"也是合理的，而事实上也的确越来越普遍。请看下例。

【例13】

17.4 Consequences of Employer's Risks

If and to the extent that any of the risks listed in Sub-Clause 17.3 above results in loss or damage to the Works, Goods or Contractor's Documents, the Contractor _shall_ promptly give notice to the Engineer and _shall_ rectify this loss or damage to the extent required by the Engineer.

—Conditions of Contract for Construction

本例节选自《施工合同条件》第 17.4 款。由于该条各款规定的是风险（risk）与责任（responsibility）（张水波、何伯森，2003: 148），因此合同范本的制定者选择"shall"来施加义务。我国规定性法律文件中与之相对应的能愿动词则是"应当"（孙懿华，2006: 121）。

【推荐译文】

17.4 雇主风险的后果

前文**第 17.3 款**列举的任何风险对**工程、货物**或**承包商文件**造成了损失或损害的，**承包商**应当立即通知**工程师**，并应当在**工程师**要求的范围内弥补该损失或损害。

就表述方式而言，实质性条款中义务部分较之权利部分，除情态助动词有所不同外，并无本质差别：二者强调的都是主体的行为，无论明示还是暗示尽皆如此。读者欲进一步了解，不妨参阅 5.1.1。

此外，规定性法律文件中的"shall"还有一种较为常见的用法，应当引起译者足够的重视：该情态助动词可以用于修辞，使这些法律文件的语气显得更为正式，更具权威性（陶博，2004: 119）。当然在这种情况下，"shall"表述的并非特定主体的义务，不同于我国常用的法律术语"应当"，实际上其在汉语译文中的体现通常不必借助词汇手段。

1. "shall"出现在表示担保或者承诺等的名词性从句之中

很多法律文本，还有合同文本，都制定了担保或者承诺条款。这类条款中用于表述担保或承诺内容的名词性从句如果包含"shall"，那么其修辞作用在于强调担保人或承诺人的决心，而不是向当事人施加义务。

【例 14】

§2-312 **Warranty of Title and Against Infringement; Buyer's Obligation Against Infringement.**

(1) Subject to subsection (2) there is in a contract for sale a <u>warranty</u> by the seller that

(a) the title conveyed *shall* be good, and its transfer rightful; and

(b) ...

—U.C.C. ARTICLE 2 SALES (2002)

【例 14】第（1）款规定的是买卖合同中卖方的法定担保义务。从语言学的角度分析，该款的各项条文实际上是相互并列的同位语从句，与其同位的名词中心词即"warranty（担保）"，所以，法典的制定者使用"shall"表述担保的内容，只是为了彰显担保人的意志。由于汉语并无相应的表达方式，因此笔者以为不必强译。

【推荐译文】

第 2-312 条 所有权担保和无侵权行为担保；买方无侵权行为的义务

（1）在不违反第（2）款规定的条件下，买卖合同中的卖方担保

（a）被转让的所有权完整，所有权的转移合法；且

（b）……

2. "shall"出现在表示享有权利或者负有义务的短语之前

英美规定性法律文件中表示享有权利或负有义务的短语很多，如"have the authority/

jurisdiction/option/power/right of""be at liberty to""be authorized to""be entitled to""have the obligation of""bear/take cost/liability/responsibility for""be obliged to""be liable for" "be responsible for"等。这些短语既可单独使用，也可与"shall"搭配，其作用相当于表述权利与义务的情态助动词。

李克兴与张新红两位学者在讨论实质性条款中"shall"的翻译时提出：如果"shall"与表示享有权利或者负有义务的短语共同使用，那么该情态助动词根本就无须翻译（2006: 168）。笔者以为其原因就在于此时"shall"并非表示义务，只具有修辞性的效果。

【例15】

2.5　Employer's Claims

This amount may be included as a deduction in the Contract Price and Payment Certificates. The Employer *shall* only be entitled to set off against or make any deduction from an amount certified in a Payment certificate, or to otherwise claim against the Contractor, in accordance with this Sub-Clause.

—Conditions of Contract for Construction

该例中"shall"与"be entitled to"相结合。由于"be entitled to"本身表述的就是授权，因而此处"shall"无论如何也不能被理解为义务——它并不强制当事人的任何行为，其作用仅限于凸显法律文件的权威性。所以，笔者认为呆板地将"应当"插入【推荐译文】，实属画蛇添足。因此，笔者在【推荐译文】中将其作省略处理。

【推荐译文】

2.5　雇主的索赔

上述金额可以作为扣减额列入合同价格和付款证书。雇主仅有权根据本款的规定冲销或扣减付款证书确认的金额，或者另行向承包商提出索赔。

3.　"shall"用于宣布某种事实状态为法律规定或合同约定

"shall"渲染法律文件的另一种修辞性用法，在于宣布某种与当事人意思表示无关的事实状态为法律规定或合同约定。

【例16】

3.3　Instructions of the Engineer

... If the Engineer or a delegated assistant:

(a) gives an oral instruction,

(b) receives a written confirmation of the instruction, from (or on behalf of) the Contractor, within two working days after giving the instruction, and

(c) does not reply by issuing a written rejection and/or instruction within two working days after receiving the confirmation,

then the confirmation *shall* constitute the written instruction of the Engineer or delegated assistant (as the case may be).

—Conditions of Contract for Construction

《施工合同条件》第3.3款涉及工程师或其托付的助手如何向承包商发出指示，这也是工程师或其托付的助手管理承包商的重要手段（张水波、何伯森, 2003: 37）。根据该款规定，工程师或其托付的助手签发指示原则上应当采用书面形式；至于口头指示，除非必要不得滥用。

而上例节选部分条文规定的就是在何种条件下口头指示方才构成书面指示。虽然其中也使用了"shall"，却并未向当事人施加任何义务，只为提升法律文件的权威性。所以，笔者推荐以下译文。

【推荐译文】

3.3　工程师的指示

……**工程师**或其托付的助手

（a）发出口头指示，

（b）在发出该指示后的两个工作日内收到**承包商**（或代表**承包商**）发来的对该指示的书面确认，且

（c）在收到该确认后的两个工作日内，未发出书面拒绝和/或指示进行答复的，

那么该确认构成**工程师**或其托付的助手（视情况而定）的书面指示。

需要强调的是，修辞性的"shall"不仅适用于肯定句，在否定句中也很常见。

【例 17】

4.1　Contractor's General Obligations

... Except to the extent specified in the Contract, the Contractor (1) *shall* be responsible for all Contractor's Documents, Temporary Works, and such design of each item of Plant and Materials as is required for the item to be in accordance with the Contract, and (2) *shall not* otherwise be responsible for the design or specification of the Permanent Works.

—Conditions of Contract for Construction

【推荐译文】

4.1　承包商的一般义务

……**承包商**（1）对所有**承包商文件、临时工程**，以及根据合同要求完成的各项**生产设备和材料**的设计负责；且（2）不对其他**永久工程**的设计或规范负责，但合同另有规定的除外。

当然，我们在翻译规定性法律文件的过程中遭遇的实际情况要复杂得多："shall"的几种用法很可能同时出现在某个具体条款中。这就需要译者仔细辨别了，绝不可一概而论。请看【例 18】。

【例 18】

3.2　Delegation by the Engineer

... The assignment, delegation or revocation *shall* be in writing and *shall* not take effect until copies have been received by both Parties.

—Conditions of Contract for Construction

虽然本例只节选了短短一句话，但它的句法结构比较复杂：不仅包含两个并列分句，而且其中后者还内嵌了状语从句。仔细分析这两个分句，我们不难发现，前者虽未使用

当事人作主语，但根据其上下文，该分句意在要求工程师采用书面形式进行指派、托付或者撤销先前的指派、托付，故此处"shall"表示的是义务；而后者则不然——工程师的指派、托付或者撤销何时生效与当事人的意思表示无关，完全取决于合同文本的具体规定，故此处"shall"仅用于修辞。

【推荐译文】

3.2　工程师的托付

……该指派、托付或者撤销应当采用书面形式，而且直到双方**当事人**都收到抄件后方才生效。

不过，"shall"在法律环境中用于修辞与表示义务的二分法不应绝对化，时常两种含义兼而有之。如【例19】。

【例19】

§2-328　Sale by Auction.

(4) ... This subsection *shall not* apply to any bid at a forced sale.

——U.C.C. ARTICLE 2　SALES (2002)

【推荐译文】

第2-328条　拍卖

（4）……本款不（得）适用于强制性销售中的任何竞价。

此外，英美规定性法律文件还常用另一情态助动词"must"来施加义务。不过，"must"较之"shall"语气更为强烈，我国规定性法律文件中与之相对应的能愿动词则是"必须"（孙懿华, 2006: 120）。

【例20】

§2-311　Options and Cooperation Respecting Performance.

(1) ... Any such specification *must* be made in good faith and within limits set by commercial reasonableness.

——U.C.C. ARTICLE 2　SALES (2002)

【推荐译文】

第2-311条　关于履行的选择权与协作义务

（1）……上述任何规定都必须出于善意，且不得超越商业上的合理限度。

应当引起注意的是，"must"在表示义务的同时，有时还用于设置隐含条件（implied condition），相关论述请读者参阅第6章。

5.2.2　不得这样行为：may not (cannot)/shall not

在规定性法律文件中，"may"用于表述可以这样行为，"shall"用于表述应当这样行为，但是这两个情态助动词的否定形式均表示禁为性义务，其内涵几乎没有差别（李克兴、张新红, 2006: 177），绝大多数情况下都可以译成相应的中文法律术语"不得"。

1. "may"的否定形式

授权性情态助动词"may"的否定形式可以表述禁止当事人这样行为，如【例21】。

【例 21】

§2-319　F.O.B and F.A.S. Terms.

(4) Under the term F.O.B vessel or F.A.S. unless otherwise agreed the buyer must make payment against tender of the required documents and the seller *may not* tender *nor* the buyer demand delivery of the goods in substitution for the documents.

—U.C.C. ARTICLE 2　SALES (2002)

【推荐译文】

第 2-319 条　FOB 和 FAS 条款

（4）依据 FOB vessel（船上交货）或 FAS（船边交货）条款，买方必须在卖方按照要求提交单据的同时支付货款；且卖方<u>不得</u>请求买方受领货物，买方也<u>不得</u>请求卖方交付货物，以此替代单据的交付与受领，但当事人另有约定的除外。

从语法角度分析，使用情态助动词"may"表示禁为性义务必须通过助动词的否定（auxiliary negation），也就是说"not"否定的必须是"may"本身，其含义近似"be not allowed to do ..."（夸克等，1998: 1097）。相反，如果"not"针对的是主动词，即主动词的否定（main verb negation），那么其表述的不是禁为性义务，而是不作为的权利，含义近似"be allowed not to do ..."。

【例 22】

2.1　Right of Access to the Site

... The right and possession *may not* be exclusive to the Contractor.

—Conditions of Contract for Construction

【推荐译文】

2.1　现场进入权

……<u>可以不</u>排他性地授予承包商该权利和占有。

当然，"may"的否定形式并非只有"not"一种，其他表示否定意义的短语也可起到同样的作用。

【例 23】

§2-205　Firm Offers.

..., but *in no event may* such period of irrevocability exceed three months; ...

—U.C.C. ARTICLE 2　SALES (2002)

【推荐译文】

第 2-205 条　不可撤销要约

……，但在任何情况下，上述不可撤销的期间<u>不得超过</u> 3 个月；……

正如前文所述，规定性法律文件有时也会使用"can"表示授权，而它的否定形式也可以用于表述禁为性义务。

【例 24】

§2-401　Passing of Title; Reservation for Security; Limited Application of This Section.

(1) Title to goods *cannot* pass under a contract for sale prior to their identification to the

contract (Section 2-501), and unless otherwise explicitly agreed the buyer acquires by their identification a special property as limited by this Act. ...

—U.C.C. ARTICLE 2　SALES (2002)

【推荐译文】

第 2-401 条　所有权的转移；担保权益的保留；本条的有限适用

（1）在货物特定于买卖合同（第 2-501 条）之前，<u>不得</u>依据该合同的约定转移该货物的所有权。该货物的特定化使买方取得了一项受本法规定限制的特殊财产权，但当事人另有明确约定的除外。

2. "shall"的否定形式

表示义务的情态助动词"shall"，其否定形式也可用于表述禁止当事人这样行为，如【例 25】。

【例 25】

4.3　Contractor's Representative

The Contractor *shall not*, without the prior consent of the Engineer, revoke the appointment of the Contractor's Representative or appoint a replacement.

—Conditions of Contract for Construction

【推荐译文】

4.3　承包商代表

……非经**工程师**事先同意，**承包商**<u>不得</u>撤销**承包商代表**的任命或者替换**承包商代表**。

"shall"表示禁为性义务的其他否定形式还有很多，如以下两例。

【例 26】

4.1　Contractor's General Obligations

... <u>No</u> significant alteration to these arrangements and methods *shall* be made without this having previously been notified to the Engineer.

—Conditions of Contract for Construction

【推荐译文】

4.1　承包商的一般义务

……非经事先通知工程师，<u>不得</u>对这些安排和方法做出任何重大改变。

【例 27】

§2-402　Rights of Seller's Creditors Against Sold Goods.

(3) <u>Nothing</u> in this Article *shall* be deemed to impair the rights of creditors of the Seller:

—U.C.C. ARTICLE 2　SALES (2002)

【推荐译文】

第 2-402 条　卖方债权人对已售货物的权利

（3）<u>不得</u>认为本编中的任何规定旨在损害卖方债权人享有的下列权利：

尽管含情态助动词的否定句多有歧义——其否定的既可以是助动词也可以是主动词（夸克等，1998：1097），但对于表示义务的"shall"来说，"应当不这样行为"与"不应当这样行为"并无差别，无须译者过虑。译者应当警惕的是，法律环境下的"shall"也可用于修辞，此时其否定形式表示的不再是禁为性义务，而是为了加强规定性法律文件的权威性。关于这个问题，前文已然述及，此处就不再重复了。

◎思考题◎

1. 如何理解实质性条款行为模式的正当性与应当性？
2. 怎样辨析英文实质性条款中"may"的各类用法？
3. 怎样辨析英文实质性条款中"shall"的各类用法？
4. 怎样辨析英文实质性条款中"may not"的各类用法？
5. 怎样辨析英文实质性条款中"shall not"的各类用法？

第6章
实质性条款的前提条件

◎学习目标◎

1. 比较停止条件与解除条件的法律内涵；

2. 理解表述停止条件的各种英语结构；

3. 掌握停止条件的汉译技巧；

4. 理解表述解除条件的各种英语结构；

5. 掌握解除条件的汉译技巧；

6. 辨析英文实质性条款中表述条件的特殊结构。

6.1　条件分类

前提条件是实质性条款的另一结构要素，其作用在于限定行为模式的适用范围，也就是当事人行使权利或者履行义务必须满足的事实状态（Haggard, 2004: 422），或者说当事人在何种事实状态下才享有权利或者负有义务（刘作翔, 2005: 72）。

6.1.1　积极条件与消极条件

条件要素的内容纷繁复杂，既可能涉及当事人的行为，也可能涉及外部事件。由于其成就与否关系到当事人行为的正当性与应当性，因此学者们将之划分为**积极条件**与**消极条件**：前者即以某事实之<u>发生</u>为条件之成就；而后者则以某事实之<u>不发生</u>为条件之成就。表现在语言上，前者多采用肯定句式；而后者多采用否定句式。如【例1】就十分典型。

【例1】

14.4　Schedule of Payments

If the Contract <u>includes</u> a schedule of payments specifying the installments in which the Contractor Price will be paid, then unless otherwise stated in this schedule:

(a) the installments quoted in this schedule of payments shall be the estimated contract values for the purpose of sub-paragraph (a) of Sub-Clause 14.3 [Application for Interim Payment Certificates];

(b) ...

(c) ...

If the Contract <u>does not include</u> a schedule of payments, the Contractor shall submit non-binding estimates of the payments which he expects to become due during each quarterly period. ...

—Conditions of Contract for Construction

【推荐译文】

14.4 付款计划表

合同<u>包含</u>规定分期支付合同价格数额的付款计划表<u>的</u>，除该付款计划表另行写明外，

（a）该付款计划表所列分期付款额应当是为了施行**第14.3款**[期中付款证书的申请]（a）项而估算的合同价值；

（b）……

（c）……

合同<u>没有包含</u>付款计划表<u>的</u>，**承包商**应当每个季度提交对其预计到期的付款额的估算，但上述估算并无约束力。……

本例由两项规定组成，其中第1项的肯定式"if"状语从句属于积极条件；而第2项的否定式"if"条件状语从句属于消极条件。二者一正一反，相互配合，涵盖了该款所述事项的各种可能性，充分体现了法律语言的严密逻辑。

当然，互为表里的积极条件与消极条件并非必须配合使用。这是译者应当注意的，更不能随意依据某项规定进行逆向推定。

6.1.2 停止条件与解除条件

再究其功能，条件要素又可分为停止条件（condition precedent）与解除条件（condition subsequent）两类：所谓**停止条件**是指决定行为模式的正当性或应当性<u>发生</u>法律效力的条件；所谓**解除条件**是指决定行为模式的正当性或应当性<u>丧失</u>法律效力的条件。

笔者想要特别强调的是，停止条件与解除条件不仅功能有异，其法律后果也迥然不同，特别是在私法领域。大致而言，如果当事人就适用**附停止条件**的实质性条款发生争议，那么应当由<u>享有权利</u>的当事人承担条件已经成就的举证责任；如果当事人就适用**附解除条件**的实质性条款发生争议，那么应当由<u>负有义务</u>的当事人承担条件已经成就的举证责任（Haggard, 2004: 424）。

在此需要说明的是，举证责任通常有行为与结果两层含义：行为意义上的举证责任通常是指按照法律规定或者依据合同约定，举证证明案件事实的责任；而结果意义上的举证责任通常是指负责举证的当事人不能证明案件事实时应当承担的不利后果（齐树洁、王振志，2004: 29）。无论如何，承担举证责任的当事人通常在诉讼中处于劣势。请看以下节选自《施工合同条件》的两个条款。

【例2】

2.1 Right of Access to the Site

If no such time is stated in the Appendix to Tender, the Employer shall give the Contractor right of access to, and possession of, the Site within such times as may be required to enable the Contractor to proceed in accordance with the programme submitted under Sub-Clause 8.3 [Programme].

—Conditions of Contract for Construction

【值得商榷的译文】

2.1　现场进入权

雇主应当在**承包商**根据**第 8.3 款**[**进度计划**]规定的进度计划进行施工所需要的时间内，授予**承包商**进入和占用**现场**的权利，<u>但</u>**投标书附录**中写明了上述时间的<u>除外</u>。

【例 3】

4.3　Contractor's Representative

Unless the Contractor's Representative is named in the Contract, the Contractor shall prior to the Commencement Date, submit to the Engineer for consent the name and particulars of the person the Contractor proposes to appoint as Contractor's Representative. ...

—Conditions of Contract for Construction

【值得商榷的译文】

4.3　承包商代表

合同中没有写明**承包商代表**姓名<u>的</u>，**承包商**应当在**开工日期**前，将其建议任命为**承包商代表**的人员姓名和详细资料提交**工程师**同意。……

比较【例 2】与【例 3】的条件从句，二者规定的内容虽极为相似，但采取的句式却截然不同，这绝非制定者一时兴之所致。

为什么【例 2】将其条件设为"If no such time is stated in the Appendix to Tender"，而不写成"Unless such time is stated in the Appendix to Tender"？原因在于二者的字面意思虽无甚差异，但其法律意义却大相径庭。若按前者规定，则属于停止条件：如果条件成就，雇主应当承担义务；若按后者规定，则属于解除条件：除非条件成就，方解除雇主的义务。因此，一旦发生争议，前者应当由主张享有权利的承包商承担证明条件已经成就的责任；而后者则应当由本来负有义务的雇主承担证明条件已经成就的责任。所以，缔约者为该款规定选择停止条件，旨在将举证责任分配给权利主体（承包商）。

【例 3】则恰恰相反。该条款放弃类似【例 2】的停止条件"If no Contractor's Representative is named in the Contract"，却选择了解除条件"Unless the Contractor's Representative is named in the Contract"。其理由正如前文所述，不过此时缔约者希望将举证责任分配给义务主体（承包商）。

因此，笔者以为，我们在翻译过程中处理条件部分内容，绝不能只求语言流畅，随兴改易停止条件与解除条件的设置。

【推荐译文】

2.1　现场进入权

投标书附录中没有写明上述时间<u>的</u>，**雇主**应当在**承包商**根据**第 8.3 款**[**进度计划**]规定的进度计划进行施工所需要的时间内，授予**承包商**进入和占用**现场**的权利。

【推荐译文】

4.3　承包商代表

承包商应当在**开工日期**前，将其建议任命为**承包商代表**的人员姓名和详细资料提交**工程师**同意，但合同中写明了**承包商代表**姓名的除外。……

鉴于停止条件与解除条件划分的重要性，下文将分别予以深入讨论。

6.2　停止条件

6.2.1　"if"条件

1. "if"引导从句结构

英美规定性法律文件中表述停止条件的结构首推"if"引导的状语从句。

【例 4】

3.4　Replacement of the Engineer

If the Employer intends to replace the Engineer, the Employer shall, not less than 42 days before the intended date of replacement, give notice to the Contractor of the name. ...

——Conditions of Contract for Construction

【推荐译文】

3.4　工程师的替换

雇主打算替换**工程师**的，应当至少在拟替换之日 42 日前通知**承包商**，告知拟替换工程师的姓名。……

如【例 4】，利用"if"从句设定主体行使权利或承担义务的前提，是实质性条款最为常见的表述方式之一。我国规定性法律文件中与之相对应的主要句式是"……的"（刘红婴，2007: 131），不过多重条件的设置除外。在此情况下，必须交替使用"如果……"，才能避免混淆。如《中华人民共和国民法典》（2020 年）第一千零七十九条规定：

人民法院审理离婚案件，应当进行调解；如果感情确已破裂，调解无效的，应当准予离婚。

依据形式逻辑的规则，此类条款意为：如果条件（X）成就，那么总有结果（Y），即 "If X, then Y"。换言之，X 是 Y 的充分条件（sufficient condition）。但是，X 并非 Y 的必要条件（necessary condition）。我们绝不能武断地据此推定 "If no X, then no Y"。也就是说，条件（X）未能成就，并不意味着结果（Y）必然不会发生。若是立法者有意将 X 设定为 Y 的充要条件，则应使用 "only if"（Haggard, 2004: 293）。请看【例 5】。

【例 5】

§2-502　Buyer's Right to Goods on Seller's Insolvency.

(2) If the identification creating his special property has been made by the buyer he acquires the right to recover the goods *only if* they conform to the contract for sale.

——U.C.C. ARTICLE 2　SALES (2002)

【推荐译文】

第 2-502 条　卖方无力清偿债务时买方对货物享有的权利

（2）买方将货物特定化为其特殊财产权的，<u>只有</u>当该货物符合买卖合同约定时才能取得该货物的追索权。

本款中的"only if"从句就是一个典型的充要条件。它不同于"if"引导的状语：只要条件（X）未能成就，那么结果（Y）必然不会发生。

笔者从逻辑学的角度分析实质性条款的停止条件，旨在说明修饰"if"状语的"only"并非仅仅用于强调，而是具有更为深远的法律意义，我们不能随意变更原文的遣词造句。

2. "if"引导短语结构

除从句外，"if"还可用于连接短语。

【例 6】

§2-305　Open Price Term.

(4) ... In such a case the buyer must return any goods already received or *if* unable so to do must pay their reasonable value at the time of delivery and the seller must return any portion of the price paid on account.

——U.C.C. ARTICLE 2　SALES (2002)

【推荐译文】

第 2-305 条　价格待定条款

（4）……在上述情形下，买方必须返还任何已经收到的货物，不能返还<u>的</u>，必须支付该货物交付时的合理价值；卖方必须返还因此收取的任何价款。

【例 7】

§2-606　What Constitutes Acceptance of Goods.

(1) Acceptance of goods occurs when the buyer

(a) ...

(b) ...

(c) does any act inconsistent with the seller's ownership; but if such act is wrongful as against the seller it is an acceptance *only if* ratified by him.

——U.C.C. ARTICLE 2　SALES (2002)

【推荐译文】

第 2-606 条　构成接受货物的情形

（1）下列情形视为接受货物：

（a）……

（b）……

（c）买方实施了任何与卖方的所有权相抵触的行为；但上述行为是不利于卖方的违法行为的，<u>只有</u>经过卖方追认，才视为接受货物。

与之相关的固定搭配中，常见的主要有"if (not) agreed upon ..." "if (not) allowed/provided/specified/stated/stipulated in ..."等。请看下例。

【例 8】

§2-309　Absence of Specific Time Provisions; Notice of Termination.

(1) The time for shipment or delivery or any other action under a contract *if not provided in* this Article or agreed upon shall be a reasonable time.

—U.C.C. ARTICLE 2　SALES (2002)

【推荐译文】

第 2-309 条　没有规定具体时间；终止合同的通知

（1）本编没有规定或当事人没有约定的，应当在合理的时间内依据合同约定装运货物、交付货物或实施其他行为。

6.2.2　"when (whenever)/where (wherever)" 条件

1. "when / where" 引导条件状语结构

英美规定性法律文件还常用"when / where"引导的状语从句来表述停止条件。

【例 9】

§2-505　Seller's Shipment Under Reservation.

(1) *Where* the seller has identified goods to the contract by or before shipment:

(a) his procurement of a negotiable bill of lading to his own order or otherwise reserves in him a security interest in the goods. ...

(b) ...

(2) *When* shipment by the seller with reservation of a security interest is in violation of the contract for sale it constitutes an improper contract for transportation within the preceding section ...

—U.C.C. ARTICLE 2　SALES (2002)

【推荐译文】

第 2-505 条　卖方在保留权益的条件下发运货物

（1）卖方在发运货物时或在发运货物前，已将合同项下的货物特定化的：

（a）卖方取得根据自己或他人指示付款的可流通提单，保留他对该货物享有的担保权益。……

（b）……

（2）卖方在保留担保权益的条件下发运货物违反买卖合同约定的，该发运构成前条规定的不适当运输合同……

【例 9】第 1 款中的"where"从句与第 2 款中的"when"从句均为条件状语。尽管日常英语中，"when (whenever) / where (wherever)"一般用于表述重复出现的条件（夸克等，1998: 1506），但规定性法律文件中的实质性条款大多可以反复适用，因而与"if"从句并无本质差别（李克兴、张新红，2006: 123）。此类从句也可译为"如果……"；但译成"……的"更符合我国规定性法律文件的行文习惯。

2. "whenever / wherever" 引导条件状语结构

相对于 "when / where" 而言，"whenever / wherever" 的语气更为强烈，多译为 "凡"，如【例 10】。

【例 10】

12.1　Works to be Measured

Whenever the Engineer requires any part of the Works to be measured, reasonable notice shall be given to the Contractor's Representative, who shall:

...

Except as otherwise stated in the Contract, *wherever* any Permanent Works are to be measured from records, these shall be prepared by the Engineer. ...

—Conditions of Contract for Construction

【推荐译文】

13.2　待测量工程

凡工程师要求测量工程任何部分的，应当向承包商代表发出合理的通知，而承包商代表应当：

……

凡需要根据记录测量任何永久工程的，应当由工程师准备这些记录，但合同另行写明的除外。……

3. "when / where" 引导其他从句结构

当然，普通英语中 "when" 多表述时间，而 "where" 多表述地点，既可用于状语从句，也可用于定语从句。这在规定性法律文件中也有所体现。

【例 11】

§2-401　Passing of Title; Reservation for Security; Limited Application of This Section.

(3) Unless otherwise explicitly agreed *where* delivery is to be made without moving the goods,

(a) if the seller is to deliver a document of title, title passes at the time *when* and the place *where* he delivers such documents; or

(b) if the goods are at the time of contracting already identified and no documents are to be delivered, title passes at the time and place of contracting.

—U.C.C. ARTICLE 2　SALES (2002)

【推荐译文】

第 2-401 条　所有权的转移；担保权益的保留；本条的有限适用

（3）交付时无须移动货物的，

（a）卖方交付所有权凭证的，所有权于卖方交付上述凭证的时间和地点发生转移；或

（b）货物在订立合同时已经特定化且不交付凭证的，所有权于订立合同的时间和地点发生转移，但当事人另有明确约定的除外。

【例 11】第（3）款（a）项中 "when / where" 引导的都是定语从句，其表述的当然不可能为条件状语，而是为了限定所有权转移的时间和地点，其功能与（b）项中的 "at the time and place of contracting" 没有差别。它不同于句首的 "where delivery is to be made without moving the goods"，后者是典型的条件状语，不可能合理地被解释为对地点的限定。

6.2.3 "must" 条件

此外，英美规定性法律文件还可以暗示方式设置停止条件，其中最常见的就是借用表示义务的情态助动词 "must"。就内容而言，这类隐含条件普遍涉及当事人的行为，而条件之成就与否则影响到该当事人的权利（Haggard, 2004: 425）。

【例 12】

§2-706 Seller's Resale Including Contract for Resale.

(3) Where the resale is at private sale the seller *must* give the buyer reasonable notification of his intention to resell.

—U.C.C. ARTICLE 2 SALES (2002)

上例所引第（3）款规定，表面看来似乎是要求卖方承担特定的必为性义务，然而参阅该条第（1）款规定：

(1) Under the conditions stated in Section 2-703 on seller's remedies, the seller may resell the goods concerned or the undelivered balance thereof ...

我们却发现转售实为卖方享有的救济权利。因此，第（3）款规定只能解释为卖方适用第（1）款规定，私下转售货物时必须满足的前提条件。若卖方无意行使该项权利，也就不必承担相关义务。难怪，有学者称之为 "虚假义务"（陶博，2004: 124）。

这类条款的翻译近似表述必为性行为模式的实质性条款（请参阅第 5 章）。

【推荐译文】

第 2-706 条 卖方转售及转售合同

（3）卖方私下转售货物的，<u>必须给予买方合理的通知</u>，告知其转售的意图。

尽管如此，洞察其与相关条文之间的内在逻辑联系，有助于译者从整体上更深入地领会所译规定性法律文件的精神。

6.3 解除条件

6.3.1 "unless" 条件

1. "unless" 引导从句结构

"unless" 引导的状语从句是英美规定性法律文件中表述解除条件的主要结构：专门用于强调条件的例外性质（夸克等，1998: 1512）。

【例 13】

8.3 Programme

Unless the Engineer, within 21 days after receiving a programme, gives notice to the Contractor stating the extent to which it does not comply with the Contract, the Contractor shall proceed in accordance with the programme, subject to the other obligations under the Contract. ...

—Conditions of Contract for Construction

【推荐译文 1】

8.3 进度计划

除**工程师**在收到进度计划后 21 日内向**承包商**发出通知,指明其中不符合**合同**约定的部分外,**承包商**应当根据该进度计划进行工作,并不得违反**合同**约定的其他义务。……

【推荐译文 2】

8.3 进度计划

承包商应当根据进度计划进行工作,并不得违反**合同**约定的其他义务,但是**工程师**在收到该进度计划后 21 日内向**承包商**发出通知,指明其中不符合**合同**约定部分的除外。……

类似【例 13】的"unless"从句在实质性条款中常用于就例外情形设置解除条件:一旦该条件成就,便解除主体本可行使的权利或本应承担的义务。对于此类条款的翻译,我们必须慎用"除非"。因为,汉语中含该连词的条件句多有歧义,如:

除非明天下雨,我们去游泳。

这句话不仅可以理解为"只要明天不下雨,我们就去游泳",即"除明天下雨外,我们将去游泳";还可以理解为"只有明天下雨,我们才去游泳",即"除非明天下雨,我们才去游泳"。

显然,与"unless"的句法意义完全一致的唯有前者。为免歧义,我们可以将这类条文译成"除……外",即【推荐译文 1】。特别是以解除条件起始,然后列表陈述多项行为模式的实质性条款,多采用此种译文,如【例 16】【例 17】。

不过,我国的规定性法律文件常以例外性但书的形式表述解除条件,如《中华人民共和国民法典》(2020 年)中有关法人分立的条款:

第六十七条 法人分立的,其权利和义务由分立后的法人享有连带债权,承担连带债务,但是债权人和债务人另有约定的除外。

又如《中华人民共和国公司法》(2023 年修订)中有关股东出资方式的规定:

第四十八条 股东可以用货币出资,也可以用实物、知识产权、土地使用权、股权、债权等可以用货币估价并可以依法转让的非货币财产作价出资;但是,法律、行政法规规定不得作为出资的财产除外。

类此行文不胜枚举,因而"unless"也可译成"……,但(是)……的除外",即【推荐译文 2】。这更易为熟悉法律语言的专业人士所接受,尤其是当原文中的"unless"条件出现在句尾时,这种译文更值得推荐。

应当引起译者注意的是,"unless"属于否定词(negation)。如果附加解除条件的实质性条款,其主句采用的也是否定形式,这样的双重否定可以转化为肯定句吗?请看下例。

【例 14】

17.5　**Intellectual and Industrial Property Rights**

... This other party (and its Personnel) shall *not* make any admission which might be prejudicial to the indemnifying Party, *unless* the indemnifying Party failed to take over the conduct of any negotiations, litigation or arbitration upon being requested to do so by such other Party.

—Conditions of Contract for Construction

【值得商榷的译文】

17.5　知识产权和工业产权

……保障方未根据上述另一方当事人的请求，接手任何谈判、诉讼或仲裁事宜<u>的</u>，该另一方当事人（及其人员）应当做出任何可能影响保障方的承认。

【例 14】所引条款采用的是双重否定句式"not ... unless ..."。依据逻辑学原理，命题 P 否定后成为～P，那么～～P≡P。据此而言，似乎原文可以改写为：

This other party (and its Personnel) shall make any admission which might be prejudicial to the indemnifying Party, if the indemnifying Party failed to take over the conduct of any negotiations, litigation or arbitration upon being requested to do so by such other Party.

但这两段文字果真完全等值吗？其实不然。从法律的角度分析，该项"unless"条件的成就，仅仅是解除了承包商的禁为性义务。这不一定就意味着要求承包商必须如此作为，也可能只是授权承包商可以这样作为。由于原合同文本并未就此做出明确约定，译者当然无权妄加揣测。因此，就法律翻译而言，双重否定的处理应当力求保留原文的表达方式，切不可片面追求译文的流畅。

【推荐译文】

17.5　知识产权和工业产权

……该另一方当事人（及其人员）不得做出任何可能损害保障方的承认，<u>但是</u>保障方未根据上述另一方当事人的请求，接手任何谈判、诉讼或仲裁事宜的<u>除外</u>。

2.　"unless"引导短语结构

除从句外，"unless"还可与短语一起使用。

【例 15】

17.1　**Indemnities**

(a) ..., *unless* attributable to any negligence, willful act or breach of the Contract by the Employer, the Employer's Personnel, or any of their respective agents, ...

—Conditions of Contract for Construction

【推荐译文】

17.1　保障

（a）……，<u>但是</u>该损害是由**雇主、雇主人员**或他们各自的任何代理人的任何过失行为、故意行为或违约行为造成的<u>除外</u>；……

比较常见的固定搭配有"unless otherwise agreed""unless otherwise allowed/provided/

specified/stated/stipulated in ..."等。

【例 16】

§2-308   Absence of Specified Place for Delivery.

Unless otherwise agreed

...

—U.C.C. ARTICLE 2   SALES (2002)

【推荐译文】

第 2-308 条   没有规定具体交货地点

除当事人另有约定外：

……

【例 17】

4.4   Subcontractors

... *Unless* otherwise stated in the Particular Conditions:

...

—Conditions of Contract for Construction

【推荐译文】

4.4   分包商

……除专用条件中另行写明外：

……

6.3.2   "except (save)"条件

1. "except"引导状语结构

另一类表述解除条件的状语是由"except"引导的。从语言学的角度分析，它与"unless"（还有现代规定性法律文件中已不太使用的"save"）都可以同时表示例外和条件（夸克等, 1998: 1508）。反映在规定性法律文件中，实质性条款用于设置解除条件的结构即相当于例外性但书。

只是"except"多与短语连用，其结构也较"unless"繁复，如以下三例。

【例 18】

§2-615   Excuse by Failure of Presupposed Conditions.

Except so far as a seller may have assumed a greater obligation and subject to the preceding section on substituted performance:

...

—U.C.C. ARTICLE 2   SALES (2002)

【推荐译文】

第 2-615 条   先决条件未成就时免责

除卖方可能承担了更多的义务且不违反前条有关替代履行的规定外：

……

【例 19】

4.2　Performance Security

The Employer shall not make a claim under the Performance Security, *except* for amounts to which the Employer is entitled under the Contract in the event of:

—Conditions of Contract for Construction

【推荐译文】

4.2　履约担保

雇主不得依据**履约担保**提出索赔，<u>但是</u>在下列情况下**雇主**依据**合同**约定有权取得的金额<u>除外</u>：

【例 20】

7.8　Royalties

(2) the disposal of material from demolitions and excavations and of other surplus material (whether natural or man-made), *except* to the extent that disposal areas within the Site are specified in the Contract.

—Conditions of Contract for Construction

【推荐译文】

7.8　不动产使用费

（2）弃置拆除、开挖的材料和其他剩余材料（无论是天然的还是人造的），<u>但</u>弃置在合同约定的**现场**内弃置区域的<u>除外</u>。

而相关的固定搭配则主要有"except as (is) agreed with ..."及"except as (is) otherwise allowed/provided/specified/stated/stipulated in ..."两种。

【例 21】

3.1　Engineer's Duties and Authority

..., *except* <u>as agreed with</u> the Contractor.

...

Except <u>as otherwise stated in</u> these Conditions:

...

—Conditions of Contract for Construction

【推荐译文】

3.1　工程师的职责和权力

……，<u>但**承包商**同意的除外</u>。

……

<u>除本**条件**中另行写明外</u>：

……

2.　"except that"引导状语结构

尽管如此，"except that"引导的从句却不完全等同于"unless"条件状语，其目的并不在于明确特定行为模式的例外情形，而是为了设置专门的限制；且这类从句多出现在句尾，更近似我国规定性法律文本中的限制性但书，因而一般不宜译成"除……外"，最直接明确的译法是"……，但是……"。

【例22】

11.6　Further Tests

These tests shall be carried out in accordance with the terms applicable to the previous tests, *except that* they shall be carried out at the risk and cost of the Party liable, under Sub-Clause 11.2 [Cost of Remedying Defects], for the cost of the remedial work.

—Conditions of Contract for Construction

如【例22】中"except that"引导的从句，就不应视为单纯的解除条件，而是为了做出限制性规定：应当由特定当事人承担"the risk and cost（风险与费用）"。

翻译该从句的难点在于如何处理其插入语"under Sub-Clause 11.2 [Cost of Remedying Defects]"：它修饰的是整个状语从句呢？还是仅限于"the Party liable"？为此，译者不妨参阅该合同范本第11.2款（11.2　Cost of Remedying Defects）的具体规定：

All work referred to in sub-paragraph (b) of Sub-Clause 11.1 [Completion of Outstanding Work and Remedying Defects] shall be executed at the risk and cost of the Contractor, if and to the extent that the work is attributable to:

(a) any design for which the Contractor is responsible,

(b) Plant, Materials or workmanship not being in accordance with the Contract, or

(c) Failure by the Contractor to comply with any other obligation.

If and to the extent that such work is attributable to any other cause, the Contractor shall be notified promptly by (or on behalf of) the Employer, and Sub-Clause 13.3 [Variation Procedure] shall apply.

显然，该条款规定的是当事人之间应当如何分配修补缺陷的风险与费用，并没有涉及相关试验的问题。由此我们不难判断【例22】中插入语修饰的仅仅是"the Party liable"。

【推荐译文】

11.6　进一步试验

这些试验应当根据先前试验适用的条款进行，<u>但是应当由按照**第11.2款【修补缺陷的费用】**</u>的规定负责支付修补工作费用的一方当事人承担风险与费用。

顺便提一句，法律文件中也有使用 save 来替代 except 的。该词源于法语，其含义及句法功能均类似于"except"，只是现已不太多见（李克兴、张新红，2006: 143）。

6.4　表述条件的其他结构

研究英美实质性条款的前提条件，除上两节中讨论的典型句式外，还有其他表述条件的结构也值得我们重视。

6.4.1　"provided that"

"provided that"引导的从句在普通英语中用得很少，但常见于英美规定性法律文件中（136）。其含义主要有二：位于句首则如同"if"；位于句尾则如同"except that"。

【例 23】

§111　Repeals as evidence of prior effectiveness

No inference shall be raised by the enactment of the Act of March 3, 1933 (ch. 202, 47 Stat. 1431), that the sections of the Revised Statues repealed by such Act were in force or effect at the time of such enactment: *Provided, however, that* any rights or liabilities existing under such repealed sections shall not be affected by their repeal.

—U.S. Code

【推荐译文】

第 111 条　废止作为此前有效的证据

不得根据 1933 年 3 月 3 日制定的**法律**（ch. 202, 47 Stat. 1431），推定修订后的成文法中被上述**法律**废止的条款在上述**法律**制定时有效：**但是**按照被废止的条款享有的权利或承担的责任不受其废止的影响。

尽管"provided that"这类措辞有助于渲染规定性法律文件的专业风格，但现代法律写作通俗平易的要求使得"if"与"except that"的运用更为普遍。

6.4.2　"subject to"

"subject to＋n."是规定性法律文件中常用的英文短语结构，就其本身的含义而言，意为"由……决定的""视……而定的""取决于……的"（陆谷孙，1993: 1874）。但在规定性法律文件中，该短语主要有两种译文：位于句首时，多译成"在不违反……的条件下"；位于句尾时，多译成"不得违反……"。

【例 24】

8.3　Programme

..., *subject to* his other obligations under the Contract. ...

—Conditions of Contract for Construction

【推荐译文】

8.3　进度计划

……，并**不得违反**合同约定的其他义务。……

常见固定搭配如下例所示。

【例 25】

§2-316　Exclusion or Modification of Warranties.

(1) ...; but *subject to* the provisions of this Article on parol or extrinsic evidence ...

(2) *Subject to* subsection (3), ...

—U.C.C. ARTICLE 2　SALES (2002)

【推荐译文】

第 2-316 条　担保的排除或变更

（1）……；但不得违反本编有关口头或外部证据的规定……

（2）在不违反第（3）款规定的条件下，……

6.4.3　"without prejudice to"

"without prejudice to＋*n.*"也是英美规定性法律文件中的常用短语结构。根据《布莱克法律词典》的解释：

Without loss of any rights; in a way that does not harm or cancel the legal rights or privileges of a party.（Garner, 2019: 1919）

该短语位于句首时多译为"在不影响……的情况下"，位于句尾时则多译成"不影响……"。

【例 26】

11.4　Failure to Remedy Defects

(c) ... *Without prejudice to* any other rights, under the Contract or otherwise, ...

—Conditions of Contract for Construction

【推荐译文】

11.4　未能修补缺陷

（c）……在不影响依据合同或其他规定享有的任何其他权利的情况下，……

6.4.4　"notwithstanding"

在此我们有必要提及另一个常见的短语结构，即"notwithstanding＋*n.*"。此短语的内涵与前两类结构恰恰相反：前两类结构实际上意味着其他规定应当优先适用，而该结构则意味着本规定更具优先性。

就翻译而言，该结构的处理与"although""though""even if"等引导的让步状语从句差别甚微，大多可以译为"即使……""尽管……"等（李克兴、张新红，2006: 141）。

【例 27】

7.6　Remedial Work

Notwithstanding any previous test or certification, ...

—Conditions of Contract for Construction

【推荐译文】

7.6　修补工作

即使先前已经过试验或已取得证书，……

常见固定搭配如下例所示。

【例 28】

19.7　Release from Performance under the Law

Notwithstanding any other provision of this Clause, ...

—Conditions of Contract for Construction

【推荐译文】

19.7 按照法律规定免除履行

即使本条有任何其他规定，……

◎常见条件短语结构翻译实践题◎

1. if (not) agreed upon ...

2. if (not) allowed/provided/specified/stated/stipulated in ...

3. unless otherwise agreed/stated in ...

4. except as (is) agreed with .../otherwise allowed/provided/specified/stated/stipulated in ...

5. provided that

6. subject to

7. without prejudice to

8. notwithstanding

◎思考题◎

1. 如何理解停止条件与解除条件的法律意义？

2. 怎样确定英文实质性条款中"when (whenever) / where (wherever)"引导的停止条件？

第7章

实质性条款的复杂长句

◎学习目标◎

1. 理解实质性条款中连接词"and"表示的两种并列关系；

2. 掌握"and"表示结合并列关系与分离并列关系时的汉译技巧；

3. 理解实质性条款中连接词"or"表示的两种并列关系；

4. 掌握"or"表示"排他性"与"包含性"并列关系时的汉译技巧；

5. 理解实质性条款中连接词"but"表示的转折关系；

6. 掌握"but"表示转折关系时的汉译技巧。

由于规定性法律文件涉及现代社会的各个领域，因而很多条款中前提条件、行为模式的设置相对比较复杂，为此常常采用列表的形式。这就牵涉到"and""or""and/or"及"but"等并列连接词（linker）的使用。尽管这些连接词本身大都易于翻译，但值得我们探究的是其所揭示的各个连接部分的内在逻辑关系。

7.1　"and"

英语中表示并列的连接词"and"主要有两种含义："共同（joint）"或"分别（several）"（Haggard, 2004: 259），亦可称之为"结合（combinatory）并列"或"分离（segregatory）并列"（夸克等, 1998: 1314）。两者的差别在于前者的连接部分总是作为一个整体发挥作用，而后者却不具有此类特征。当然，这种歧义性更多地体现于名词短语或其修饰语的并列。至于下文重点讨论的列表式条文则多为分句，因而"and"大都只用于表示结合并列关系。

7.1.1　"and"连接前提条件

就条件而言，"and"通常只表示被连接的多个句子成分结合起来，共同限止特定法律条款的适用范围。

【例1】

8.5　Delays Caused by Authorities

If the following conditions apply, namely:

(a) the Contractor has diligently followed the procedures laid down by the relevant legally constituted public authorities in the Country,

(b) these authorities delay or disrupt the Contractor's work, <u>and</u>

(c) the delay or disruption was Unforeseeable,

Then this delay or disruption will be considered as a cause of delay under sub-paragraph (b) of Sub-Clause 8.4 [Extension of Time for Competition].

—Conditions of Contract for Construction

【推荐译文】

8.5 部门造成的延误

符合下列条件<u>的</u>：

（a）**承包商**已经勤勉地遵守了**工程所在国**依法成立的相关公共部门设置的程序；

（b）这些部门延误或中断了**承包商**的工作；<u>且</u>

（c）该延误或中断**不可预见**，

那么该延误或中断将被视为符合**第 8.4 款**[**竣工时间的延长**]（b）项规定的延误理由。

【例 1】中的"if"状语从句，以同位语的方式并置了三项条件，且末两项条件之间由"and"相连接。与总起式的"If the following conditions apply"联系起来（请比较【例6】的总起句），我们完全可以推断制定者意在表明：必须同时满足所有条件，才可适用该款规定。

此类情况下的"and"多译为"且"，而非"和"或"以及"。这不仅是出于语言通顺方面的考虑，更是因为汉语中的"且"具有递进的意思，恰好反映了原文多个条件层层推进的内涵。相反，"和"与"以及"等则不常用于连接分句（陶博，2004: 307-312）。

当然，英美规定性法律文件中表述必须同时适用的数项条件，还有另一种更为常见的方式，即将这些条件通过几个状语从句直接并列起来，如【例 2】。

【例 2】

8.10 Payment for Plant and Materials in Event of Suspension

The Contractor shall be entitled to payment of the value (as at the date of suspension) of Plant and/or Materials which have not been delivered to Site, <u>*if*</u>:

(a) the work on Plant or delivery of Plant and/or Materials has been suspended for more than 28 days, <u>and</u>

(b) the Contractor has marked the Plant and/or Materials as the Employer's property in accordance with the Engineer's instructions.

—Conditions of Contract for Construction

【推荐译文 1】

8.10 暂停期间生产设备和材料的付款

符合下列条件<u>的</u>，**承包商**有权取得尚未运到现场的**生产设备**和/或**材料**的付款，其数额为上述**生产设备**和/或**材料**（在暂停开始之日）的价值：

（a）暂停**生产设备**的生产或者**生产设备**和/或**材料**的交付超过 28 日；<u>且</u>

（b）**承包商**已经按照**工程师**的指示，将该**生产设备**和/或**材料**标注为**雇主**的财产。

【推荐译文 2】

8.10　暂停期间生产设备和材料的付款

<u>如果</u>

（a）暂停**生产设备**的生产或者**生产设备**和/或**材料**的交付超过 28 日；<u>且</u>

（b）**承包商**已经按照**工程师**的指示，将该**生产设备**和/或**材料**标注为**雇主**的财产，则**承包商**有权得到尚未运到现场的**生产设备**和/或**材料**的付款，其数额为上述**生产设备**和/或**材料**（在暂停开始之日）的价值。

处理此类条款，笔者以为至少有两种模式可资参考：既可构造总起式的"符合下列条件的"作为句首，再将具体条件分列于句尾，即【推荐译文 1】；也可按日常汉语的表述习惯，将条件状语分句置于句首，即【推荐译文 2】。究其含义，两者并无差别，但考虑到中文规定性法律文件的行文习惯，本例前一译文似乎更为妥当。

7.1.2　"and"连接行为模式

行为模式列表中的"and"，多表示数项规定层层递进，如【例 3】。

【例 3】

§2-327　Special Incidents of Sale on Approval and Sale or Return.

(1) …

(2) Under a sale or return <u>unless</u> otherwise agreed

(a) the option to return extends to the whole or any commercial unit of the goods while in substantially their original condition, but must be exercised seasonally; <u>and</u>

(b) the return is at the buyer's risk and expense.

—U.C.C. ARTICLE 2　SALES (2002)

【推荐译文】

第 2-327 条　接受成交买卖和余货退回买卖中的特殊事项

（1）……

（2）在余货退回买卖中，<u>除当事人另有约定外</u>，

（a）退货的选择权扩展至实质上处于原状的全部货物或任何商业单位的货物，但该权利必须及时行使；<u>且</u>

（b）由买方承担退货的风险与费用。

此类"and"与连接并列条件的"and"功能极为相似：表示多项规定同时适用，还隐含着逻辑上的递进关系，自然也应当译为"且"。但有时"and"也用于连接词汇短语，仅表示数项规定简单并列，而无意义上的递进，如【例 4】。

【例 4】

13.6　Daywork

<u>Except for</u> any items for which the Daywork Schedule specifies that payment is not due, the Contractor shall deliver each day to the Engineer accurate statements in duplicate which shall include the following details of the resources used in executing the previous day's work:

(a) the names, occupations and time of Contractor's Personnel,

(b) the identification, type and time of Contractor's Equipment and Temporary Works, <u>and</u>

(c) the Quantities and types of Plant and Materials used.

—Conditions of Contract for Construction

【推荐译文】

13.6　计日工作

除计日工作计划表中指明的任何未到付款期的项目<u>外</u>，**承包商**应当每日向**工程师**提交精确报表一式两份，该报表应当包括前一日实施工作过程中所用各项资源的下列详细信息：

（a）**承包商人员**的姓名、职位和使用时间，

（b）**承包商设备**和**临时工程**的标识、型号和使用时间，<u>以及</u>

（c）所用**生产设备**与**材料**的数量和型号。

本例中"and"连接的是多项名词短语，相互之间并无逻辑上的递进关系，因此，该处"and"不宜译为"且"。笔者以为将之译成"和"或"以及"更忠实于原文。

7.1.3　"and"表示分离并列关系

值得译者注意的还有下例中"and"表示分离并列关系的特殊用法。

【例5】

§2-613　Casualty to Identified Goods.

<u>Where</u> the contract requires for its performance goods identified when the contract is made, and the goods suffer casualty without fault of either party before the risk of loss passes to the buyer, or in a proper case under a "no arrival, no sale" term (Section 2-324) then

(a) <u>if</u> the loss is total the contract is avoided; <u>and</u>

(b) <u>if</u> the loss is partial or the goods have so deteriorated as no longer to conform to the contract the buyer may nevertheless demand inspection and at his option either treat the contract as avoided or accept the goods with due allowance from the contract price for the deterioration or the deficiency in quantity but without further right against the seller.

—U.C.C. ARTICLE 2　SALES (2002)

【推荐译文】

第2-613条　已特定货物的毁损

如果合同要求以订立合同时就已特定的货物为履行标的，且在损失风险转移给买方前，或适用"货不到，不成交"条款的情况下，该货物非因任何一方当事人的过错而遭受毁损，那么：

（a）货物全部毁坏<u>的</u>，合同无效；（<u>而</u>）

（b）货物部分毁坏或货物严重受损以致不符合合同约定<u>的</u>，买方仍可以要求检验，并可以自行选择视合同无效或接受货物。买方接受货物的，卖方应当根据货物变质或数量短少的情况适当降低合同价格，但买方不享有对抗卖方的其他权利。

【例 5】中（a）（b）两项规定的次级条件相互抵触，绝不可能同时成就，而该处 "and" 旨在强调两种截然相反情形之间的对比关系，因此，笔者以为在汉语译文中应当译成 "而"，或者干脆省略。

7.2 "or"

"or" 也是常用于表示并列的英语连接词，含义有二："排他性（exclusive）" 与 "包含性（inclusive）"，但前者是较为一般性的用法（夸克等，1998: 1286）。

7.2.1 "or" 连接前提条件

正如第 6 章所述，"if" 状语多为充分条件，而非必要条件。换言之，多个相互独立的前提条件的成就，可能导致同一行为模式的适用。因此，由 "or" 连接数个条件，表示成就其一，就应适用该条款。这在规定性法律文件中也是屡见不鲜。请看【例 6】。

【例 6】

20.3 Failure to Agree Dispute Adjudication Board

<u>If</u> any of the following conditions apply, namely:

(a) the Parties fail to agree upon the appointment of the sole member of the DAB by the date stated in the first paragraph of Sub-Clause 20.2,

(b) either Party fails to nominate a member (for approval by the other Party) of a DAB of three persons by such date,

(c) the Parties fail to agree upon the appointment of the third member (to act as chairman) of the DAB by such date, <u>or</u>

(d) the Parties fail to agree upon the appointment of a replacement person within 42 days after the date on which the sole member or one of the three members declines to act or is unable to act as a result of death, resignation or termination of appointment,

then the appointing entity or official named in the Appendix to Tender shall, upon the request of either or both of the Parties and after due consultation with both Parties, appoint this member of the DAB. ...

—Conditions of Contract for Construction

【推荐译文】

20.3 未能就争端裁决委员会达成一致意见

符合下列条件之一<u>的</u>：

（a）双方**当事人**未在第 **20.2** 款第一项写明的日期前就 DAB 唯一成员的任命达成一致意见；

（b）任何一方**当事人**未在上述日期前提名 DAB 三位成员中的一人（供另一方**当事人**认可）；

（c）双方**当事人**未在上述日期前就 DAB（将担任主席的）第三位成员的任命达成

一致意见；或

　　（d）在 DAB 的唯一成员或三位成员中的一人拒绝履行职责或者因死亡、辞职或任期届满而不能履行职责之日起 42 日内，双方**当事人**未能就替代人员的任命达成一致意见，那么**投标书附录**中指明的任命机构或官员应当根据任何一方**当事人**或双方**当事人**的请求，与双方**当事人**经过适当协商后，任命该 DAB 成员。……

　　本例与【例 1】不同，尽管其"if"状语从句也以同位语的方式并置了多项条件，然末两项条件之间却由"or"相连接，且该处的总起句为"if any of the following conditions apply"。由此，我们可以断定制定者意在表明：所引文本中的各项条件之间相互排斥，只需成就任何一项，便应适用该款规定。此类情况下的"or"多译为"或"。

　　这是选择停止条件的表述方式之一，而另一种更为常见的方式则如【例 7】所示。

【例 7】

§2-305　Open Price Term.

(1) ... In such a case the price is a reasonable price at the time for delivery <u>if</u>

(a) nothing is said as to price; <u>or</u>

(b) the price is left to be agreed by the parties and they fail to agree; <u>or</u>

(c) the price is to be fixed in terms of some agreed market or other standard as set or recorded by a third person or agency and it is not so set or recorded.

—U.C.C. ARTICLE 2　SALES (2002)

【推荐译文 1】

第 2-305 条　价格待定条款

　　（1）……在上述情况下，符合下列条件之一<u>的</u>，价格为交货时的合理价格：

　　（a）当事人未提到价格；<u>或</u>

　　（b）价格留待当事人协议确定，当事人未达成协议；<u>或</u>

　　（c）价格将根据第三人或机构制定或者记录的某个双方约定的市场或其他标准确定，第三人或机构未能制定或者记录该标准。

【推荐译文 2】

第 2-305 条　价格待定条款

　　（1）……在上述情况下，<u>如果</u>

　　（a）当事人未提到价格；<u>或</u>

　　（b）价格留待当事人协议确定，当事人未达成协议；<u>或</u>

　　（c）价格将根据第三人或机构制定或者记录的某个双方约定的市场或其他标准确定，第三人或机构未能制定或者记录该标准，

则价格为交货时的合理价格。

　　如【例 7】设置的三项条件不仅由"or"相连接，且连接方式不同于前例：除末尾两项条件之间使用了选择词外，第一、第二项条件之间也使用了选择词，其目的当然在于避免歧义：任何一项条件都不是必选的，只要满足其中之一即可适用该款规定。

　　类似于【例 2】，该款也有两种译法。就本例而言，笔者更倾向于前一译文。因为，仔

细分析上述三个条件，我们不难发现它们相互之间是排他性的关系：满足其中任何一个条件，就意味着绝不可能出现其他两种情况。而【推荐译文 1】中总起式的"符合下列条件之一的"，不仅符合我国规定性法律文件的行文习惯，而且使原文的意图更为明确。

但是译者必须注意，如果原文中的"or"是"包容性"的含义，或者很难判断其准确内涵，那么似乎【推荐译文 2】更可取。

此外，数个相互并列的"unless"从句通常只用"or"连接。如【例 8】便是如此。

【例 8】

6.5　Working Hours

No work shall be carried out on the Site on locally recognized days of rest, or outside the normal working hours stated in the Appendix to Tender, <u>unless</u>:

(a) otherwise stated in the Contract,

(b) the Engineer gives consent, <u>or</u>

(c) the work is unavoidable, or necessary for the protection of life or property or for the safety of the Works, in which case the Contractor shall immediately advise the Engineer.

—Conditions of Contract for Construction

【推荐译文 1】

6.5　工作时间

<u>除有下列情形外</u>，当地公认的休息日或**投标附录书**中写明的正常工作时间以外的其他时间不得在**现场**工作：

（a）合同中另行写明；

（b）**工程师**同意；<u>或</u>

（c）该工作是保护生命或财产或者维护**工程**安全所不可避免或必需的。在此情况下，**承包商**应当立即通知**工程师**。

【推荐译文 2】

6.5　工作时间

当地公认的休息日或**投标附录书**中写明的正常工作时间以外的其他时间不得在**现场**工作，<u>但有下列情形的**除外**</u>：

（a）合同中另行写明；

（b）**工程师**同意；<u>或</u>

（c）该工作是保护生命或财产或者维护**工程**安全所不可避免或必需的。在此情况下，**承包商**应当立即通知**工程师**。

本例中的解除条件共包含三项规定，以"or"相连接，只要满足其一，即可适用该法律条款。

翻译这类条款通常也有两种处理方式：既可构造总起式的"除有下列情形外"作为句首，并将具体条件列在句末，即【推荐译文 1】；也可运用转折句式，将之译成"但有下列情形的除外"，随后分列具体条件，即【推荐译文 2】。显然，后者更符合我国规定性法律文件的行文习惯（请参阅第 6 章中的相关内容）。

7.2.2 "or" 连接行为模式

通过"or"连接数个行为模式，则是为当事人提供多种选择的可能性，当然其中某些行为模式的适用，还必须同时满足其他特定的次级条件，如【例9】。

【例9】

9.4 Failure to Pass Tests on Completion

<u>If</u> the Works, or a Section, fail to pass the Tests on Completion repeated under Sub-Clause 9.3 [Retesting], the Engineer shall be entitled to:

(a) order further repetition of Tests on Completion under Sub-Clause 9.3;

(b) <u>if</u> the failure deprives the Employer of substantially the whole benefit of the Works or Section, reject the Works or Section (as the case may be), in which event the Employer shall have the same remedies as are provided in sub-paragraph (c) of Sub-Clause 11.4 [Failure to Remedy Defects]; <u>or</u>

(c) issue a Taking-Over Certificate, <u>if</u> the Employer so requests.

—Conditions of Contract for Construction

【推荐译文】

9.4 未能通过竣工试验

工程或某**部分工程**未通过按照第 **9.3 款**[**重新试验**]的规定重新进行的**竣工试验的**，那么：

（a）**工程师**有权下令按照第 **9.3 款**的规定再次进行**竣工试验**；

（b）如果未通过试验使**雇主**实质上丧失了**工程**或**部分工程**全部利益，**工程师**有权拒收**工程**或**部分工程**（视情况而定）。在此情况下，**雇主**应当采取与第 **11.4 款**[**未能修补缺陷**]（c）项规定相同的补救措施；<u>或</u>

（c）如果**雇主**要求颁发**接收证书**，**工程师**有权颁发该证书。

本例中（b）（c）两项的选择适用，就必须分别以两项条文中专门规定的次级条件的成就为前提。而该处"or"的作用在于强调行为模式的可选择性，不妨将之译成"或"。

而下例则更为复杂。

【例10】

§2-319 F.O.B. and F.A.S. Terms.

(1) <u>Unless</u> otherwise agreed the term F.O.B. (which means "free on board") at a named place, even though used only in connection with the stated price, is a delivery term under which

(a) <u>when</u> the term is F.O.B. the place of shipment, the seller must at that place ship the goods in the manner provided in this Article (Section 2-504) and bear the expense and risk of putting them into the possession of the carrier; <u>or</u>

(b) <u>when</u> the term is F.O.B. the place of destination, the seller must at his own expense and risk transport the goods to that place and there tender delivery of them in the manner provided in this Article (Section 2-503);

(c) <u>when</u> under either (a) or (b) the term is also F.O.B. vessel, car or other vehicle, the seller must in addition at his own expense and risk load the goods on board. ...

——U.C.C. ARTICLE 2　SALES (2002)

【推荐译文】

第 2-319 条　FOB 和 FAS 条款

（1）除当事人另有约定<u>外</u>，指明地点的 FOB 条款（即"运输工具上交货"）即使只在写明价格时使用，也是交货条款。依据该条款：

（a）该条款为 FOB 装运地交货<u>的</u>，卖方必须在该地以本编（**第 2-504 条**）规定的方式装运货物，并承担将货物交由承运人占有的费用与风险；<u>或</u>

（b）该条款为 FOB 目的地交货<u>的</u>，卖方必须自担费用与风险将货物运至该地，并在该地以本编（**第 2-503 条**）规定的方式请求受领货物；

（c）适用（a）项或（b）项规定的同时，该条款还是 FOB 船上、火车上或其他运输工具上交货<u>的</u>，卖方必须自担费用与风险将货物装上轮船、火车或其他运输工具。……

请译者特别注意，上例中的三项条文，其中前两项之间由"or"连接，而后两项之间却没有任何连接词。从语言学的角度分析，制定者的意图很明显：前两项规定只能择其一，第三项规定则为补充，必须与前两项之一协同适用。所以，笔者认为译文中的"或"绝不可省。

7.3　"and/or"

【例 11】

8.6　Rate of Progress

<u>If</u>, at any time:

(a) actual progress is too slow to complete within the Time for Completion, <u>and/or</u>

(b) progress has fallen (or will fall) behind the current programme under Sub-Clause 8.3 [Programme],

other than as a result of a cause listed in Sub-Clause 8.4 [Extension of Time for Completion], then the Engineer may instruct the Contractor to submit, under Sub-Clause 8.3 [Programme], a revised programme and supporting report describing the revised methods which the Contractor proposes to adopt in order to expedite progress and complete within the Time for Completion.

——Conditions of Contract for Construction

【推荐译文】

8.6　工程进度

在任何时候：

（a）实际工程进度过于迟缓，无法在**竣工时间**内完工的；<u>且/或</u>

（b）进度已经（或将要）落后于**第 8.3 款**[**进度计划**]规定的现行进度计划的，

工程师可以指示**承包商**按照**第 8.3 款**[**进度计划**]的规定提交一份经过修改的进度计划及

补充报告，说明**承包商**为加快进度以便在**竣工时间**内完工而建议采用的修改方法，但上述情况是由**第 8.4 款**[**竣工时间的延长**]中列举的某项原因造成的除外。

特别值得译者注意的是"and/or"这种特殊用法。它不同于表示"共同"的"and"：所列数个条件无须同时成就；也不同于表示"排他性"的"or"：所列数个条件可以同时成就。现代规定性法律文件不太使用"and/or"，原因在于"and"与"or"本身就具有歧义，联合使用显然其内涵更为混淆。所以，很多法学家建议使用："... or any combination of these ..."或"... any one or more of the following ..."这类句式来明确表述制定者的意图（陶博，2004: 301-302）。

然而迄今为止，"and/or"这类连接词的使用还是较为普遍，其含义相当于"包含性"的"or"（288）。因此，规定性法律文件中使用了"and/or"作连接词，那么该文件中的"or"一般就只能表示排他性了。本书引为实例的《统一商法典》及《施工合同条件》便是如此。将【例 11】中的"and/or"译成"且/或"，显然可取。

7.4 "but"

列表式条文中的"but"常用于表示转折，相当于汉语中的补充性但书，其含义近似"'and'加'yet'表示的对立"（夸克等，1998: 1289）。请看【例 12】。

【例 12】

§2-509   Risk of Loss in the Absence of Breach.

(1) Where the contract requires or authorizes the seller to ship the goods by carrier

(a) if it does not require him to deliver them at a particular destination, the risk of loss passes to the buyer when the goods are duly delivered to the carrier even though the shipment is under reservation (Section 2-505); but

(b) if it does require him to deliver them at a particular destination and the goods are there duly tendered while in the possession of the carrier, the risk of loss passes to the buyer when the goods are there duly so tendered as to enable the buyer to take delivery.

—U.C.C. ARTICLE 2   SALES (2002)

【推荐译文】

第 2-509 条   无违约情形下的损失风险

（1）合同要求或授权卖方委托承运人发运货物的，

（a）如果合同不要求卖方在特定目的地交付货物，则损失风险于货物适当交付承运人时转移给买方，即使货物是在卖方保留权益的条件下发运的（**第 2-505 条**）；**但是**

（b）如果合同要求卖方在特定目的地交付货物，且承运人占有的货物在该地适当请求受领，则损失风险于货物在该地适当请求受领以便买方接受交付时转移给买方。

所引条款中的两项规定设置的次级条件与【例 5】相似——不可能同时成就。事实上，两者之间的差别仅在于"but"较"and"更强调后一项规定的出乎意料性。笔者以为将其译成"但（是）"即可。

7.5　综合性条款

还有更为复杂的条款：无论前提条件，还是行为模式，都有多项设置。其译文的处理，尤需译者谨慎。

【例13】

§2-311　**Options and Cooperation Respecting Performance.**

(3) <u>Where</u> such specification would materially affect the other party's performance but is not seasonably made <u>or</u> where one party's cooperation is necessary to the agreed performance of the other but is not seasonably forthcoming, the other party in addition to all other remedies

(a) is excused for any resulting delay in his own performance; <u>and</u>

(b) may also either proceed to perform in any reasonable manner or after the time for a material part of his own performance treat the failure to specify or to cooperate as a breach by failure to deliver or accept the goods.

—U.C.C. ARTICLE 2　SALES (2002)

【推荐译文】

第2-311条　关于履行的选择权与协助

（3）上述细节将实质性影响另一方当事人履约却没有及时明确<u>的</u>或一方当事人的协助是另一方当事人履约所必须却没有及时提供<u>的</u>，另一方当事人除其他救济外<u>还享有下列权利</u>：

（a）对因此导致的任何迟延履行免责；<u>且</u>

（b）还可以任何合理的方式继续履行，或在其实质部分义务的履行期限过后，将未明确的细节或未提供的协助视为没有交付或接受货物造成的违约。

本例的前提条件由"or"连接的两个并列的"where"状语从句构成；而行为模式部分则包括"and"连接的两项权利。显然，原法律文件的制定者意图表明成就任何一项前提条件，就应授予相关当事人全部两项权利。

总之，译者在着手处理此类复杂冗长的综合性条款前，必须厘清其内在逻辑关系，方能通过译文准确传递原文本的全部信息。

◎思考题◎

1. "and"作为连接词可以表示哪些关系，各有什么特点？如何区分？

2. "and"表示结合并列关系与分离并列关系的法律内涵有什么差别？

3. "or"作为连接词可以表示哪些关系，各有什么特点？如何区分？

4. "or"表示排他并列关系与包含并列关系的法律内涵有什么差别？

5. "but"作为连接词可以表示哪些关系，各有什么特点？如何区分？

6. "but"引导的分句与我国法律文件中的但书之间有什么相同点和不同点？

◆第三编翻译实践练习

●英译汉

1. Objection to Nomination

The Contractor shall not be under any obligation to employ a nominated Subcontractor against whom the Contractor raises reasonable objection by notice to the Engineer as soon as practicable, with supporting particulars. An objection shall be deemed reasonable if it arises from (among other things) any of the following matters, unless the Employ agrees to indemnify the Contractor against and from the consequences of the matter:

(a) there are reasons to believe that the Subcontractor does not have sufficient competence, resources or financial strength;

(b) the subcontract does not specify that the nominated Subcontractor shall indemnify the Contractor against and from any negligence or misuse of Goods by the nominated Subcontractor, his agents and employees; or

(c) the subcontract does not specify that, for the subcontracted work (including design, if any), the nominated Subcontractor shall:

　(i) undertake to the Contractor such obligations and liabilities as will enable the Contractor to discharge his obligations and liabilities under the Contract, and

　(ii) indemnify the Contractor against and from all obligations and liabilities arising under or in connection with the Contract and from the consequences of any failure by the Subcontractor to perform these obligations or to fulfill these liabilities.

2. Payments to Nominated Subcontractors

The Contractor shall pay to the nominated Subcontractor the amounts which the Engineer certifies to be due in accordance with the subcontract. These amounts plus other charges shall be included in the Contractor Price in accordance with subparagraph (b) of Sub-Clause 13.5 [Provisional Sums], except as stated in Sub-Clause 5.4 [Evidence of Payments].

3. Evidence of Payments

Before issuing a Payment Certificate which includes an amount payable to a nominated Subcontractor, the Engineer may request the Contractor to supply reasonable evidence that the nominated Subcontractor has received all amounts due in accordance with previous Payment Certificates, less applicable deductions for retention or otherwise. Unless the Contractor:

(a) submits this reasonable evidence to the Engineer, or

(b) (i) satisfies the Engineer in writing that the Contractor is reasonably entitled to withhold or refuse to pay these amounts, and

　(ii) submits to the Engineer reasonable evidence that the nominated Subcontractor has been notified of the Contractor's entitlement, then the Employer may (at his sole discretion) pay, direct to the nominated Subcontractor, part or all of such amounts previously certified (less applicable deductions) as are due to the nominated Subcontractor and for which the Contractor has failed to submit the evidence described in sub-paragraphs (a) or (b) above. The Contractor shall then repay, to the Employ, the amount which the nominated Sub-contractor was directly paid by the Employer.

4. Taking Over of the Works and Sections

The Engineer shall, within 28 days after receiving the Contractor's application:

(a) issue the Taking-Over Certificate to the Contractor, stating the date on which the Works or Section were completed in accordance with the Contract, except for any minor outstanding work and defects which will not substantially affect the use of the Works or Section for their intended purpose (either until or whilst this work is completed and these defects are remedied); or

(b) reject the application, giving reasons and specifying the work required to be done by the Contractor to enable the Taking-Over Certificate to be issued. The Contractor shall then complete this work before issuing a further notice under this Sub-Clause.

If the Engineer fails either to issue the Taking-Over Certificate or to reject the Contractor's application within the period of 28 days, and if the Works or Section (as the case may be) are substantially in accordance with the Contract, the Taking-Over Certificate shall be deemed to have been issued on the last day of that period.

5. Taking Over of Parts of the Works

The Employer shall not use any part of the Works (other than as a temporary measure which is either specified in the Contract or agreed by both Parties) unless and until the Engineer has issued a Taking-Over Certificate for this part. However, if the Employer does any part of the Works before the Taking-Over Certificate is issued:

(a) the part which is used shall be deemed to have been taken over as from the date on which it is used,

(b) the Contractor shall cease to be liable for the care of such part as from this date, when responsibilities shall pass to the Employer, and

(c) if requested by the Contractor, the Engineer shall issue a Taking-Over Certificate for this part.

6. Interference with Tests on Completion

If the Contractor suffers delay and/or incurs Cost as a result of this delay in carrying out the Tests on Completion, the Contractor shall give notice to the Engineer and shall be entitled subject to Sub-Clause 20.1 [Contractor's Claims] to:

(a) an extension of time for any such delay, if completion is or will be delayed, under Sub-Clause 8.4 [Extension of Time for Completion], and

(b) payment of any such Cost plus reasonable profit, which shall be included in the Contract Price.

7. Termination by Employer

The Employer shall be entitled to terminate the Contractor if the Contractor:

(a) fails to comply with Sub-Clause 4.2 [Performance Security] or with a notice under Sub-Clause 15.1 [Notice to Correct],

(b) abandons the Works or otherwise plainly demonstrates the intention not to continue performance of his obligations under the Contract,

(c) without reasonable excuse fails:

(i) to proceed with the Works in accordance with Clause 8 [Commencement, Delays and Suspension], or

(ii) to comply with a notice issued under Sub-Clause 7.5 [Rejection] or Sub-Clause 7.6 [Remedial Work], within 28 days after receiving it,

(d) subcontracts the whole of the Works or assigns the Contract without the required agreement,

(e) becomes bankrupt or insolvent, goes into liquidation, has a receiving or administration order made against him, compounds with his creditors, or carries on business under a receiver, trustee or manager for the benefit of his creditors, or if any act is done or event occurs which (under applicable Laws) has a similar effect to any of these acts or events, or

(f) gives or offers to give (directly or indirectly) to any person any bribe, gift, gratuity, commission or other thing of value, as an inducement or reward:

(i) for doing or forbearing to do any action in relation to the Contract, or

(ii) for showing or forbearing to show favor or disfavor to any person in relation to the Contract,

or if any of the Contractor's Personnel, agents or Subcontractors gives or offers to give (directly or indirectly) to any person any such inducement or reward as is described in this sub-paragraph (f). However, lawful inducements and rewards to Contractor's Personnel shall not entitle termination.

8. Payment after Termination

After a notice of termination under Sub-Clause 15.2 [Termination by Employer] has taken effect, the Employer may:

(a) proceed in accordance with Sub-Clause 2.5 [Employer's Claims],

(b) withhold further payments to the Contractor until the costs of execution, completion and remedying of any defects, damages for delay in completion (if any), and all other costs incurred by the Employer, have been established and/or

(c) recover from the Contractor any losses and damages incurred by the Employer and any extra costs of completing the Works, after allowing for any sum due to the Contractor under Sub-Clause 15.3 [Valuation at Date of Termination]. After recovering any such losses, damages and extra costs, the Employer shall pay any balance to the Contractor.

第四编

法律句法编下：

刑事实质性条款（汉译英）◆◆

第 8 章
犯罪的客观方面：罪体

◎学习目标◎

1. 掌握行为犯法条的汉语表述结构及其英译句法；

2. 掌握危险犯法条的汉语表述结构及其英译句法；

3. 掌握情节犯法条的汉语表述结构及其英译句法；

4. 掌握数额/数量犯法条的汉语表述结构及其英译句法；

5. 掌握结果犯法条的汉语表述结构及其英译句法。

《中华人民共和国刑法》的实质性条款主要出现在分则部分。所谓刑法分则（specific provisions），是关于具体犯罪及其法定刑的规范体系（陈兴良，2001：10）。我国刑法典的分则编总计规定了十类犯罪。当然，这是依据犯罪的同类客体进行划分的结果，而犯罪客体是指刑法所保护却为犯罪所侵害的特定社会关系。它并不直接体现于具体条文，故对我们讨论规定性法律文件的翻译技巧助益有限。笔者以为，我们应当先从犯罪的客观方面入手展开研究，因为刑法分则各条款之间变化最为繁复的内容就是具体犯罪的外在表现形式即罪体。脱离罪体，我们就无法限定犯罪的范围并使之与其他犯罪相区别（226-227）。据此，犯罪可分为行为犯、危险犯、情节犯、数额犯/数量犯及结果犯。

8.1 行为犯

所谓<u>行为犯</u>，是指以法定行为作犯罪构成必备要件的犯罪，只要实施了该行为，犯罪即告成立，至于其危害结果则在所不问。请看【例 1】。

【例 1】

　　第二百零二条　以暴力、威胁方法<u>拒不缴纳税款的</u>，处三年以下有期徒刑或者拘役，并处拒缴税款一倍以上五倍以下罚金；<u>情节严重的</u>，处三年以上七年以下有期徒刑，并处拒缴税款一倍以上五倍以下罚金。

　　【对照译文】

Article 202 Whoever <u>refuses to pay taxes</u> by means of violence or threat shall be sentenced to fixed-term imprisonment of not more than three years or criminal detention and shall also be fined not less than one time but not more than five times the amount he refuses to pay; if the circumstances are serious, he shall be sentenced to fixed-term imprisonment of not less than three years but not more than seven years and shall also be fined not less than one time but not more than five times the amount he refuses to pay.

【例1】所引抗税罪的前段就是典型的行为犯：只要行为人实施了"以暴力、威胁方法拒不缴纳税款的"行为即构成此罪，并不涉及行为的危害结果。至于该款后段则补充设置"情节严重的"要件构成情节加重犯。

我们应当注意的是，前段有关实行行为的规定为二者的共同构成要件，但后段有关情节的规定仅为派生的犯罪构成要件，故笔者认为，译文应当将情节要件以条件状语从句的形式后置于主句，方可将主语相同的前后两段条文更好地融为一体。

【推荐译文】

Section 202 Whoever refuses to pay taxes by means of violence or threat shall be sentenced to pay a fine not less than one time nor more than five times the amount of taxes that he refuses to pay in addition to a sentence of imprisonment for a term not more than three years; or shall be sentenced to pay a fine not less than one time nor more than five times the amount of taxes that he refuses to pay in addition to a sentence of imprisonment for a term not less than three years nor more than seven years, if the circumstances thereof are serious.

与此类似的是，有些结果犯的条款行文也未明言其结果，如【例2】。

【例2】

第二百三十四条　故意伤害他人身体的，处三年以下有期徒刑、拘役或者管制。

犯前款罪，致人重伤的，处三年以上十年以下有期徒刑；致人死亡或者以特别残忍手段致人重伤造成严重残疾的，处十年以上有期徒刑、无期徒刑或者死刑。本法另有规定的，依照规定。

【对照译文】

Article 234 Whoever intentionally inflicts injury upon another person shall be sentenced to fixed-term imprisonment of not more than three years, criminal detention or public surveillance.

Whoever commits the crime mentioned in the preceding paragraph, thus causing severe injury to another person, shall be sentenced to fixed-term imprisonment of not less than three years but not more than 10 years; if he causes death to the person or, by resorting to especially cruel means, causes severe injury to the person, reducing the person to utter disability, he shall be sentenced to fixed-term imprisonment of not less than 10 years, life imprisonment or death, except as otherwise specifically provided in this Law.

该例第一款规定的是故意伤害罪的普通构成要件，尽管其文字止于行为，但他人因此受到伤害的结果为该罪既遂所必需，故属结果犯。至于第二款则补充了两类结果加重犯的派生构成要件，分别为"致人重伤的"与"致人死亡或者以特别残忍手段致人重伤造成严重残疾的"。由于"致人重伤的"仅为第一句前段的要件，"致人死亡或者以特别残忍手段致人重伤造成严重残疾的"仅为第一句后段的要件，故译文将之分别后置以避免歧义；而该款第二句的例外性规定针对的是整个第一句，只有前置才能明确其适用范围。

【推荐译文】

Section 234　<u>Whoever intentionally injures another person's body</u> shall be sentenced to imprisonment for a term not more than three years, criminal detention or public surveillance.

<u>Except as otherwise specifically provided in this Law</u>, whoever commits against another person the crime described in the preceding paragraph shall be sentenced to imprisonment for a term not less than three years nor more than ten years, <u>if serious bodily injury is thus caused to such person</u>; or shall be sentenced to imprisonment for a term not less than ten years, life imprisonment or death, <u>if death is thus caused to such person or serious bodily injury is thus caused by especially cruel means which reduces such person to utter disability</u>.

8.2　危险犯

所谓**危险犯**，是指以达到特定的危险状态作为构成要件的犯罪。刑法上的危险相对于实害而言只是一种可能性。尽管如此，危害结果的出现与否虽不影响定罪，却大抵具有量刑意义，故我国刑法典通常采取危险犯与其派生的实害犯相对应的立法模式。

8.2.1　同款表述危险犯与其派生的实害犯

【例3】

第一百二十三条　对飞行中的航空器上的人员使用暴力，<u>危及飞行安全</u>，<u>尚未造成严重后果的</u>，处五年以下有期徒刑或者拘役；<u>造成严重后果的</u>，处五年以上有期徒刑。

【对照译文】

Article 123　Whoever uses violence against any person on board an aircraft and <u>thereby endangers air safety</u>, <u>if there are no serious consequences</u>, shall be sentenced to fixed-term imprisonment of not more than five years or criminal detention; <u>if there are serious consequences</u>, he shall be sentenced to fixed-term imprisonment of not less than five years.

【例3】所引条款规定的是暴力危及飞行安全罪。该行为以"危及飞行安全"作为其构成犯罪所必须达到的危险状态，故属于典型的危险犯；而此条款中"尚未造成严重后果的"（即构成危险犯）与"造成严重后果的"（派生为实害犯）规定只是法院据以确定量刑档次的前提条件。

参照《美国模范刑法典》第220.2条（SECTION 220.2　CAUSING OR RISING CATASTROPHE）第（1）款：

(1) CAUSING CATASTROPHE. A person who causes a catastrophe by explosion, fire, flood, avalanche, collapse of building, release of poison gas, radioactive material or other harmful or destructive force or substance, or by any other means of causing potentially widespread injury or damage, commits a felony of the second degree if he does so purposely or knowingly, or a felony of the third degree if he does so recklessly.

笔者以为，本例的译文亦可调整如下。

【推荐译文】

Section 123　Whoever <u>endangers air safety</u> by means of violence against any person on board an aircraft in flight shall be sentenced to imprisonment for a term not more than five years or criminal detention, <u>if no serious consequences are thus caused</u>; or shall be sentenced to imprisonment for a term not less than five years, <u>if serious consequences are thus caused</u>.

值得注意的是前例中规定的危险状态仅是该行为构成犯罪的共同要件，而有些条款中的危险状态却同时影响量刑幅度，直接与加重结果相对应，如【例4】。

【例4】

　　第一百四十五条　生产不符合保障人体健康的国家标准、行业标准的医疗器械、医用卫生材料，或者销售明知是不符合保障人体健康的国家标准、行业标准的医疗器械、医用卫生材料，足以严重危害人体健康的，处三年以下有期徒刑或者拘役，并处销售金额百分之五十以上二倍以下罚金；对人体健康造成严重危害的，处三年以上十年以下有期徒刑，并处销售金额百分之五十以上二倍以下罚金；后果特别严重的，处十年以上有期徒刑或者无期徒刑，并处销售金额百分之五十以上二倍以下罚金或者没收财产。

【对照译文】

Article 145　Whoever produces medical apparatuses and instruments or medical hygiene materials that are not up to the national or industrial standards for safeguarding human health or sells such things while clearly knowing the fact, and <u>if it is serious enough to endanger human health</u>, shall be sentenced to fixed-term imprisonment of not more than three years or limited incarceration and shall also be fined not less than half but not more than two times the sales revenue; <u>if it causes serious harm to human health</u>, he shall be sentenced to fixed-term imprisonment of not less than three years but not more than 10 years and shall also be fined not less than half but not more than two times the sales revenue; <u>if the consequence is especially serious</u>, he shall be sentenced to fixed-term imprisonment of not less than 10 years or life imprisonment, and shall also be fined not less than half but not more than two times the sales revenue or be sentenced to confiscation of property.

本例规定的是生产、销售不符合标准的医用器材罪。其中，"足以严重危害人体健康的"既是"生产、销售不符合标准的医用器材"行为构成犯罪的要件，同时又与"对人体健康造成严重危害的""后果特别严重的"分别充当法院确定量刑档次的依据，因此，笔者以为，【推荐译文】后置结构相似的条件分句，较之【对照译文】更能体现三项要件在逻辑上的对应性。

【推荐译文】

Section 145　Whoever produces medical apparatuses and instruments or medical hygiene materials that are not up to the national or industrial standards for safeguarding human health or whoever sells such things with knowledge that they are not up to the national or industrial standards for safeguarding human health shall be sentence to pay a fine not less than half nor more than two times the amount of sales only or in addition to a sentence of imprisonment for a term not more than three years or criminal detention, <u>if it seriously endangers human health;</u> or shall be sentenced to pay a fine not less than half nor more than two times the amount of sales in addition to a sentence of imprisonment for a term not less than three years nor more than ten years, <u>if it causes serious harm to human health;</u> or shall be sentenced to pay a fine not less than half nor more than two times the amount of sales or be sentenced to confiscation of property, in addition to a sentence of imprisonment for a term not less than ten years or life imprisonment, <u>if the consequences thus caused are especially serious.</u>

8.2.2　异款表述危险犯与其派生的实害犯

当然，危险犯与其派生的实害犯也可通过不同条款分别表述，如以下两例。

【例5】

第一百一十四条　放火、决水、爆炸以及投放毒害性、放射性、传染病病原体等物质或者以其他危险方法危害公共安全，<u>尚未造成严重后果的</u>，处三年以上十年以下有期徒刑。

【例6】

第一百一十五条　放火、决水、爆炸以及投放毒害性、放射性、传染病病原体等物质或者以其他危险方法<u>致人重伤、死亡或者使公私财产遭受重大损失的</u>，处十年以上有期徒刑、无期徒刑或者死刑。

前引条款共涉及五项犯罪：放火罪、决水罪、爆炸罪、投放危险物质罪、以危险方法危害公共安全罪。其中，【例5】为危险犯；而【例6】则为其派生的实害犯。

我国刑法典为简化条文，将五项犯罪合并规定，其差异仅体现于犯罪的行为方式，而作为构成要件的危险状态与危害结果却是一致的。且罪名相同的危险犯与其派生的实害犯虽在语言上具有相似性，但异款表述的形式使译文得以更为自由地展开。

【推荐译文】

Section 114　Whoever <u>endangers public security</u> by fire, flood, explosion, spread of poisonous or radioactive material, infectious disease pathogens or other substance, or by other dangerous means, shall be sentenced to imprisonment for a term not less than three years nor more than ten years <u>if no serious consequences are thus caused.</u>

【推荐译文】

Section 115　Whoever <u>causes serious injury or death to human or heavy losses to public or private property</u> by fire, flood, explosion, spread of poisonous or radioactive material, infectious disease pathogens or other substance, or by other dangerous means, shall be sentenced to imprisonment for a term not less than ten years, life imprisonment or death.

8.2.3　具体危险犯与抽象危险犯

在法理上，危险犯可分为具体危险犯与抽象危险犯两类。对具体危险犯而言，其行为的具体危险状态属于犯罪的构成要件，需要法院认定，如上述数例；对抽象危险犯而言，其行为的抽象危险状态并非犯罪的构成要件，无须法院认定，如【例7】。但在立法上，我国刑法典对危险要件所作的规定是概括性的（赵秉志，2004：88），其语言表述没有任何差别。

【例7】

　　第一百一十条　有下列间谍行为之一，<u>危害国家安全的</u>，处十年以上有期徒刑或者无期徒刑；情节较轻的，处三年以上十年以下有期徒刑：

　　（一）参加间谍组织或者接受间谍组织及其代理人的任务的；

　　（二）为敌人指示轰击目标的。

　　本例所引条款规定的间谍罪就是抽象危险犯。由于此类犯罪行为本身就包含严重侵害法益的可能性，因而只需符合构成要件的危害行为存在即成立犯罪（陈兴良，2001：275）。当然，究其行文，与规定具体危险犯的条款并无差别，故通常情况下可以等同处理。

【推荐译文】

Section 110　Whoever <u>endangers the security of the People's Republic of China</u> by

(1) joining an espionage organization or accepting a mission assigned by or on behalf of such organization; or

(2) directing enemies to bomb or shell a target,

shall be sentenced to imprisonment for a term not less than ten years or life imprisonment; or shall be sentenced to imprisonment for a term not less than three years nor more than ten years if the circumstances thereof are minor.

8.3　情节犯

　　所谓**情节犯**，是指以特定严重或恶劣的情节作为构成要件的犯罪。请看【例8】。

【例8】

　　第二百六十条　虐待家庭成员，<u>情节恶劣的</u>，处二年以下有期徒刑、拘役或者管制。

　　【例8】规定的虐待罪便是情节犯。此类犯罪中的"情节"是指共同构成要件以外影响定罪的一系列主客观事实情状，即定罪情节（393）。虽因其涉及定罪而必须由刑法明文规定，但鉴于其在各种犯罪中的表现不同，分则条款只能以"情节"这个概念加以涵括。

　　依据《布莱克法律词典》的定义：

Aggravating circumstance: 1. A fact or situation that increases the degree of liability or culpability for a criminal act.

Mitigating circumstance: 1. A fact or situation that does not justify or excuse a wrongful act or offense but that reduces the degree of culpability ...（Garner, 2019: 306）

可见英美法中的"aggravating circumstance""mitigating circumstance"分别对应我国刑法术语"加重情节""减轻情节"，因此，笔者以为"情节"亦可译成"circumstance"。

【推荐译文】

Section 260　Whoever maltreats a member of his family shall be sentenced to imprisonment for a term not more than two years, criminal detention or public surveillance, <u>if the circumstances thereof are flagrant</u>.

尽管有时犯罪与刑罚具有单一的对等关系（如前例），但定罪情节的存在是以罪刑阶梯的立法方式为前提的（陈兴良，2001: 394），所以我国刑法典中规定情节犯的条文多数针对同一犯罪在情节严重程度上的差别，并分置了相应的法定刑。请看【例9】。

【例9】

第二百四十九条　煽动民族仇恨、民族歧视，<u>情节严重的</u>，处三年以下有期徒刑、拘役、管制或者剥夺政治权利；<u>情节特别严重的</u>，处三年以上十年以下有期徒刑。

【对照译文】

Article 249　Whoever incites national enmity or discrimination, <u>if the circumstances thereof are serious</u>, shall be sentenced to fixed-term imprisonment of not more than three years, criminal detention, public surveillance or deprivation of political rights; <u>if the circumstances thereof are especially serious</u>, he shall be sentenced to fixed-term imprisonment of not less than three years but not more than ten years.

该例所引条款规定的是煽动民族仇恨、民族歧视罪。为突显原文体现的罪刑均衡原则，笔者主张译文应当将条款中影响量刑幅度的情节要件后置。

【推荐译文】

Section 249　Whoever incites national enmity or discrimination shall be sentenced to imprisonment for a term not more than three years, criminal detention, public surveillance or deprivation of political rights, <u>if the circumstances thereof are serious</u>; or shall be sentenced to imprisonment for a term not less than three years nor more than ten years, <u>if the circumstances thereof are especially serious</u>.

此外，我国刑法典中尚有一类情节减轻犯/情节加重犯：犯罪情节虽非其普通犯罪构成的要件，却是法院减轻或者加重处罚的派生要件，本章【例1】便是如此。再请看【例10】。

【例10】

第一百五十一条　……

走私国家禁止出口的文物、黄金、白银和其他贵重金属或者国家禁止进出口的珍贵动物及其制品的，处五年以上十年以下有期徒刑，并处罚金；<u>情节特别严重的</u>，处十年以上有期徒刑或者无期徒刑，并处没收财产；<u>情节较轻的</u>，处五年以下有期徒刑，并处罚金。

走私珍稀植物及其制品等国家禁止进出口的其他货物、物品的，处五年以下有期徒刑或者拘役，并处或者单处罚金；<u>情节严重的</u>，处五年以上有期徒刑，并处罚金。

【推荐译文】

Section 151　...

Whoever smuggles cultural relics, gold, silver or other precious metals, the export of which are forbidden by the State, or precious and rare species of wildlife or the products thereof, the import and export of which are forbidden by the State, shall be sentenced to pay a fine in addition to a sentence of imprisonment for a term not less than five years nor more than ten years; or shall be sentenced to confiscation of property in addition to a sentence of imprisonment for a term not less than ten years or life imprisonment, if the circumstances thereof are especially serious; or shall be sentenced to pay a fine in addition to a sentence of imprisonment for a term not more than five years, if the circumstances thereof are minor.

Whoever smuggles other goods or articles such as precious and rare species of plants or the products thereof, the import and export of which are forbidden by the State, shall be sentenced to pay a fine only or in addition to imprisonment for a term not more than five years or criminal detention; or shall be sentenced to pay a fine in addition to imprisonment for a term not less than five years, if the circumstances thereof are serious.

8.4　数额犯/数量犯

所谓**数额犯/数量犯**，是指以特定数额/数量作为构成要件的犯罪。如以下两例。

【例 11】

第一百七十三条　变造货币，数额较大的，处三年以下有期徒刑或者拘役，并处或者单处一万元以上十万元以下罚金；数额巨大的，处三年以上十年以下有期徒刑，并出二万元以上二十万元以下罚金。

【对照译文】

Article 173　Whoever alters currencies shall, if the amount involved is relatively large, be sentenced to fixed-term imprisonment of not more than three years or criminal detention and shall also, or shall only, be fined not less than 10,000 *yuan* but not more than 100,000 *yuan*; if the amount involved is huge, he shall be sentenced to fixed-term imprisonment of not less than three years but not more than 10 years and shall also be fined not less than 20,000 *yuan* but not more than 200,000 *yuan*.

【例 12】

第三百四十五条　盗伐森林或者其他林木，数量较大的，处三年以下有期徒刑、拘役或者管制，并处或者单处罚金；数量巨大的，处三年以上七年以下有期徒刑，并处罚金；数量特别巨大的，处七年以上有期徒刑，并处罚金。

【对照译文】

Article 345　Whoever stealthily fells trees, bamboo, etc., in forest or woods, if the amount involved is relatively large, shall be sentenced to fixed-term imprisonment of not more than three years, criminal detention or public surveillance and shall also, or shall only, be fined; if the amount involved is huge, he shall be sentenced to fix-termed imprisonment of not less than three years but not more than seven years and shall also be fined; <u>if the amount involved is especially huge</u>, he shall be sentenced to fixed-term imprisonment of not less than seven years and shall also be fined.

【例 11】【例 12】分别规定变造货币罪与盗伐林木罪。此类条款与前文所述情节犯近似，亦大都设置了等级各异的法定刑，与犯罪行为所涉数额/数量上的差别相互对应，故笔者以为其译文同样应当将条款中的数额/数量要件后置。

值得译者注意的是"数额"与"数量"的翻译。【对照译文】将二者一概处理为"amount"，似乎考虑欠周。当然，我国刑法分则中的"数额"均指金额，将之译成"amount"显然无可厚非。

【推荐译文】

Section 173　Whoever alters currencies shall be sentenced to pay a fine not less than RMB 10,000 nor more than RMB 100,000 only or in addition to a sentence of imprisonment for a term not more than three years or criminal detention, <u>if the amount involved is relatively large</u>; or shall be sentenced to pay a fine not less than RMB 20,000 nor more than RMB 200,000 in addition to a sentence of imprisonment for a term not less than three years nor more than 10 years, <u>if the amount involved is huge</u>.

而"数量"则不同，涉及此术语的条款所指各有不同。如【例 12】，依据《最高人民法院关于审理破坏森林资源刑事案件具体应用法律若干问题的解释》（2000 年）第四条规定：

第四条　盗伐林木"数量较大"，以二至五立方米或者幼树一百至二百株为起点；盗伐林木"数量巨大"，以二十至五十立方米或者幼树一千至二千株为起点；盗伐林木"数量特别巨大"，以一百至二百立方米或者幼树五千至一万株为起点。

可见此处"数量"既指盗伐林木的体积，也指盗伐林木的株数。

至于刑法第三百四十二条非法占用农用地罪中规定的"数量"则显然是指非法占用的农用地面积：

第三百四十二条　违反土地管理法规，非法占用耕地、林地等农用地，改变被占用土地用途，数量较大，造成耕地、林地等农用地大量毁坏的，处五年以下有期徒刑或者拘役，并处或者单处罚金。

此外，我国刑法典中尚有其他两类多以"数量"为要件的条款。一类为走私、贩卖、运输、制造毒品罪（分则第六章第七节），其中"数量"指的无非是涉罪毒品的重量或者原植物的株数；另一类更能说明问题的是危害税收征管罪（分则第三章第六节）。

就以该节第二百零七条为例。

第二百零七条　非法出售增值税专用发票的，处三年以下有期徒刑、拘役或者管制，并处二万元以上二十万元以下罚金；<u>数量较大</u>的，处三年以上十年以下有期徒刑，并处五万元以上五十万元以下罚金；<u>数量巨大</u>的，处十年以上有期徒刑或者无期徒刑，并处五万元以上五十万元以下罚金或者没收财产。

该条款中所谓"数量"就不同于同节第二百零四条中所谓"数额"：

第二百零四条 以假报出口或者其他欺骗手段,骗取国家出口退税款,数额较大的,处五年以下有期徒刑或者拘役,并处骗取税款一倍以上五倍以下罚金……

后者的"数额"显然是指骗取出口退税款的金额;可依据《关于适用〈全国人民代表大会常务委员会关于惩治虚开、伪造和非法出售增值税专用发票犯罪的决定〉的若干问题的解释》(1996 年):

二、根据《决定》第二条规定,伪造或者出售伪造的增值税专用发票的,构成伪造、出售伪造的增值税专用发票罪。

……

伪造或者出售伪造的增值税专用发票 100 份以上或者票面额累计 50 万元以上的,属于"数量较大"……

……

三、根据《决定》第三条规定,非法出售增值税专用发票的,构成非法出售增值税专用发票罪。

非法出售增值税专用发票案件的定罪量刑数量标准按照本解释第二条第二、三、四款的规定执行。

前者的"数量"是指非法出售增值税专用发票的份数或累计票面金额。故笔者以为第二百零七条中的"数量"不应与第二百零四条中的"数额"同样译成"amount",否则读者就无法理解原文中两术语之间的差别。

但若根据各相关条款的具体情况,将"数量"译成不同英文词汇,又有悖于规定性法律文件的一致性风格而非最佳选择。不若将之统一译成"quantity",也可适用于各种情形。请看【例 12】的【推荐译文】。

【推荐译文】

Section 345 Whoever stealthily fells trees in forest or woods shall be sentenced to pay a fine only or in addition to a sentence of imprisonment for a term not more than three years, criminal detention or public surveillance, if the quantity involved is relatively large; or shall be sentenced to pay a fine in addition to a sentence of imprisonment for a term not less than three years nor more than seven years, if the quantity involved is huge; or shall be sentenced to pay a fine in addition to a sentence of imprisonment for a term not less than seven years, if the quantity involved is especially huge.

再者,我国刑法分则中有的条款还规定了"数额"的具体所指,包括"销售金额(the amount of sales)"(如第一百四十条)与"非法所得数额(the amount of illegal gains)"(如第二百一十四条),以及第二百零一条中的"逃避缴纳税款数额(the amount of tax evaded)"。后者甚至将定罪量刑的具体数字都明确化了。

【例 13】

第二百零一条 纳税人采取欺骗、隐瞒手段进行虚假纳税申报或者不申报,逃避缴纳税款数额较大并且占应纳税额百分之十以上的,处三年以下有期徒刑或者拘役,并处罚金;数额巨大且占应纳税额百分之三十以上的,处三年以上七年以下有期徒刑,并处罚金。

【推荐译文】

Section 201   A taxpayer who files false tax returns by means of cheating or concealing or fails to file his tax returns shall be sentenced to pay for a fine in addition to a sentence of imprisonment for a term not more than three years or criminal detention, <u>if the amount of tax evaded is relatively large and accounts for not less than 10 percent of his taxes payable</u>; or shall be sentenced to pay for a fine in addition to a sentence of imprisonment for a term not less than three years nor more than seven years, <u>if the amount of tax evaded is huge and accounts for not less than 30 percent of his taxes payable</u>.

当然，其他涉及"数额"或"数量"的条款，虽以"较大""巨大""特别巨大"泛指，但也大都由最高人民法院的司法解释阐明具体数字，以方便实施。

8.5 结果犯

所谓<u>结果犯</u>，是指以发生特定的危害结果作为构成要件的犯罪。请看下例。

【例 14】

第一百二十八条   ……

依法配备公务用枪的人员，非法出租、出借枪支的，依照前款的规定处罚。

依法配置枪支的人员，非法出租、出借枪支，<u>造成严重后果的</u>，依照第一款的规定处罚。

【推荐译文】

Section 128   ...

A person lawfully equipped with a gun for discharge of his official duties who illegally leases or loans his gun shall be punished pursuant to the provisions of the preceding paragraph.

A person lawfully provided with a gun who illegally leases or loans his gun shall be punished pursuant to the provisions of the first paragraph <u>if serious consequences are thus caused</u>.

【例 14】所引法条第二、三款规定的非法出租、出借枪支罪，最好地体现了行为犯与结果犯的区别。其中，第二款针对依法配备公务用枪的人员而设，属行为犯：其行为无须造成严重后果即构成犯罪；而第三款则针对依法配置枪支的人员而言，属结果犯，其行为只有造成严重后果才构成犯罪。显然，二者之别就在于结果是否为犯罪必备构成要件。

结果犯也与情节犯、数额犯/数量犯相似，常依据结果的严重程度设置等级各异的法定刑，如【例 15】。笔者以为其译文与前两类犯罪条款的处理无异，应当将平行的结果要件后置。

【例 15】

第一百六十七条   国有公司、企业、事业单位直接负责的主管人员，在签订、履行合同过程中，因严重不负责任被诈骗，<u>致使国家利益遭受重大损失的</u>，处三年以下有期徒刑或者拘役；<u>致使国家利益遭受特别重大损失的</u>，处三年以上七年以下有期徒刑。

【推荐译文】

Section 167   A person directly in charge of a State-owned company, enterprise or institution who, during negotiation or performance of a contract, is defrauded due to serious neglect of his duty, shall be sentenced to imprisonment for a term not more than three years or criminal detention, <u>if heavy losses are thus caused to the interests of the State</u>; or shall be sentenced to imprisonment for a term not less than three years nor more than seven years, <u>if especially heavy losses are thus caused to the interests of the State</u>.

常用于表述结果要件的行文还有以下几种：

（1）"造成重大安全事故的（cause a serious accident）"（如第一百三十七条）；

（2）"致使发生重大伤亡事故的（cause an accident with heavy casualties）"（如第一百三十八条）；

（3）"后果特别严重的（if the consequences thus caused are especially serious）"；

（4）"造成（较大、重大、特别重大）损失的[if (relatively/especially) heavy losses are thus caused]"（如第一百八十六条）。

此外，规定结果犯的条款中也有叠用两项结果要件的，如下例。

【例 16】

第一百三十二条　铁路职工违反规章制度，<u>致使发生铁路运营安全事故</u>，<u>造成严重后果的</u>，处三年以下有期徒刑或者拘役；<u>造成特别严重后果的</u>，处三年以上七年以下有期徒刑。

【对照译文】

Article 132   Any railway worker who operates in violation of rules and regulations and <u>thereby causes a railway operational accident</u>, <u>if there are serious consequences</u>, shall be sentenced to fixed-term imprisonment of not more than three years or criminal detention; <u>if there are especially serious consequences</u>, he shall be sentenced to fixed-term imprisonment of not less than three years but more than seven years.

笔者以为，【例 16】中的两项结果要件地位不同："致使发生铁路运营安全事故"仅为定罪要件；而"造成严重后果的"与"造成特别严重后果的"相对应，涉及量刑幅度。所以，二者在译文中的处理也应当有所差别。

【推荐译文】

Section 132   A railway worker who <u>causes a railway operational accident</u> due to his violation of rules and regulations concerned shall be sentenced to imprisonment for a term not more than three years or criminal detention, <u>if serious consequences are thus caused</u>; or shall be sentenced to imprisonment for a term not less than three years nor more than seven years, <u>if especially serious consequences are thus caused</u>.

更为复杂的则如【例 17】。

【例 17】

第三百三十九条　……

未经国务院有关主管部门许可，擅自进口固体废物用作原料，<u>造成重大环境污染事故，致使公私财产遭受重大损失或者严重危害人体健康的</u>，处五年以下有期徒刑或者拘役，并处罚金；<u>后果特别严重的</u>，处五年以上十年以下有期徒刑，并处罚金。

【推荐译文】

Section 339　...

Whoever <u>causes a major accident of environmental pollution</u> due to his import of solid waste as raw material without permission of the competent administration under the State Council, shall be sentenced to pay a fine in addition to a sentence of imprisonment for a term not more than five years or criminal detention, <u>if heavy losses are thus caused to public or private property or serious harm is thus caused to human health</u>; or shall be sentenced to pay a fine in addition to a sentence of imprisonment for a term not less than five years nor more than ten years, <u>if the consequences thus caused are especially serious</u>.

＊　　　　　　　　　　＊　　　　　　　　　　＊

综上，本章所引各例的【推荐译文】总是将影响量刑幅度的犯罪构成要件置于相应各段条文的尾部。原因在于此类要件与构成该罪名的共同要件有所不同，笔者以为，只有将之译成后置条件状语从句才能明确其修饰范围，从而突出罪行大小与刑罚轻重相互对应的关系，贯彻我国刑法总则规定的罪刑均衡原则。此外，还有些定罪要件的成文化表述如"情节恶劣的"（【例 8】）、"造成严重后果的"（【例 14】）等也应仿照行文相同的派生要件后置处理，从而保持规定性法律文件的一致性风格。

◎翻译实践题◎

1. 数额与结果

1) 数额较大的/巨大的/特别巨大的

2) 情节较轻的/严重的/特别严重的

3) 后果严重的/特别严重的

4) 造成严重后果的/特别严重后果的

5) 造成较大/重大/特别重大损失的

6) 致使公私财产遭受重大损失或者严重危害人体健康的

7) 造成重大安全事故的

8) 致使发生重大伤亡事故的

2. 刑事处罚

1) 处三年以下有期徒刑、拘役或者管制

2) 处三年以上十年以下有期徒刑

3) 处十年以上有期徒刑、无期徒刑或者死刑

4) 处五年以下有期徒刑或者拘役

5) 处五年以上十年以下有期徒刑

6) 处十年以上有期徒刑或者无期徒刑

7) 并处或者单处罚金

8) 并处罚金

9) 并处没收财产

第9章
犯罪的客观方面：其他情节

◎学习目标◎

1. 掌握犯罪方式手段的汉语表述特征；

2. 掌握犯罪方式手段的英译句法；

3. 掌握犯罪客观随附情状的汉语表述特征；

4. 掌握犯罪客观随附情状的英译句法；

5. 掌握犯罪准用性罪状的汉语表述特征；

6. 掌握犯罪准用性罪状的英译句法。

第 8 章我们详细讨论了翻译过程中应当如何恰当处理《中华人民共和国刑法》（2023年修正）分则条款中规定的犯罪客观要素：行为、危险、情节、数额/数量、结果等。此外，还有犯罪的方式手段、客观附随情状及准用性罪状，也是译者需要谨慎关注的。

9.1　方式手段

《中华人民共和国刑法》（2023 年修正）分则描述的罪体中有些条款还规定了特殊的犯罪行为方式或手段。此类方式手段多表述为"以/使用/采取……方法/手段"，因其涉及定罪而更需译者引起重视。请看【例 1】。

【例 1】

第二百零四条　以假报出口或者其他欺骗手段，骗取国家出口退税款，数额较大的，处五年以下有期徒刑或者拘役，并处骗取税款一倍以上五倍以下罚金；……

本例所引的是骗取出口退税罪，其中"以假报出口或者其他欺骗手段"便是该罪的法定行为方式。笔者以为，该条款的处理可参照《美国模范刑法典》第 220.2 条（SECTION 220.2　CAUSING OR RISING CATASTROPHE）第（1）款：

(1) CAUSING CATASTROPHE. A person who causes a catastrophe by explosion, fire, flood, avalanche, collapse of building, release of poison gas, radioactive material or other harmful or destructive force or substance, or by any other means of causing potentially widespread injury or damage, commits a felony of the second degree if he does so purposely or knowingly, or a felony of the third degree if he does so recklessly.

【推荐译文】

Section 204 Whoever defrauds the State of tax refunded for export <u>by false export declaration or by any other deceptive means</u> shall be sentenced to pay a fine not less than one time but less than five times the amount of tax defrauded, in addition to a sentence of imprisonment for a term not more than five years or criminal detention, if the amount of tax defrauded is relatively large; ...

再如【例 2】规定的非法获取国家秘密罪，也是"以窃取、刺探、收买方法"为该罪成立所必备的客观构成要件，其译文亦可作类似处理。

【例 2】

　　第二百八十二条　以窃取、刺探、收买方法，非法获取国家秘密的，处三年以下有期徒刑、拘役、管制或者剥夺政治权利；情节严重的，处三年以上七年以下有期徒刑。

　　【推荐译文】

Section 282 Whoever unlawfully obtains State secrets <u>by stealing, spying or buying</u> shall be sentenced to imprisonment for a term not more than three years, criminal detention, public surveillance or deprivation of political rights; or shall be sentenced to imprisonment for a term not less than three years nor more than seven years, if the circumstances thereof are serious.

在分则条款中为表述犯罪方式或手段而反复出现的行文尚有如下两类：

（1）"以暴力、胁迫或者其他方法/手段（by means of violence or coercion or by any other means）"或者"以暴力、威胁方法/手段（by means of violence or threat）"；

（2）"使用诈骗方法/欺骗手段（by means of fraud）"。

9.2　客观附随情状

　　所谓客观附随情状，是指犯罪的时间与地点（陈兴良, 2001: 295）。尽管时间与地点是任何具体犯罪行为存在的基础，但这些客观附随情状通常并非犯罪成立的前提，故罕见于刑法条款的明文规定。不过也有某些犯罪例外：特定的时间与地点为其成立的必备构成要件。此类犯罪的客观附随情状必须由分则法条加以具体描述，因而值得译者注意。

9.2.1　时　间

　　有些分则条款规定特定时间为具体犯罪成立的要件。此类时间要素在法条中的表现形式虽多种多样，但大致上可分为两类。

1. 限定犯罪行为的时间要素

【例 3】

　　第三百一十一条　明知他人有间谍犯罪或者恐怖主义、极端主义犯罪行为，<u>在司法机关向其调查有关情况、收集有关证据时</u>，拒绝提供，情节严重的，处三年以下有期徒刑、拘役或者管制。

　　【对照译文】

Article 311　Whoever, while clearly knowing that another person has committed the crime of espionage, terrorism or extremism, refuses to provide relevant particulars or relevant evidence <u>when an officer from a judicial authority asks him to do so</u>, if the circumstances are serious, shall be sentenced to fixed-term imprisonment of not more than three years, criminal detention or public surveillance.

【例3】规定的是拒绝提供间谍犯罪、恐怖主义犯罪、极端主义犯罪证据罪。该罪体中时间要素的作用在于限定犯罪行为，即"拒绝提供"的行为必须发生"在司法机关向其调查有关情况、收集有关证据时"方为犯罪。

笔者以为，【对照译文】将之处理成"when an officer from a judicial authority asks him to do so"值得商榷。原因在于"ask him to do so"看似简练，实则语焉不详，可能引起歧义："do"是指"refuse"呢？还是"provide"呢？比较而言，【推荐译文】的处理似乎更为准确。

【推荐译文】

Section 311　Whoever, with knowledge that another person has committed the criminal conduct of espionage, terrorism or extremism, refuses to provide relevant information or evidence <u>when the judiciary authority requires him of such information or evidence</u>, shall be sentenced to imprisonment for a term not more than three years, criminal detention or public surveillance, if the circumstances thereof are serious.

2. 非限定犯罪行为的时间要素

【例4】

第三百九十四条　国家工作人员<u>在国内公务活动或者对外交往中</u>接受礼物，依照国家规定应当交公而不交公，数额较大的，依照本法第三百八十二条、第三百八十三条的规定定罪处罚。

【对照译文】

Article 394　Any State functionary who, <u>in his activities of domestic public service or in his contacts with foreigners</u>, accepts gifts and does not hand them over to the State as is required by State regulations, if the amount involved is relatively large, shall be convicted and punished in accordance with the provisions of Articles 382 and 383 of this Law.

【例4】所引法条是对贪污罪的补充。该罪体中时间要素的作用在于限定犯罪对象，即"应当交公"的"礼物"必须是"在国内公务活动或者对外交往中接受"的。

事实上，此要素的正确理解不能脱离认定该罪所必须依照的"国家规定"，主要包括《国家行政机关及其工作人员在国内公务活动中不得赠送和接受礼品的规定》《国务院关于在对外活动中不赠礼、不受礼的决定》《国务院关于对党和国家机关工作人员在国内外交往中收受的礼品实行登记制度的规定》等。由此可见，所谓"在国内公务活动或者对外交往中"，即国家工作人员因公务活动与国内外人士交往期间，故笔者以为，译成"in his activities of domestic public service or in his contacts with foreigners"失之累赘，不如【推荐译文】更为简洁。

【推荐译文】

Section 394　A state employee who fails to hand over to the State gifts <u>accepted during his official contact with people at home or abroad</u>, as is required by State regulations, shall be convicted and sentenced to a punishment pursuant to the provisions in Sections 382 and 383 of this Law if the amount involved is relatively large.

3. 补　充

正如前两例所述，时间要素的翻译讲究精确简洁，故译者对原文的理解不可拘泥于语言形式，而应斟酌其实质。请看【例 5】。

【例 5】

第一百六十七条　国有公司、企业、事业单位直接负责的主管人员，<u>在签订、履行合同过程中</u>，因严重不负责任被诈骗，致使国家利益遭受重大损失的，处三年以下有期徒刑或者拘役；致使国家利益遭受特别重大损失的，处三年以上七年以下有期徒刑。

【对照译文】

Article 167　If a person who is directly in charge of a State-owned company, enterprise or institution, <u>when signing or fulfilling a contract</u>, is defrauded due to serious neglect of responsibility and thus causes heavy losses to the interests of the State, he shall be sentenced to fixed-term imprisonment of not more than three years or criminal detention; if especially heavy losses are caused to the interests of the State, he shall be sentenced to fixed-term imprisonment of not less than three years but not more than seven years.

本例规定的是签订、履行合同失职被骗罪。该法条采用叙明罪状，其中"在签订、履行合同过程中"为此罪成立的必备时间要件，重要性当然不言而喻。

"在……过程中"的短语结构表明"签订"与"履行"并非指行为人的瞬间动作，而是指合同当事人协商并实施合同的全部互动过程。所谓合同的签订，即当事人各方就某一民事法律关系达至合意的行为；所谓合同的履行，即当事人各方实施履行合同标的的行为（刘家琛, 2002: 715）。

因此，笔者以为【对照译文】将"签订"译成"signing"，限缩了成立犯罪的时间要素，故而不妥。

【推荐译文】

Section 167　A person directly in charge of a State-owned company, enterprise or institution who, <u>during negotiation or performance of a contract</u>, is defrauded due to serious neglect of his duty, shall be sentenced to imprisonment for a term not more than three years or criminal detention, if heavy losses are thus caused to the interests of the State; or shall be sentenced to imprisonment for a term not less than three years nor more than seven years, if especially heavy losses are thus caused to the interests of the State.

我国刑法分则中时间要素的常用行文还有以下几类：

（1）"在金融业务活动中（in financial activities）"；

（2）"在经济往来中（in economic activities）"；

（3）"在刑事诉讼中（in criminal proceedings）"；

（4）"在民事、行政审判活动中（in civil or administrative proceedings）"。

至于出现频率最高的当属"战时"，请看我国刑法第四百三十四条及其【推荐译文】。

【例6】

　　第四百三十四条　战时自伤身体，逃避军事义务的，处三年以下有期徒刑；情节严重的，处三年以上七年以下有期徒刑。

　　【推荐译文】

Section 434　Whoever, <u>during wartime</u>, injures himself to evade his military obligation, shall be sentenced to imprisonment for a term not more than three years; or shall be sentenced to imprisonment for a term not less than three years nor more than seven years, if the circumstances thereof are serious.

9.2.2　地　点

有些分则条款规定特定地点为具体犯罪成立的要件。此类地点要素在法条中的表现形式不如时间要素种类繁多，但大致上也可分为两类。

1. 限定犯罪行为的地点要素

【例7】

　　第四百四十六条　战时<u>在军事行动地区</u>，残害无辜居民或者掠夺无辜居民财物的，处五年以下有期徒刑；情节严重的，处五年以上十年以下有期徒刑；情节特别严重的，处十年以上有期徒刑、无期徒刑或者死刑。

　　【对照译文】

Article 446　Any serviceman who, during wartime, cruelly injures innocent residents <u>in an area of military operation</u> or plunders their money or property shall be sentenced to fixed-term imprisonment of not more than five years; if the circumstances are serious, he shall be sentenced to fixed-term imprisonment of not less than five years but not more than 10 years; if the circumstances are especially serious, he shall be sentenced to fixed-term imprisonment of not less than 10 years, life imprisonment or death.

　　【例7】规定的是战时残害居民、掠夺居民财物罪。该罪体中地点要素的作用在于限定犯罪行为，即"残害无辜居民或者掠夺无辜居民财物"的行为必须发生"在军事行动地区"。

　　笔者以为，【对照译文】的处理不妥："in an area of military operation"修饰的不仅是"cruelly injures innocent residents"，还包括"plunders their money or property"，故应将之前置。

　　【推荐译文】

Section 446　A serviceman who, <u>in an area of military operation</u> during wartime, cruelly injures innocent residents or plunders their properties, shall be sentenced to imprisonment for a term not more than five years; or shall be sentenced to imprisonment for a term not less than five years nor more than ten years, if the circumstances thereof are serious; or shall be sentenced to imprisonment for a term not less than ten years, life imprisonment or death, if the circumstances thereof are especially serious.

2. 非限定犯罪行为的地点要素

【例 8】

第三百一十六条 ……

劫夺押解途中的罪犯、被告人、犯罪嫌疑人的，处三年以上七年以下有期徒刑；情节严重的，处七年以上有期徒刑。

【对照译文】

Article 316 ...

Whoever rescues the criminal, defendant or criminal suspect <u>under escort</u> shall be sentenced to fixed-term imprisonment of not less than three years but not more than seven years; if the circumstances are serious, he shall be sentenced to fixed-term imprisonment of not less than seven years.

【例 8】规定的是劫夺被押解人员罪。该罪体中地点要素的作用在于限定犯罪对象，即"劫夺"的"罪犯、被告人、犯罪嫌疑人"必须是"押解途中的"。

所谓"押解途中"，即被依法关押的人员自押解出关押场所后直至押解入关押场所前的途中，故笔者以为，译成"under escort"不足以尽显原文之意。

【推荐译文】

Section 316 ...

Whoever seizes the offender, defendant or criminal suspect <u>being sent under escort</u> shall be sentenced to imprisonment for a term not less than three years nor more than seven years; or shall be sentenced to imprisonment for a term not less than seven years, if the circumstances thereof are serious.

3. 补 充

我国刑法分则中地点要素的常用行文还有以下两类：

（1）"在公共场合/公众场合（in a public place）"；

（2）"在境外的（abroad）"。

出现频率较高的还有"在战场上"，请看我国刑法第四百二十三条及其【推荐译文】。

【例 9】

第四百二十三条 在战场上贪生怕死，自动放下武器投降敌人的，处三年以上十年以下有期徒刑；情节严重的，处十年以上有期徒刑或者无期徒刑。

【对照译文】

Article 423 Any serviceman who cares for nothing but his skin <u>on the battlefield</u> voluntarily lays down his arms and surrenders to the enemy shall be sentenced to fixed-term imprisonment of not less than three years but not more than 10 years; if the circumstances are serious, he shall be sentenced to fixed-term imprisonment of not less than 10 years or life imprisonment.

本例规定的是投降罪。该法条中的地点要素"在战场上"限定的是"自动放下武器投降敌人的"行为。就此而言，【对照译文】的处理显属含糊其词。更何况将"贪生怕死"译成富有文学色彩的"cares for nothing but his skin"，不符合规定性法律语言的消极修辞原则，故笔者推荐如下译文。

【推荐译文】

Section 423　A serviceman who, <u>on the battlefield</u>, cowardly lays down his weapon and surrenders to the enemy, shall be sentenced to imprisonment for a term not less than three years nor more than ten years; or shall be sentenced to imprisonment for a term not less than ten years or life imprisonment, if the circumstances thereof are serious.

9.3　准用性罪状

所谓准用性罪状是指没有直接规定犯罪构成要件的全部内容，空缺部分需要其他刑法条款或者非刑法条款予以填充的罪状（刘志远，2003: 168），主要分为引证罪状与空白罪状两类。

9.3.1　引证罪状

所谓引证罪状是指空缺部分需要其他刑法条款予以填充的准用性罪状（168）。如【例10】。

【例10】

第三百九十七条　……

国家机关工作人员徇私舞弊，<u>犯前款罪的</u>，处五年以下有期徒刑或者拘役；情节特别严重的，处五年以上十年以下有期徒刑。本法另有规定的，依照规定。

【对照译文】

Article 397　...

Any functionary of a State organ who engages in malpractice for personal gain and <u>commits the crime mentioned in the preceding paragraph</u> shall be sentenced to fixed-term imprisonment of not more than five years or criminal detention; if the circumstances are especially serious, he shall be sentenced to fixed-term imprisonment of not less than five years but not more than 10 years, except as otherwise specifically provided in this law.

本例所引条款是对该法条第一款规定的滥用职权罪与玩忽职守罪的补充。此款采用引证罪状"犯前款罪的"保持刑法语言的简洁性，而"徇私舞弊"则是较前款加重处罚的构成要件。【对照译文】将"徇私舞弊"译成"engages in malpractice for personal gain"，笔者以为过分拘泥于原文，违背了避免赘言原则。事实上，所谓"engages in malpractice"指的是"commits the crime mentioned in the preceding paragraph"，故推荐如下译文。

【推荐译文】

Section 397　...

Except as otherwise specifically provided in this Law, an employee of a State agency who commits the crime mentioned in the preceding paragraph out of personal consideration, shall be sentenced to imprisonment for a term not more than five years or criminal detention; or shall be sentenced to imprisonment for a term not less than five years nor more than ten years, if the circumstances thereof are especially serious.

9.3.2　空白罪状

所谓空白罪状是指空缺部分需要其他非刑法条款予以填充的准用性罪状（169）。

1. 绝对空白罪状

所谓绝对空白罪状，是指刑法分则条文仅仅规定应当参照其他有关法律法规，而未对具体犯罪构成的行为要件做出类型化表述（169）。

【例11】

第四百三十六条　违反武器装备使用规定，情节严重，因而发生责任事故，致人重伤、死亡或者造成其他严重后果的，处三年以下有期徒刑或者拘役；后果特别严重的，处三年以上七年以下有期徒刑。

本例所引的武器装备肇事罪，采用的就是绝对空白罪状。该罪的行为要件只由"违反武器装备使用规定"涵盖，故笔者以为将之译成动宾结构更为恰当。

【推荐译文】

Section 436　Whoever violates the regulations on the use of weapons and equipment, the circumstances of which are serious, and thus causes an accident, shall be sentenced to imprisonment for a term not more than three years or criminal detention, if such accident causes serious injury or death to human or other serious consequences; or shall be sentenced to imprisonment for a term not less than three years nor more than seven years, if the consequences thus caused are especially serious.

2. 相对空白罪状

所谓相对空白罪状，是指刑法分则条文不仅规定应当参照其他有关法律法规，还针对具体犯罪构成的行为要件做出类型化表述（169）。

【例12】

第四百三十七条　违反武器装备管理规定，擅自改变武器装备的编配用途，造成严重后果的，处三年以下有期徒刑或者拘役；造成特别严重后果的，处三年以上七年以下有期徒刑。

本例所引的擅自改变武器装备编配用途罪，采用的就是相对空白罪状。与上例不同，该款的行为要件除"违反武器装备管理规定"外，还包括"擅自改变武器装备的编配用途"。从整体而言，前者仅为限定后者的行为性质，故笔者以为将之译成介宾结构作状语更为恰当。

【推荐译文】

Section 437　Whoever, <u>in violation of the regulations on control of weapons and equipment</u>, alters without authorization the allocation and use of weapons and equipment, shall be sentenced to imprisonment for a term not more than three years or criminal detention, if serious consequences are thus caused; or shall be sentenced to imprisonment for a term not less than three years nor more than seven years, if especially serious consequences are thus caused.

与上例近似的是刑法分则中的另一类条款，如【例 13】。该类条款虽非相对空白罪状，但"未经……批准"与"违反……规定/法规"的功能是同一的，也用于限定犯罪行为的性质，故亦可采取相同的处理方式。

【例 13】

第一百七十四条　未经国家有关主管部门批准，擅自设立商业银行、证券交易所、期货交易所、证券公司、期货经纪公司、保险公司或者其他金融机构的，处三年以下有期徒刑或者拘役，并处或者单处二万元以上二十万元以下罚金；情节严重的，处三年以上十年以下有期徒刑，并处五万元以上五十万元以下罚金。

【推荐译文】

Article 174　Whoever, <u>without the approval of the competent authorities of the State</u>, establishes a commercial bank, a securities exchange, a futures exchange, a securities company, a futures Brokerage company, an insurance company or any other banking institution, shall be sentenced to pay a fine not less than 20,000 *yuan* nor more than 200,000 *yuan* only or in addition to a sentence of imprisonment for a term not more than three years or criminal detention; or shall be sentenced to pay a fine not less than 50,000 *yuan* nor more than 500,000 *yuan* in addition to a sentence of imprisonment for a term not less than three years nor more than 10 years, if the circumstances thereof are serious.

9.4　综　合

前文所举范例各就犯罪客观方面的某一要素展开分析。而事实上，分则中的条款多数具有综合性。请看以下两例。

【例 14】

第三百四十条　违反保护水产资源法规，在禁渔区、禁渔期或者使用禁用的工具、方法捕捞水产品，情节严重的，处三年以下有期徒刑、拘役、管制或者罚金。

【对照译文】

Article 340　Whoever, <u>in violation of the law or regulations on protection of aquatic resources</u>, catches aquatic products <u>in an area or during a season closed to fishing</u>, or <u>uses prohibited fishing gear or methods for the purpose</u>, if the circumstances are serious, shall be sentenced to fixed-term imprisonment of not more than three years, criminal detention or public surveillance or be fined.

【例 15】

第三百四十一条 ……

违反狩猎法规，在禁猎区、禁猎期或者使用禁用的工具、方法进行狩猎，破坏野生动物资源，情节严重的，处三年以下有期徒刑、拘役、管制或者罚金。

【对照译文】

Article 341 Whoever, in violation of the law or regulations on hunting, hunts wildlife in an area or during a season closed to hunting, or uses prohibited hunting gear or methods for the purpose, thus damaging wildlife resources, if the circumstances are serious, shall be sentenced to fixed-term imprisonment of not more than three years, criminal detention or public surveillance or be fined.

上述两例所引条款虽然简短，但丝毫不影响其罪体的综合性。其中，"违反保护水产资源法规"与"违反狩猎法规"均属相对空白罪状，"禁渔区"与"禁猎区"均属地点要素，"禁渔期"与"禁猎期"均属时间要素，"使用禁用的工具、方法"则属行为方式。笔者以为，这些客观要素的功能旨在限定构成犯罪的行为性质、行为方式及附随情状，因而译文应当将其全部处理为状语。故【对照译文】将"使用禁用的工具、方法"特别处理为"uses prohibited fishing gear or methods for the purpose"与"uses prohibited hunting gear or methods for the purpose"不如【推荐译文】更符合原文的主旨。

【推荐译文】

Section 340 Whoever, in violation of the laws or regulations on protection of aquatic resources, catches aquatic products in an area or during a season closed to fishing or with prohibited gears or by prohibited methods, shall be sentenced to imprisonment for a term not more than three years, criminal detention or public surveillance or to pay a fine, if the circumstances thereof are serious.

【推荐译文】

Section 341 Whoever, in violation of the laws or regulations on hunting, hunts wildlife in an area or during a season closed to hunting or with prohibited gears or by prohibited means, and thus damages wildlife resources, shall be sentenced to imprisonment for a term not more than three years, criminal detention or public surveillance or to pay a fine, if the circumstances thereof are serious.

再如【例 16】，所引欺诈发行证券罪的行为要件虽无上述状语限定，但其定罪量刑涉及数额、结果与情节要件。

【例 16】

第一百六十条 在招股说明书、认股书、公司、企业债券募集办法等发行文件中隐瞒重要事实或者编造重大虚假内容，发行股票或者公司、企业债券、存托凭证或者国务院依法认定的其他证券，数额巨大、后果严重或者有其他严重情节的，处五年以下有期徒刑或者拘役，并处或者单处罚金；数额特别巨大、后果特别严重或者有其他特别严重情节的，处五年以上有期徒刑，并处罚金。

【对照译文】

Article 160　Whoever issues any shares of stock, corporate or enterprise bonds, depositary receipts, or other securities determined by the State Council in accordance with the law by concealing any material fact or falsifying any major content in the share offering prospectus, share subscription form, corporate or enterprise bond offering prospectus, or any other offering document shall, <u>if the amount involved is huge, the consequences are serious</u>, or there is any other serious circumstance, be sentenced to imprisonment of not more than five years or limited incarceration and a fine or be sentenced to a fine only; or <u>if the amount involved is especially huge, the consequences are especially serious, or there is any other especially serious circumstance</u>, shall be sentenced to imprisonment of not less than five years and a fine.

本例中的"数额巨大""后果严重"与"有其他严重情节"相互平行，具体行为只需符合其一即构成犯罪。这不仅是分析原文语言结构所得的结果，可引为旁证的还有《最高人民检察院、公安部关于经济犯罪案件追诉标准的规定》（2001 年 4 月 18 日）中的第四条：

四、欺诈发行股票、债券案（刑法第一百六十条）

在招股说明书、认股书、公司、企业债券募集办法中隐瞒重要事实或者编造重大虚假内容，发行股票或者公司、企业债券，涉嫌下列情形之一的，应予追诉：

1. 发行数额在一千万元以上的；
2. 伪造政府公文、有效证明文件或者相关凭证、单据的；
3. 股民、债权人要求清退，无正当理由不予清退的；
4. 利用非法募集的资金进行违法活动的；
5. 转移或者隐瞒所募集资金的；
6. 造成恶劣影响的。

正如本书第 8 章所述，本例也应处理为条件状语置于句末。更重要的是，笔者以为还应使之维持平行结构。而我国刑法第七次修正（2009 年）前该要件的译文"if the amount of the falsely registered capital is huge, and the consequences are serious, or if there are other serious circumstances"，则意味着要么同时满足数额要件与结果要件，要么满足情节要件，方才构成犯罪，这显然背离了原文的意思。

【推荐译文】

Section 160　Whoever issues any shares of stock, corporate or enterprise bonds, depositary receipts, or other securities determined by the State Council in accordance with the law by concealing important facts or falsifying major information, in the prospectus on offer of shares, forms of subscription for shares or measures for offer of company or enterprise bonds, or any other offering documents, shall be sentenced to pay a fine only or in addition to a sentence of imprisonment for a term not more than five years or criminal detention, <u>if the amount of such fund is huge, the consequences thus caused are serious, or other circumstances thereof are serious</u>; or shall be sentenced to pay a fine in addition to a sentence of imprisonment for a term not less than five years, <u>if the amount of such fund is especially huge, the consequences thus caused are especially serious, or other circumstances thereof are especially serious.</u>

而【例 17】则代表了另一类综合性条款。该例所引战时临阵脱逃罪的普通构成要件"战时临阵脱逃"并不复杂，仅有时间要素为其客观附随情状；可另有两项派生要件"情节严重的""致使战斗、战役遭受重大损失的"分别构成"情节加重犯"与"结果加重犯"。

【例 17】

第四百二十四条　战时临阵脱逃的，处三年以下有期徒刑；<u>情节严重的</u>，处三年以上十年以下有期徒刑；<u>致使战斗、战役遭受重大损失的</u>，处十年以上有期徒刑、无期徒刑或者死刑。

【推荐译文】

Section 424　A serviceman who, <u>during wartime</u>, deserts from the battlefield shall be sentenced to imprisonment for a term not more than three years; or shall be sentenced to imprisonment for a term not less than three years nor more than ten years, <u>if the circumstances thereof are serious</u>; or shall be sentenced to imprisonment for a term not less than ten years, life imprisonment or death, <u>if heavy losses are thus caused to a battle or campaign.</u>

◎翻译实践题◎

1. 方式手段

1) 以假报出口或者其他欺骗手段

2) 以窃取、刺探、收买方法

3) 以暴力、胁迫或者其他方法/手段

4) 以暴力、威胁方法/手段

2. 附随情状

1) 在司法机关向其调查有关情况、收集有关证据时

2) 在国内公务活动或者对外交往中

3) 在签订、履行合同过程中

4) 在金融业务活动中

5) 在经济往来中

6) 在刑事诉讼中

7) 在民事、行政审判活动中

8) 战时

9) 在战场上

10) 在军事行动地区

11) 押解途中

12) 在公共场合/公众场合

13) 在境外的

3. 准用性罪状

1) 犯前款罪的

2) 违反武器装备使用规定

3) 违反武器装备管理规定

4) 未经国家有关主管部门批准

第 10 章
犯罪的主体及主观方面

◎学习目标◎

1. 掌握犯罪主体的汉语表述结构；

2. 掌握犯罪主体的英译句法；

3. 掌握犯罪主观方面的汉语表述结构；

4. 掌握犯罪主观方面的英译句法。

10.1 犯罪的主体

所谓犯罪主体，是指实施危害社会行为的具有刑事责任能力的自然人与单位（陈兴良，2001: 203）。《中华人民共和国刑法》（2023 年修正）分则条款中有关犯罪主体的表述多隐含或明示于"的"字短语构建的罪体部分。

10.1.1 自然人犯罪

1. 一般主体

我国刑法分则中规定的犯罪主体大都是自然人，且以一般主体为多。如下例。

【例1】

第一百五十一条 走私武器、弹药、核材料或者伪造的货币的，处七年以上有期徒刑，并处罚金或者没收财产；情节特别严重的，处无期徒刑，并处没收财产；情节较轻的，处三年以上七年以下有期徒刑，并处罚金。

本例所引条款规定的是走私武器、弹药罪，走私核材料罪与走私假币罪。此三种犯罪构成要件中的主体均为一般主体，只要是达到刑事责任年龄、具备刑事责任能力的自然人实施了该款所规定的行为，即构成犯罪。

从语言形式上分析，我国刑法分则中以一般主体为犯罪构成要件的条款，多省略行为主体（隐含于"的"字短语中）。而英美刑法则常将此类条款表述为如下两种句式：

SECTION 210.5 CAUSING OR AIDING SUICIDE.

(1) *Causing Suicide as Criminal Homicide.* A person may be convicted of criminal homicide for causing another to commit suicide only if he purposely causes such suicide by force, duress or deception.

(2) *Aiding or Soliciting Suicide as an Independent Offense.* A person who purposely aids or solicits another to commit suicide is guilty of a felony of the second degree if his conduct causes such suicide or an attempted suicide, and otherwise of a misdemeanor.

—Model Penal Code

上引第一款因涉及罪名"criminal homicide"而在形式上不同于第二款。由于我国刑法分则条款通常只描述罪体，罕有直接规定罪名的，因此其译文套用后者的句式更为贴切。该句式还有多种变体，如"anyone who ..."、"everyone who ..."、"whoever ..."等。

【推荐译文】

Section 151 Whoever smuggles weapons, ammunition, nuclear material or counterfeit currency, shall be sentenced to pay a fine or be sentenced to confiscation of property, in addition to a sentence of imprisonment for a term not less than seven years; or shall be sentenced to confiscation of property in addition to a sentence of life imprisonment, if the circumstances thereof are especially serious; or shall be sentenced to pay a fine in addition to a sentence of imprisonment for a term not less than three years nor more than seven years, if the circumstances thereof are minor.

2. 特殊主体

我国刑法分则中也有些条款规定的是身份犯，即仅有具备特定身份或职务的特殊主体才能成立的犯罪。其中，最常见的就是以"国家工作人员"或"国家机关工作人员"为主体，如【例 2】。

【例 2】

　　第三百九十七条　国家机关工作人员滥用职权或者玩忽职守，致使公共财产、国家和人民利益遭受重大损失的，处三年以下有期徒刑或者拘役；情节特别严重的，处三年以上七年以下有期徒刑。本法另有规定的，依照规定。

【对照译文】

Article 397 Any functionary of a State organ who abuses his power or neglects his duty, thus causing heavy losses to public money or property or the interests of the State and the people, shall be sentenced to fixed-term imprisonment of not more than three years or criminal detention; if the circumstances are especially serious, he shall be sentenced to fixed-term imprisonment of not less than three years but not more than seven years, except as otherwise specially provided in this Law.

本例引用的是规定滥用职权罪与玩忽职守罪的条款。此两罪的特殊主体即"国家机关工作人员"。该主体不同于"国家工作人员"：

第九十三条　本法所称国家工作人员，是指国家机关中从事公务的人员。

国有公司、企业、事业单位、人民团体中从事公务的人员和国家机关、国有公司、企业、事业单位委派到非国有公司、企业、事业单位、社会团体从事公务的人员，以及其他依照法律从事公务的人员，以国家工作人员论。

根据上述规定，"国家机关工作人员"虽属"国家工作人员"，但仅为其主要组成部分而非全部。笔者以为，将"国家工作人员"译成"a State functionary"不是十分恰当。根据《布莱克法律辞典》的定义，"functionary"是指"a public officer or employee; esp., one whose job involves unimportant or mundane duties"（Garner, 2019: 815）。换言之，"functionary"这个词的使用具有一定的局限性，多指级别较低、职责不太重要的公务人员，故建议将之译成更为常见的"a public official"或者"a government employee"，也可以效仿中共中央党史和文献研究院提供的《中华人民共和国宪法》英文版，译作"a State employee"。

再者，【对照译文】将"国家机关"译成"State organ"也有不妥。实际上，"organ"并非法律术语。英美法中与之相对应的是"agency"，《布莱克法律辞典》将其解释为"an official body, esp. within the government, with the authority to implement and administer particular legislation"（77），故笔者推荐如下译文。

【推荐译文】

Section 397 Except as otherwise specially provided in this Law, <u>an employee of a State agency</u> who abuses his power or neglects his duty, and thus causes heavy losses to public property or the interests of the State and people, shall be sentenced to imprisonment for a term not more than three years or criminal detention; or shall be sentenced to imprisonment for a term not less than three years nor more than seven years, if the circumstances thereof are especially serious.

更需引起译者注意的是，有些条款貌似省略犯罪主体要件而成为无主句，但是必须由特殊主体方能构成犯罪。请看下例。

【例3】

第四百三十八条 盗窃、抢夺武器装备或者军用物资的，处五年以下有期徒刑或者拘役；情节严重的，处五年以上十年以下有期徒刑；情节特别严重的，处十年以上有期徒刑、无期徒刑或者死刑。

【对照译文】

Article 438 <u>Whoever</u> steals or forcibly seizes weapons, equipment or military supplies shall be sentenced to fixed-term imprisonment of not more than five years or criminal detention; if the circumstances are serious, he shall be sentenced to fixed-term imprisonment of not less than five years but not more than 10 years; if the circumstances are especially serious, he shall be sentenced to fixed-term imprisonment of not less than 10 years, life imprisonment or death.

【例3】规定的是盗窃、抢夺武器装备、军用物资罪。该款条文也未指明行为主体，若仅以此论之，当然应将其主体要件理解为一般主体。但此条款属刑法分则第十章"军人违反职责罪"，而该章首条便规定：

第四百二十条 军人违反职责，危害国家军事利益，依照法律应当受刑罚处罚的行为，是军人违反职责罪。

可见军人违反职责罪的犯罪主体必须是军人，自然前例所引第四百三十八条也不例外。

而【对照译文】以"whoever"起首，不如【推荐译文】更符合立法者的意图。

【推荐译文】

Section 438 <u>A serviceman</u> who steals or forcibly seizes weapons, equipment or military supplies, shall be sentenced to imprisonment for a term not more than five years or criminal detention; or shall be sentenced to imprisonment for a term not less than five years nor more than ten years, if the circumstances thereof are serious; or shall be sentenced to imprisonment for a term not less than ten years, life imprisonment or death, if the circumstances thereof are especially serious.

10.1.2 单位犯罪

单位犯罪不同于自然人犯罪，其主体为单位，包括公司、企业、事业单位、机关和团体，对此，我国刑法总则第二章第四节有明确规定。

较之英美法术语"corporate crime"，两个概念显然并不完全一致。依据《布莱克法律词典》的解释，"corporate crime"是指"a crime committed by a corporation's representatives acting on its behalf"（467），故《元照英美法词典》将该术语译成法人犯罪（薛波，2003:325）。而单位犯罪的主体除法人外，还涉及非法人团体。

但以下【对照译文】将"单位"译为"unit"也是不妥的。作为法律术语，"unit"仅指"a single thing, group, or person viewed as an individual or as one of several things"（Garner, 2019: 1568）。

笔者以为，译成"organizational crime"更为恰当。尽管英美法中此术语与"corporate crime"表示同一概念，可"organization"本意是指组织，不同于指示法人的"corporation"。结合我国刑法第三十条有关单位负刑事责任的范围：

第三十条 公司、企业、事业单位、机关、团体实施的危害社会的行为，法律规定为单位犯罪的，应当负刑事责任。

"organizational crime"的约定定义应当不会被译文读者所误解。如以下两例。

【例4】

第一百五十条 单位犯本节第一百四十条至第一百四十八条规定之罪的，对单位判处罚金，并对其直接负责的主管人员和其他直接责任人员，依照各该条的规定处罚。

【对照译文】

Article 150 Where <u>a unit</u> commits the crime as mentioned in Articles 141 through 148 of this Section, it shall be fined, and the persons who are directly in charge and the other persons who are directly responsible for the crime shall be punished in accordance with the provisions of the Articles respectively.

【例5】

第一百五十一条 ……

<u>单位</u>犯本条规定之罪的，对单位判处罚金，并对其直接负责的主管人员和其他直接责任人员，依照本条各款的规定处罚。

【对照译文】

Article 151 ...

Where <u>a unit</u> commits the crime as mentioned in this Article, it shall be fined, and the persons who are directly in charge and the other persons who are directly responsible for the crime shall be punished in accordance with the provisions of the paragraphs in this Article respectively.

【例 4】【例 5】便是我国刑法分则中最典型的规定单位犯罪的条款。前者为第三章第一节"生产、销售伪劣商品罪"的最后一款法条，补充该节规定的各项犯罪也可为单位犯罪；而后者为第三章第二节"走私罪"首条最后一款，补充该条规定的各项犯罪也可为单位犯罪。二者行文亦相似，译文处理也相近。

【推荐译文】

Section 150 Where <u>an organization</u> commits a crime as mentioned in Sections 141 through 148 of this Article, the organization shall be sentenced to pay a fine, and persons who are directly in charge of it and other persons who are directly responsible for the crime shall be punished pursuant to the provisions of these sections respectively.

【推荐译文】

Section 151 ...

Where <u>an organization</u> commits a crime as mentioned in this Section, the organization shall be sentenced to pay a fine, and persons who are directly in charge and other persons who are directly responsible for the crime shall be punished pursuant to the provisions of the paragraphs in this Section respectively.

当然，我国刑法分则中也有些条款不采用概括性的法律术语"单位"，而是具体列举了可以构成单位犯罪的主体，如【例 6】。【例 7】则是与主体相对应的自然人犯罪。

【例 6】

第一百六十二条 <u>公司、企业</u>进行清算时，隐匿财产，对资产负债表或者财产清单作虚伪记载或者在未清偿债务前分配公司、企业财产，严重损害债权人或者其他人利益的，<u>对其直接负责的主管人员和其他直接责任人员</u>，处五年以下有期徒刑或者拘役，并处或者单处二万元以上二十万元以下罚金。

【对照译文】

Article 162 Where, in the process of its liquidation, <u>a company or enterprise</u> conceals its assets, records false information in its balance sheet or inventory of assets, or distributes the company or enterprise assets prior to full payment of its debts, thus causing serious harm to the interests of the creditors or others, <u>the persons who are directly in charge and the other persons who are directly responsible for the crime</u> shall be sentenced to fixed-term imprisonment of not more than five years or criminal detention and shall also, or shall only, be fined not less than 20,000 *yuan* but not more than 200,000 *yuan*.

【例 7】

第一百六十三条 **公司、企业或者其他单位的工作人员**，利用职务上的便利，索取他人财物或者非法收受他人财物，为他人谋取利益，数额较大的，处三年以下有期徒刑或者拘役，并处罚金；数额巨大或者有其他严重情节的，处三年以上十年以下有期徒刑，并处罚金；数额特别巨大或者有其他特别严重情节的，处十年以上有期徒刑或者无期徒刑，并处罚金。

【对照译文】

Article 163 Where, by taking advantage of his or her position, <u>any staff member of a company, an enterprise, or any other entity</u> solicits or illegally accepts any money or property from any other person in order to seek benefits for such other person, the staff member shall be sentenced to imprisonment of not more than three years or limited incarceration and a fine if the amount involved is relatively large; shall be sentenced to imprisonment of not less than three years nor more than ten years and a fine if the amount involved is huge or there is any other serious circumstance; or shall be sentenced to imprisonment of not less than ten years or life imprisonment and a fine if the amount involved is especially huge or there is any other especially serious circumstance.

【例 7】规定的公司、企业人员受贿罪，其主体为公司、企业的工作人员；而【例 6】规定的妨害清算罪，其主体则为公司、企业。尽管我国刑法总则第三十一条规定单位犯罪应采用双罚制，但本条却采用单罚制——仅处罚"直接负责的主管人员和其他直接责任人员"。

所谓"直接负责的主管人员"，是指对单位犯罪负有直接责任的主要领导人员，如厂长、副厂长、经理、副经理、部门经理等等；所谓"其他直接责任人员"，是指除直接负责的主管人员之外其他对单位犯罪负有直接责任的人员，即单位犯罪的直接实施者（刘家琛，2002: 147）。

笔者以为，此类条款中的"主管人员"实际上与英美法术语 "high managerial agent" 相对应。依据《布莱克法律词典》的定义，该术语意为：

An agent of a corporation or other business who has authority to formulate corporate policy or supervise employees. —Also termed *superior agent*. （Garner, 2019: 80）

也有些英美成文法延伸了其概念，如《美国模范刑法典》第 2.07 条（SECTION 2.07 LIABILITY OF CORPORATIONS, UNINCORPORATED ASSOCIATIONS AND PERSONS ACTING, OR UNDER A DUTY TO ACT, IN THEIR BEHALF）第（4）款（b）（c）项规定：

(b) "agent" means any director, officer, servant, employee or other person authorized to act in behalf of the corporation or association and, in the case of an unincorporated association, a member of such association;

(c) "<u>high managerial agent</u>" means an officer of a corporation or an unincorporated association, or, in the case of a partnership, a partner, or any other agent of a corporation or association having duties of such responsibility that his conduct may fairly be assumed to represent the policy of the corporation or association.

故而如下译文值得推荐。

【推荐译文】

Section 162　Where <u>a company or enterprise</u>, under liquidation, conceals its assets, records false information in its balance sheet or inventory of assets, or distributes its assets prior to full payment of its debts, and thus causes serious harm to the interests of its creditors or other persons, <u>high managerial and other agents of the company or enterprise who are directly responsible for its criminal conduct</u> shall be sentenced to pay a fine not less than 20,000 *yuan* nor more than 200,000 *yuan*, in addition to a sentence of imprisonment for a term not more than five years or criminal detention.

【推荐译文】

Section 163　<u>An agent of a company, enterprise or other organization</u> who takes advantage of his position, and demands property from another person or illegally accepts another person's property in return for the benefit he seeks for such person, shall be sentenced to pay a fine in addition to a sentence of imprisonment for a term not more than three years or criminal detention, if the amount involved is relatively large; or shall be sentenced to pay a fine in addition to a sentence of imprisonment for a term not less than three years nor more than ten years, if the amount involved is huge or other circumstances thereof are serious; or shall be sentenced to pay a fine in addition to a sentence of imprisonment for a term not less than ten years or life imprisonment, if the amount involved is especially huge or other circumstances thereof are especially serious.

10.1.3　必要共同犯罪

所谓必要共同犯罪，是指在构成要件的性质上，刑法条款本身就规定必须由数个行为人才能实施的犯罪（大谷实, 2003: 296）。如以下两例。

【例 8】

第一百零四条　组织、策划、实施武装叛乱或者武装暴乱的，对<u>首要分子或者罪行重大的</u>，处无期徒刑或者十年以上有期徒刑；对<u>积极参加的</u>，处三年以上十年以下有期徒刑；对<u>其他参加的</u>，处三年以下有期徒刑、拘役、管制或者剥夺政治权利。

【例 9】

第二百九十条　……

聚众冲击国家机关，致使国家机关工作无法进行，造成严重损失的，对<u>首要分子</u>，处五年以上十年以下有期徒刑；对<u>其他积极参加的</u>，处五年以下有期徒刑、拘役、管制或者剥夺政治权利。

【例 8】【例 9】之类的条款是我国刑法分则中最典型的必要共同犯罪。【例 8】规定的武装叛乱、暴乱罪，其行为要件表现为"组织、策划、实施武装叛乱或者武装暴乱"；【例 9】规定的聚众冲击国家机关罪，其行为要件表现为"聚众冲击国家机关"。显然，两罪均非单个犯罪分子可以实施的，必须由数人共同完成。对于此类犯罪，我国刑法的量刑原则是针对行为人在共同犯罪中所起的作用分别设定刑罚种类及幅度。具体而言，就是要区别"首要分子""积极参加的""其他参加的"等各自惩处，不过犯罪的客观要件仍是由上述行为人共同实施的。故笔者以为，处理此类条款，译文应当体现犯罪的共同性，以"among those who ..."起首，是比较恰当的。

【推荐译文】

Section 104 <u>Among those who</u> organize, plot or carry out armed rebellion or armed riot, <u>ringleaders or whoever commits major criminal conduct</u> shall be sentenced to life imprisonment or imprisonment for a term not less than ten years; a<u>ctive participants</u> shall be sentenced to imprisonment for a term not less than three years nor more than ten years; and <u>other participants</u> shall be sentenced to imprisonment for a term not more than three years, criminal detention, public surveillance or deprivation of political rights.

【推荐译文】

Section 290 ...

<u>Among those who</u> are gathered to assault a State agency and make such agency unable to deal with its work and thus cause heavy losses, <u>ringleaders</u> shall be sentenced to imprisonment for a term not less than five years nor more than ten years; and <u>other active participants</u> shall be sentenced to imprisonment for a term not more than five years, criminal detention, public surveillance or deprivation of political rights.

10.2　犯罪的主观方面

所谓犯罪主观方面，是指行为人对于危害社会结果的心理状态（陈兴良，2001: 204）。

10.2.1　故意/过失

故意与过失乃是我国刑法理论中的重要术语，因而《中华人民共和国刑法》（2023年修正）总则中的条款对此有着明确定义：

第十四条　明知自己的行为会发生危害社会的结果，并且希望或者放任这种结果发生，因而构成犯罪的，是<u>故意犯罪</u>。

故意犯罪，应当负刑事责任。

第十五条　应当预见自己的行为可能发生危害社会的结果，因为疏忽大意而没有预见，或者已经预见而轻信能够避免，以致发生这种结果的，是<u>过失犯罪</u>。

过失犯罪，法律有规定的才负刑事责任。

【例 10】

第二百三十二条　故意杀人的，处死刑、无期徒刑或者十年以上有期徒刑；情节较轻的，处三年以上十年以下有期徒刑。

【推荐译文】

Section 232　Whoever <u>intentionally</u> commits homicide shall be sentenced to death, life imprisonment or imprisonment for a term not less than ten years; or shall be sentenced to imprisonment for a term not less than three years nor more than ten years, if the circumstances thereof are relatively minor.

【例11】

第二百三十三条　<u>过失</u>致人死亡的，处三年以上七年以下有期徒刑；情节较轻的，处三年以下有期徒刑。本法另有规定的，依照规定。

【推荐译文】

Section 233　Except as otherwise specifically provided in this Law, whoever <u>negligently</u> causes death of another person shall be sentenced to imprisonment for a term not less than three years nor more than seven years; or shall be sentenced to imprisonment for a term not more than three years, if the circumstances thereof are relatively minor.

规定故意杀人罪的【例10】与规定过失致人死亡罪的【例11】就是一组对比鲜明的法条。当然，我国刑法分则中很多条款并未使用术语"故意"或者"过失"，但其原因不足为译者所虑。

10.2.2　明　知

明知作为故意犯罪主观要件中不可或缺的因素，规定于前引刑法总则第十四条："明知自己的行为会发生危害社会的结果"。此外，刑法分则中也有条款涉及明知，规定的却是危害结果以外的其他犯罪客观情状。

而英美法中的明知（knowledge）则为四种犯罪意图（mens rea）之一①。《布莱克法律词典》将之解释为：

An awareness or understanding of a fact or circumstance; a state of mind in which a person has no substantial doubt about the existence of a fact.（Garner, 2019: 1043）

具体到成文法条款，则多采用如下近似表述：

（1）《美国模范刑法典》第 2.02 条（SECTION 2.02　GENERAL REQUIREMENTS OF CULPABILITY）第（2）款（b）项：

(b) *Knowingly*. A person acts knowingly with respect to a material element of an offense when:

(i) if the element involves the nature of his conduct or the attendant circumstances, he is aware that his conduct is of that nature or that such circumstances exist; and

(ii) if the element involves a result of his conduct, he is aware that it is practically certain that his conduct will cause such a result.

（2）《美国模范刑法典》第212.4 条（SECTION 212.4　INTERFERENCE WITH CUSTODY）第（1）款：

---

① 英美法中所谓犯罪意图，包括蓄意、明知、轻率与疏忽。

(1) CUSTODY OF CHILDREN. A person commits an offense if he knowingly or recklessly takes or entices any child under the age of 18 from the custody of its parent, guardian or other lawful custodian, when he has no privilege to do so. ...

(a) ...

(b) ...

... The offense is a misdemeanor unless the actor, not being a parent or person in equivalent relation to the child, acted with knowledge that his conduct would cause serious alarm for the child's safety, ..., in which case the offense is a felony of the third degree.

前者为法典第一编（General Provisions）中的条款，规定明知的一般内容。显然，英美法中的"knowledge"作为一种独立的犯罪意图，其内容的广泛性远胜于我国刑法中仅为主观故意之要素的明知。而后者则出现于法典第二编（Definition of Specific Crimes）。其规定包括两类：一类为重申明知的一般内容；另一类则为详述明知的特殊内容。

重申一般内容的明知，因其内容已见于总则，故只需"knowingly"作状语即可；而详述特殊内容的明知，则因其内容不见于总则，故采用"with knowledge that ..."作状语，后续同位语从句也是为此而设。

比较而言，我国刑法分则条款中的明知，旨在详述不同于总则规定的特殊内容，如【例12】。故笔者认为，【对照译文】以"knowingly"为状语不妥，应当采用【推荐译文】。

【例12】

第一百四十八条　生产不符合卫生标准的化妆品，或者销售明知是不符合卫生标准的化妆品，造成严重后果的，处三年以下有期徒刑或者拘役，并处或者单处销售金额百分之五十以上二倍以下罚金。

【对照译文】

Article 148　Whoever produces cosmetics that are not up to hygiene standards or knowingly sells such cosmetics, thus causing serious consequences, shall be sentenced to fixed-term imprisonment of not more than three years or criminal detention and shall also, or shall only, be fined not less than half but not more than two times the amount of earnings from sales.

【推荐译文】

Section 148　Whoever produces cosmetics that are not up to hygiene standards or whoever sells such cosmetics with knowledge that they are not up to hygiene standards shall be sentenced to pay a fine not less than half nor more than two times the amount of sales only or in addition to a sentence of imprisonment for a term not more than three years or criminal detention, if serious consequences are thus caused.

10.2.3　目　的

所谓犯罪目的，作为主观附随情状之一，指的是犯罪人实施犯罪行为所希望达到的结果（陈兴良，2001：379）。

通常，犯罪目的为直接故意的心理内容所包含，但我国刑法分则中也有些条款特别规定了不为直接故意所包容的犯罪目的。遇此类目的犯条款，译者在处理时必须谨慎，因为犯罪目的对于直接故意犯罪行为性质的确定具有决定性意义。请看下例。

【例 13】

第二百七十六条　<u>由于泄愤报复或者其他个人目的</u>，毁坏机器设备、残害耕畜或者以其他方法破坏生产经营的，处三年以下有期徒刑、拘役或者管制；情节严重的，处三年以上七年以下有期徒刑。

【对照译文】

Article 276　Anyone who, <u>for purpose of giving vent to spite or retaliating or out of other personal motives</u>, destroys or damages machines or equipment, cruelly injures or slaughters farm animals or sabotages production and business operation by other means, shall be sentenced to fixed-term imprisonment of not more than three years, criminal detention or public surveillance; if the circumstances are serious, he shall be sentenced to fixed-term imprisonment of not less than three years but not more than seven years.

【例 13】所引条款规定的是破坏生产经营罪。"由于泄愤报复或者其他个人目的"即为该罪的主观附随情状，**【对照译文】**将"目的"译成"motive"，笔者以为不妥。依据《布莱克法律词典》的解释：

While motive is the inducement to do some act, intent is the mental resolution or determination to do it.（Garner, 2019: 964）

故该术语相当于我国刑法理论中的"动机"，即激起和推动犯罪人实施犯罪行为的心理动因（陈兴良，2001: 379）。动机虽也是犯罪的主观附随情状，却不同于目的而未具体规定在分则条款表述的罪状之中。

相反，英美法术语"purpose"依据《布莱克法律词典》的定义，意为"an objective, goal, or end"（Garner, 2019: 1493）。所以，**【推荐译文】**将"目的"译为"purpose"是极为合理的。这也符合英美成文法的行文习惯，如《美国模范刑法典》第 213.1 条（Section 213.1　Rape and Related Offenses）第（1）款（b）项：

(b) he has substantially impaired her power to appraise or control her conduct by administering or employing without her knowledge drugs, intoxicants or other means <u>for the purpose of</u> preventing resistance;

【推荐译文】

Section 276　Whoever, <u>for the purpose of venting his anger or taking his revenge or for any other purpose</u>, sabotages production by damaging machine equipment or injuring farm animals or by any other means, shall be sentenced to imprisonment for a term not more than three years, criminal detention or public surveillance; or shall be sentenced to imprisonment for a term not less than three years nor more than seven years, if the circumstances thereof are serious.

我国刑法分则中比较常见的目的主观要件之一是"为谋取不正当利益"，主要规定于构成犯罪的行贿行为，包括行贿罪、对单位行贿罪、单位行贿罪等，以及下例所引的对公司、企业人员行贿罪。

【例 14】

第一百六十四条　为谋取<u>不正当利益</u>，给予公司、企业或者其他单位的工作人员以财物，数额较大的，处三年以下有期徒刑或者拘役，并处罚金；数额巨大的，处三年以上十年以下有期徒刑，并处罚金。

【推荐译文】

Section 164　Whoever, <u>for the purpose of seeking illegitimate benefits</u>, gives property to an employee of a company, enterprise or other entity, shall be sentenced to pay a fine in addition to a sentence of imprisonment for a term not more than three years or criminal detention, if the amount of such property is relatively large; or shall be sentenced to pay a fine in addition to a sentence of imprisonment for a term not less than three years nor more ten years, if the amount of such property is huge.

而另一类常见的目的主观要件则为"以非法占有为目的"，主要规定于金融诈骗犯罪行为，如下例所引的集资诈骗罪。

【例 15】

第一百九十二条　<u>以非法占有为目的</u>，使用诈骗方法非法集资，数额较大的，处三年以上七年以下有期徒刑，并处罚金；数额巨大或者有其他严重情节的，处七年以上有期徒刑或者无期徒刑，并处罚金或者没收财产。

【推荐译文】

Section 192　Whoever, <u>for the purpose of unlawful possession</u>, unlawfully raises fund by means of fraud, shall be sentenced to pay a fine in addition to a sentence of imprisonment for a term not less than three years nor more than seven years, if the amount of fund thus raised is relatively large; or shall be sentenced to pay a fine or be sentenced to confiscation of property, in addition to a sentence of imprisonment for a term not less than seven years or life imprisonment, if the amount of fund thus raised is huge or other circumstances thereof are serious.

◎翻译实践题◎

1. 犯罪主体

1) 国家工作人员

2) 国家机关工作人员

3) 军人

4) 单位

5) 公司、企业

6) 国有公司、企业、事业单位直接负责的主管人员

7) 公司、企业或者其他单位的工作人员

8) 其直接负责的主管人员和其他直接责任人员

9) 铁路职工

10) 依法配备公务用枪的人员

11) 依法配置枪支的人员

12) 首要分子或者罪行重大的

13) 积极参加的

2. 犯罪主观方面

1) 故意

2) 过失

3) 明知……

4) 由于泄愤报复或者其他个人目的

5) 为谋取不正当利益

6) 以非法占有为目的

◆第四编翻译实践练习

●汉译英

1. 分裂国家罪

第一百零三条　组织、策划、实施分裂国家、破坏国家统一的，对首要分子或者罪行重大的，处无期徒刑或者十年以上有期徒刑；对积极参加的，处三年以上十年以下有期徒刑；对其他参加的，处三年以下有期徒刑、拘役、管制或者剥夺政治权利。

2. 非法持有宣扬恐怖主义、极端主义物品罪

第一百二十条之六　明知是宣扬恐怖主义、极端主义的图书、音频视频资料或者其他物品而非法持有，情节严重的，处三年以下有期徒刑、拘役或者管制，并处或者单处罚金。

3. 生产、销售不符合安全标准的食品罪

第一百四十三条　生产、销售不符合食品安全标准的食品，足以造成严重食物中毒事故或者其他严重食源性疾病的，处三年以下有期徒刑或者拘役，并处罚金；对人体健康造成严重危害或者有其他严重情节的，处三年以上七年以下有期徒刑，并处罚金；后果特别严重的，处七年以上有期徒刑或者无期徒刑，并处罚金或者没收财产。

4. 过失致人重伤罪

第二百三十五条　过失伤害他人致人重伤的，处三年以下有期徒刑或者拘役。本法另有规定的，依照规定。

5. 抢劫罪

第二百六十三条　以暴力、胁迫或者其他方法抢劫公私财物的，处三年以上十年以下有期徒刑，并处罚金；有下列情形之一的，处十年以上有期徒刑、无期徒刑或者死刑，并处罚金或者没收财产：……

6. 妨害公务罪

第二百七十七条 以暴力、威胁方法阻碍国家机关工作人员依法执行职务的，处三年以下有期徒刑、拘役、管制或者罚金。

以暴力、威胁方法阻碍全国人民代表大会和地方各级人民代表大会代表依法执行代表职务的，依照前款的规定处罚。

在自然灾害和突发事件中，以暴力、威胁方法阻碍红十字会工作人员依法履行职责的，依照第一款的规定处罚。

7. 聚众冲击军事禁区罪

第三百七十一条 聚众冲击军事禁区，严重扰乱军事禁区秩序的，对首要分子，处五年以上十年以下有期徒刑；对其他积极参加的，处五年以下有期徒刑、拘役、管制或者剥夺政治权利。

8. 受贿罪

第三百八十五条 国家工作人员利用职务上的便利，索取他人财物的，或者非法收受他人财物，为他人谋取利益的，是受贿罪。

国家工作人员在经济往来中，违反国家规定，收受各种名义的回扣、手续费，归个人所有的，以受贿论处。

●宪法翻译的启示 3：行为模式篇

●宪法翻译的启示 4：前提条件篇

第五编

法律语篇◆◆

第 11 章
规定性法律文件

◎学习目标◎

1. 理解规定性法律文件的十项语言推定原则；
2. 掌握检验规定性法律译文的准确性标准；
3. 掌握检验规定性法律译文的一致性标准。

导　言

　　准确翻译规定性法律文件的重要性不言而喻。无论是在英美法系国家，还是在大陆法系国家，成文法都是极为重要的法律渊源，是人们守法、执法、司法的根本依据。

　　正如本书 2.1.2 所述，规定性法律原文与译文均以内容为重。但由于两文本读者群之间存在文化差异，为使原文与译文传递的信息量实现动态对等，我们作为文化中介是否需要在译文中补充原文中隐含的背景知识呢？要回答这个问题，笔者以为必须从读者角度来考察。

　　谁才是规定性法律文件的最主要读者？不同学者对此有着不同观点：最狭隘的理解只涉及法官，而最宽泛的理解则包括一切立法、守法、执法与司法人员（陶博，2004：43-44）。

　　现代社会强调法治，普法教育方兴未艾。认为法官是法律文本的唯一读者，显然不合时宜。可普通民众又能在多大程度上理解规定性法律文件呢？考虑到法律工作的专业化程度之高，无论规范性法律文本的遣词造句多么平易简洁，普通民众也因不了解文本背后蕴含的法学传统与理论而无法真正领会其精神实质，故普通民众通常只能求助于专业人士处理法律事务。因此，笔者以为，规定性法律文件的主要读者是那些专业法律人士。

　　具体到规定性法律文件的译本，其读者必然是从事涉外法律工作的专业人士，包括法官、检察官及律师等。这些专业人士对外国法律文化的了解，较之法律文本的译者，大抵有过之而无不及。在译文文本中补充相关文化背景知识，无异于画蛇添足。

　　无论如何，法律文化的差异对于规定性法律文件的翻译，其重要性依然不可忽视，特别是法律文本的语言特色及解释原则。本章就将从这两个维度着手研究规定性法律文件翻译的一般性问题。

11.1　翻译前提：原文的理解

尽管规定性法律文件的表述以追求语言的准确性为宗旨，然而由于语言形式本身的限制，无论文本的制定者如何斟酌文字，也无法绝对避免歧义的产生。因此，译者在理解原文的过程中，必须时常借助法律解释的方法，以澄清原文中可能存在的歧义。当然，这些推理解释原则还可作为我们品评译文表述准确性程度的工具：若译文无须借助此类工具即可为读者所理解无疑最佳；若借助此类工具方可为读者所理解，但推定结果与原文内容无出入的，则为次优；而借助此类工具方可为读者所理解，且推定结果与原文内容不相符的，则不足取。

就法理而言，规定性法律文件的解释原则可分两类：法律推定与语言推定。其中法律推定主要包括**单行法优于普通法原则**（the rule that specific statutes prevail over general statutes）、**后法优于前法原则**（the rule *lex posterior derogat priori*）、**禁止默示废止原则**（the rule disfavoring repeals by implication）、**采有效性解释原则**（the rule of adopting a construction that favors validity）、**不利起草者的解释原则**（the rule of constructing a document against the drafter）、**符合公共政策原则**（the rule of public policy）等。此类解释方法虽有助于法院解决冲突法律规范或合同条款的适用问题，但大都与译者关系不大，故笔者的分析将主要针对语言推定原则。

11.1.1　避免赘言原则

避免赘言原则（the rule against tautology）体现了规定性法律文件的简洁性风格，本质在于推定此类文本中的每个词都是有意义的，都是制定者真实意图的反映，故全都不可或缺（陶博，2004: 90）。当然，这并非意味着英汉法律互译过程中，原文与译文所用词汇必须完全一一对应，毕竟英汉语言形式存在本质差别，正如下例所示。

【例1】

第九十七条　出租人在约定的受载期限内未能提供船舶的，承租人有权解除合同。但是，出租人将船舶延误情况和船舶预期抵达装货港的日期通知承租人的，承租人应当自收到通知时起四十八小时内，将是否解除合同的决定通知出租人。

——《中华人民共和国海商法》（1992 年）

【推荐译文】

Section 97　When the shipowner fails to provide the ship within the laydays as specified in the charter, the charterer shall be entitled to cancel the charter party. However, if the shipowner notifies the charterer of the delay of such ship and the expected date of its arrival at the port of loading, the charterer shall notify the shipowner whether to cancel the charter within 48 hours from the receipt of the shipowner's notice.

前引条款规定的是承租人享有的合同解除权。就词汇层面而言，原文与译文相比，不一致处颇多。较为显著的就有汉语"情况""时"，以及英语"such""shipowner's"等。

但究其整体含义，"船舶延误情况"与"the delay of such ship"、"收到通知时"与"the receipt of the shipowner's notice"实际上并无差别。

除此以外，我们在翻译过程中，绝不可率性随意删减原文词句，否则就有悖于避免赘言原则的推定。如以下两例。

【例 2】

第九十条 船舶在装货港开航前，因不可抗力或者其他不能归责于承运人和托运人的原因致使合同不能履行的，双方均可以解除合同，并互相不负赔偿责任。<u>除合同另有约定外</u>，运费已经支付的，承运人应当将运费退还给托运人；货物已经装船的，托运人应当承担装卸费用；已经签发提单的，托运人应当将提单退还承运人。

——《中华人民共和国海商法》（1992 年）

【对照译文】

Article 90 Either the carrier or the shipper may request the cancellation of the contract and neither shall be liable to the other if, due to force majeure or other causes not attributable to the fault of the carrier or the shipper, the contract could not be performed prior to the ship's sailing from its port of loading. If the freight has already been paid, it shall be refunded to the shipper, and, if the goods have already been loaded on board, the loading/discharge expenses shall be borne by the shipper. If a bill of lading has already been issued, it shall be returned by the shipper to the carrier.

【例 3】

第九十六条 出租人应当提供约定的船舶；经承租人同意，可以更换船舶。但是，<u>提供的船舶或者更换的船舶</u>不符合合同约定的，承租人有权拒绝或者解除合同。

——《中华人民共和国海商法》（1992 年）

【对照译文】

Article 96 The shipowner shall provide the intended ship. The intended ship may be substituted with the consent of the charterer. However, if <u>the ship substituted</u> does not meet the requirements of the charter party, the charterer may reject the ship or cancel the charter.

此两例的【对照译文】，较之原文缩减了些词句，但这不是出于语言形式方面的考虑。事实上，前款漏译画线部分"除合同另有约定外"，从而限制了当事人的意思自由；后款漏译画线部分"提供的船舶"，从而限制了该规范的适用条件。换言之，【对照译文】擅自篡改了原文制定者的意图，而这无疑是法律翻译的大忌。请看笔者的【推荐译文】。

【推荐译文】

Section 90 If, prior to the ship's sailing from its port of loading, the contract is not performable due to force majeure or other causes not attributable to the fault of the carrier or shipper, either the carrier or shipper may cancel the contract but neither of them shall be liable to the other. <u>Except as otherwise specified in the contract</u>, the carrier shall refund to the shipper the freight paid, and the shipper shall pay the loading/discharge expenses of the goods loaded on board and return to the carrier the bill of lading issued.

【推荐译文】

Section 96　The shipowner shall provide the intended ship, but he may replace it with the consent of the charterer. However, if <u>the ship provided or replaced</u> does not meet the requirements of the charter party, the charterer may reject the ship or cancel the charter.

11.1.2　文义解释原则与整体解释原则

规定性法律文件制定者的意图只能通过语言文字表述出来。这些语言文字依据**文义解释原则**（the plain meaning），应当按照其习惯使用的含义进行解释。一般词汇取通常含义，专业词汇取特定含义，至于篇章句子亦因根据语法规则及标点符号来诠释，除非可能产生歧义或者荒谬的结果（Haggard, 2004: 89-90）。而且所涉文本必须作为一个整体来理解，其中任何条款，甚至单个词句都不应孤立地进行诠释，即遵循**整体解释原则**（the rule that a document must be read as a whole）（陶博，2004: 91）。以下所引条款的翻译便能很好地说明这个问题。

【例 4】

第三十五条　船长负责船舶的管理和驾驶。

船长在其职权范围内发布的命令，<u>船员、旅客和其他在船人员</u>都必须执行。

——《中华人民共和国海商法》（1992 年）

【对照译文】

Article 35　The Master shall be responsible for the management and navigation of the ship.

Orders given by the Master within the scope of his functions and powers must be carried out by <u>other members of the crew, the passengers and all persons on board</u>.

上例原文画线部分共涉及三类在船人员。其中"船员"，依据<u>文义解释原则</u>，一般认为应不包括船长在内。据此而言，似乎【对照译文】"other members of the crew"是可取的。但若结合相关条款，却能发现这种理解大谬不然。按照该法第三十一条规定：

船员，是指包括船长在内的船上一切任职人员。

笔者以为，我们应当遵循<u>整体解释原则</u>，将之译为"the crew"。

【推荐译文】

Section 35　The Master shall be responsible for the management and navigation of the ship.

<u>The crew, passengers and other persons on board</u> must carry out instructions given by the Master to the extent of his functions and powers.

无疑，上述两项推定原则是译者理解原规定性法律文件所不可或缺的。而随后三项原则虽为文义解释与整体解释在特定情形下相互结合的具体细化，不过适用的前提必须是原文内容确有歧义，并且针对的只能是本身具有多种含义的词汇，以期从中选取最佳的理解。

11.1.3　否定解释原则

《布莱克法律词典》将拉丁语"*expressio unius est exclusio alterius*"即"the expression of one thing is the exclusion of another"定义为：

> A canon of construction holding that to express or include one thing implies the exclusion of the other, or of the alternative.（Garner, 2019: 726）

依据**否定解释原则**（the rule of *expressio unius est exclusio alterius*），规定性法律文件中列举具体事项的条款可推定为有排他性（Haggard, 2004: 97）。正因为如此，很多规定性法律文件才特意注明具体事项的列举不具有排他性，以避免歧义。如《施工合同条件》第 4.10 条第 2 款斜体部分：

> ... To the same extent, the Contractor shall be deemed to have inspected and examined the Site, its surroundings, the above data and other available information, and to have been satisfied before submitting the Tender as to all relevant matters, including (*without limitation*):
>
> (a) the form and nature of the Site, including sub-surface conditions,
>
> (b) the hydrological and climatic conditions,
>
> (c) the extent and nature of the work and Goods necessary for the execution and completion of the Works and the remedying of any defects,

11.1.4　类别解释原则

《布莱克法律词典》将拉丁语"*ejusdem gnenris*"即"of the same kind or class"定义如下：

> A canon of construction holding that when a general word or phrase follows a list of specifics, the general word or phrase will be interpreted to include only items of the same class as those listed.（Garner, 2019: 654）

依据**类别解释原则**（the rule of *ejusdem generis*），规定性法律文件中列举具体事项的条款若以宽泛的抽象词汇结尾的，则该词汇的确切含义可由先行事项推定（Haggard, 2004: 100）。当然，抽象词汇的推定含义必须基于具体事项的共同特征，而文本制定者亦会尽可能揭示此点，以避免歧义。如《施工合同条件》第 13.2 条第 1 款斜体部分：

> The Contractor may, at any time, submit to the Engineer a written proposal which (in the Contractor's opinion) will, if adopted, (i) accelerate completion, (ii) reduce the cost to the Employer of executing, maintaining or operating the Works, (iii) improve the efficiency or value to the Employer of the completed Works, or (iv) otherwise *be of benefit to the Employer*.

11.1.5　关联解释原则

《布莱克法律词典》将拉丁语"*noscitur a sociis*"即"it is known by its associates"定义如下：

> A canon of construction holding that the meaning of an unclear word or phrase, esp. one in

a list, should be determined by the words immediately surrounding it.（Garner, 2019: 1274）

依据**关联解释原则**（the rule of *noscitur a sociis*），规定性法律文件中意思含混不清的词汇可以通过对关联词的理解，进而推定其含义（Haggard, 2004: 102）。该原则特别适用于分析以"或/or""和/and"连接的数个在同一条款中具有类似语法及推理功能的词汇（陶博, 2004: 92）。

对于前述五项解释原则，笔者以为，在很多情况下必须综合运用，方可恰如其分地理解原文。请看下例。

【例5】

SECTION 220.2 CAUSING OR RISING CATASTROPHE

(1) <u>CAUSING CATASTROPHE</u>. A person who causes a catastrophe by explosion, <u>fire</u>[①], <u>flood</u>, <u>avalanche</u>[②], <u>collapse of building</u>[③], release of poison gas, radioactive material or <u>other harmful or destructive force or substance</u>, or by any <u>other means</u>[④] of causing potentially widespread <u>injury or damage</u>[⑤], commits a felony of the second degree if he does so purposely or knowingly, or a felony of the third degree if he does so recklessly.

—Model Penal Code

【对照译文】

第220.2条 引起灾祸的发生或者危险

（1）<u>引起灾祸</u>。行为人通过爆炸、<u>纵火</u>[①]、<u>洪水、雪崩</u>[②]、<u>建筑物倒塌</u>[③]、释放有毒气体、放射性物质或者<u>其他有害物质、破坏力</u>或者有可能引起广泛<u>伤害或者破坏</u>[⑤]的<u>其他手段</u>[④]，蓄意地、明知地引起灾祸的，成立二级重罪；轻率地引起灾祸的，成立三级重罪。

本条款所规定的犯罪，客观地列举了一组具体行为"explosion, fire, flood, avalanche, collapse of building, release of poison gas, radioactive material or other harmful or destructive force or substance"，并以兜底性短语"any other means of causing potentially widespread injury or damage"结尾。实际上，这也是我们理解原文的关键所在。

首先应当引起译者注意的无疑是"fire"，该词与"explosion"并列。依据<u>文义解释原则</u>，"explosion"当然是指行为，故可译为"爆炸"；而"fire"却有歧义，指的究竟是"火"呢？还是"放火"呢？对此，我们不妨比较该条第二款的规定：

(2) <u>RISKING CATASTROPHE</u>. A person is guilty of a misdemeanor if he recklessly creates a risk of catastrophe in the employment of <u>fire</u>, explosives or other dangerous means listed in Subsection (1).

此款中的"fire"与"explosive"并列，显然皆非行为，而是指可资利用的事物、状态，否则立法者大可不必在第（1）款所列的其他手段外，特意加以说明，并将"fire"置于"explosive"之前。据此论之，译者当可推定前面与"explosion"并列的"fire"指行为，故应译成"放火"。这是符合<u>整体解释原则</u>的。

紧接下来的便是"flood"与"avalanche"，二者通常的词典含义分别指"洪水"及"雪崩"。然以自然灾害入罪无疑极为荒谬，故不可取。鉴于这两个词汇列举在一组同类事项中，因此译者可根据其前后的关联词来加深理解，也就是借助<u>关联解释原则</u>推定。

正如前文所论，起首的"explosion"与"fire"皆指行为，而其后的"release of poison gas, radioactive material or other harmful or destructive force or substance"显然亦是名词化的动宾短语，所以，"flood"与"avalanche"应当解释成人为的自然灾害，换言之即"引发洪水、雪崩"。

亦可合并做类似处理的尚有"collapse of building"。若简单地将其理解成"推倒建筑物"，那么依据<u>否定解释原则</u>，其他导致建筑物倒塌的行为将被排除在外。这显然有悖于原文的规定，因为立法者本无意姑息任何导致建筑物倒塌的行为。故笔者以为，应当将之译成"引发建筑物倒塌"。

然后是结尾处的兜底性规定，"other means"的含义亦不甚明确。《布莱克法律词典》将"means"定义为"something that helps to attain an end; an instrument; a cause"（Garner, 2019: 1174）。而《元照英美法词典》则将之译成"手段；方法；工具"（薛波, 2003: 904）。落实到本款规定，应取何种译文呢？笔者以为应当将之与前列具体词汇理解为同一类事项，这也是<u>类别解释原则</u>的要求。既然分项列举的这些词汇皆指行为，那么"other means"就应当译成"任何其他手段/方法"。

还有原文最后一处画线短语"injury or damage"的翻译也需要译者慎重。依据《布莱克法律词典》的解释，"injury"是指"any harm or damage"（Garner, 2019: 939）；而"damage"则指"loss or injury to person or property"（488），其含义似乎并无差异。而《元照英美法词典》指出，"injury"与"damage"的区别通常在于：前者多针对人身，而后者多针对财产（薛波, 2003: 697）。二者同时使用，当然是为了使行文更加严谨。笔者以为，将之译成"人身伤害或财产毁坏"，是综合运用<u>文义解释原则</u>与<u>整体解释原则</u>的必然结果。

【推荐译文】

第220.2条　引起灾难的发生或者危险

（1）<u>引起灾难的发生</u>。行为人蓄意或明知地通过爆炸，<u>放火</u>①，<u>引发洪水、雪崩</u>②、建筑物倒塌③，排放有毒气体、放射性材料或者<u>其他有损害性或破坏性的力量或物质</u>，或者通过任何可能导致大量<u>人身伤害或财产毁坏</u>⑤的其他手段④引起灾难发生的，属于二级重罪；行为人轻率地通过上述手段引起灾难发生的，属于三级重罪。

尽管否定解释、类别解释及关联解释是英美法国家通行的法律解释原则，但汉语规定性法律文件的理解亦可如此推定，且在不少情况下，依据数个原则推定的结果完全一致，更能加深译者对原文的理解。如下例。

【例6】

第八十七条　<u>应当向承运人支付的运费、共同海损分摊、滞期费和承运人为货物垫付的必要费用以及应当向承运人支付的其他费用没有付清</u>，又没有提供适当担保的，承运人可以在合理的限度内留置其货物。

——《中华人民共和国海商法》（1992年）

【对照译文】

Article 87　If the freight, contribution in general average, demurrage to be paid to the carrier and other necessary charges paid by the carrier on behalf of the owner of the goods as well as other charges to be paid to the carrier have not been paid in full, nor has appropriate security been given, the carrier may have a lien, to a reasonable extent, on the goods.

本条款原文所列承运人有权留置货物作为担保的费用包括"应当向承运人支付的运费、共同海损分摊、滞期费和承运人为货物垫付的必要费用以及应当向承运人支付的其他费用"。比较【对照译文】，笔者以为，关键在于如何理解"承运人为货物垫付的必要费用"：该项费用是否亦应包含在"应当向承运人支付的"修饰范围之内呢？仅依据语法规则及标点符号，显然无法完全澄清其歧义。然而以法律语言推定原则论之，却是再明白不过的了。

首先依据关联解释原则，所议费用与"应当向承运人支付的运费、共同海损分摊、滞期费"及"应当向承运人支付的其他费用"并列，故可推定其性质是一致的。

再依据类别解释原则，既然结尾处的兜底性规定"其他费用"亦由"应当向承运人支付的"修饰，可见这是前列具体事项的共同性质，而所议费用理应包括在内。

最后依据整体解释原则，该法条赋予留置权的主体仅为承运人，因此先行列举的由留置货物所担保的费用必然也只限于那些应当支付给承运人的费用，这是完全符合法理的推定。

就此而言，【推荐译文】的处理显然更加贴近原文的内容。

【推荐译文】

Section 87　The carrier may have a lien, to a reasonable extent, on the goods if the following amounts which shall be paid to the carrier are neither paid in full nor given an appropriate security: freight, contribution in general average, demurrage and any necessary charges with respect to such goods paid by the carrier on behalf of their owner, as well as other charges.

11.1.6　对应解释原则

《布莱克法律词典》将拉丁语 *"reddendo singula singulis"* 即 "by rendering each to each" 定义为：

Assigning or distributing separate things to separate persons, or separate words to separate subjects. • This was used as a rule of construction designed to give effect to the intention of the parties who drafted the instrument. （Garner, 2019: 1529-1530）

依据对应解释原则（the rule of *reddendo singula singulis*），若译者遇到类似"men and women may become members of fraternities and sororities"的结构，无法在目标语言习惯允许的范围内重现其表述，便只能推定它们是一一对应的，译成"男生可以成为男生联谊会的成员，女生可以成为女生联谊会的成员"。当然，此类结构本身意义含混，罕见于严谨的规定性法律文件。

如【例5】中的"other harmful or destructive force or substance"就不应做此推定，因为"harmful"与"destructive"两限定词既修饰"force"也修饰"substance"，且此结构完全可以"有损害性或破坏性的力量或物质"的形式重现在汉语中。而【对照译文】

却将之错译成"其他有害物质、破坏力",简直是乱点鸳鸯谱。笔者以为,唯有【推荐译文】才可取。

11.1.7 修饰最后先行词的原则

依据**修饰最后先行词的原则**(the rule of last modification),英语规定性法律文件中限定成分的修饰范围在理解上若有歧义,则推定为仅修饰与之相邻的先行词,而不涉及其他距之较远的语言结构。但该原则绝不适用于汉语文本,因为中文限定成分多位于被修饰词之前,故只能推定被修饰的是紧接其后的词汇。此外,适用该原则的必要前提是基于文义解释无法判断原文制定者的本意。读者不妨仔细阅读下例所引原文。

【例7】

第一百九十四条 船舶因发生意外、牺牲或者其他特殊情况而损坏时,为了安全完成本航程,驶入避难港口、避难地点或者驶回装货地点进行必要的修理,在该港口或者地点额外停留期间所支付的港口费,船员工资、给养,船舶所消耗的燃料、物料,为修理而卸载、储存、重装或者搬移船上货物、燃料、物料以及其他财产所造成的损失、支付的费用,应当列入共同海损。

——《中华人民共和国海商法》(1992年)

【对照译文】

Article 194 When a ship, after having been damaged in consequence of accident, sacrifice or other extraordinary circumstances, shall have entered a port or place of refuge or returned to its port or place of loading to effect repairs which are necessary for the safe prosecution of the voyage, then the port charge paid, the wages and maintenance of the crew incurred and the fuel and stores consumed during the extra period of detention in such port or place, as well as the loss or damage and charges arising from the discharge, storage, reloading and handling of the goods, fuel, stores and other property on board in order to have the repairs done shall be allowed as general average.

根据该条款原文,依法应当列入共同海损的包括两类:(I)"在该港口或者地点额外停留期间所支付的港口费,船员工资、给养,船舶所消耗的燃料、物料";(II)"为修理而卸载、储存、重装或者搬移船上货物、燃料、物料以及其他财产所造成的损失、支付的费用"。

笔者如此理解原文,实则立足于对该条款主语的语法结构及标点符号的分析,即文义解释。事实上,该主语由两个偏正短语构成:前者是从动宾结构转化而成的,故原"支付"的宾语都属于限定成分"在该港口或者地点额外停留期间所支付的"修饰范围;而后者也是由两个并列的动宾结构转化过来的,其中"造成的损失"与"支付的费用"之间由顿号相连,显然均属限定成分"为修理而卸载、储存、重装或者搬移船上货物、燃料、物料以及其他财产"的修饰范围,否则就应使用逗号分隔。现将其结构分析列表如下:

I. 在该港口或者地点额外停留期间所支付的（限定成分）				
港口费	船员（限定成分）		船舶所消耗的（限定成分）	
	工资	给养	燃料	物料
II. 为修理而卸载、储存、重装或者搬移船上货物、燃料、物料以及其他财产（限定成分）				
造成的（限定成分）		支付的（限定成分）		
损失		费用		

而【对照译文】的主句主语亦可分解为两组：(i) the port charge paid, the wages and maintenance of the crew incurred and the fuel and stores consumed during the extra period of detention in such port or place; (ii) the loss or damage and charges arising from the discharge, storage, reloading and handling of the goods, fuel, stores and other property on board in order to have the repairs done shall be allowed as general average。其分类的依据当然在于"as well as"结构的使用。又因后一短语中"loss or damage and charges"由同一定冠词修饰，故皆为现在分词"arising from the discharge, storage, reloading and handling of the goods, fuel, stores and other property on board in order to have the repairs done shall be allowed as general average"的限定范围。而前一短语的限定成分"during the extra period of detention in such port or place"修饰的范围则无法凭借其语法结构或标点符号来判定，我们只能依据修饰最后先行词的原则，推定被修饰的短语仅为"the fuel and stores consumed"，这显然偏离了原文的意思。故笔者以为，应当改写成【推荐译文】：以逗号断开该限定成分，从而表明被修饰成分涵盖了"the port charge, the wages and maintenance of the crew and the fuel and stores consumed by the ship"。

> 【推荐译文】
> **Section 194** When a ship, due to its damage as a result of accident, sacrifice or other exceptional circumstances, enters a port or place of refuge or returns to its place of loading to execute the repairing work as is necessary for the safe completion of the voyage, the following amounts shall be allowed as general average: (i) the port charge, the wages and maintenance of the crew and the fuel and stores consumed by the ship, during the extra period of detention in such port or place; and (ii) the loss and charges arising from the discharging, storing, reloading and handling of the goods, fuel, stores and other property on board in order to have such repairing work done.

11.1.8　支持行政解释的原则

从严格意义上来说，**支持行政解释的原则**（the rule favoring agency interpretation）不属于语言推定，而是立足于法院的惯常做法，即尊重负责贯彻实施法律的相关行政机关对该法律的解释。因此，译者也可以参考行政机关的解释，特别是无法就文本本身理解原文时更是必须如此。同样可供参考的资料尚有司法机关的解释，即我国最高人民法院的司法解释及普通法国家的判例。

此外，对于《美国模范刑法典》或《统一商法典》的翻译，我们还可以将自己对法条的理解求证于其制定者的正式评注；对于国际组织发布的合同范本，译者亦可求证于该组织的诠释。需要提请译者注意的是，这与前文述及的不利起草者的解释原则并无矛盾。不利起草者原则只适用于解释具体的商业合同，因为起草合同的一方当事人在选择术语表述概念方面具有极大的优势，且其真实意图很难为另一方当事人所完全了解。但它并不适用于法律的解释，也不适用于合同范本的解释，原因在于这些反映制定者意图的评注及诠释与规定性法律文件一起被公之于众，故易为采纳此类文本的人所知悉。从某种意义上说，我们完全可以视之为原文本不可或缺的一部分，若采纳这些文本的人别有意图，则应清楚明晰地表述出来。

现仅以下面所引条款为例说明该推定原则的运用。

【例 8】

SECTION 2.04　IGNORANCE OR MISTAKE

(1) Ignorance or mistake as to a matter of fact or law is a defense if:

(a) the ignorance or mistake negatives the purpose, knowledge, belief, recklessness or negligence <u>required to establish a material element of the offense</u>; or

(b) the law provides that the state of mind established by such ignorance or mistake constitutes a defense.

—Model Penal Code

【对照译文】

第 2.04 条　不知或者错误

（1）存在下列情形时，对于事实或者法律的不知或者错误，可作为抗辩事由：

（a）不知或者错误否定了<u>对成立犯罪本体要件所必需的</u>蓄意、明知、确信、轻率或者疏忽；或者

（b）法律规定由不知或者错误所确立的心理状态可作为抗辩事由。

【推荐译文】

第 2.04 条　不知或者误解

（1）对于事实或者法律的不知或误解有下列情形的，属于抗辩事由：

（a）该不知或误解否定了<u>确立一项犯罪实质要件所要求的</u>蓄意、明知、确信、轻率或疏忽；或者

（b）法律规定了由上述不知或误解确立的心理状态构成抗辩事由。

该例原文的画线部分 "required to establish a material element of the offense" 作为限定词，其修饰范围若依修饰最后先行词的原则，就应推定为 "negligence"。然而，"purpose, knowledge, belief, recklessness or negligence" 属同一类具体事项，并由同一定冠词限定，故遵循文义解释原则，该限定词基于语法规则修饰的应当是所有五个词汇。那么译者应当如何抉择呢？笔者以为，文义解释应当优先采纳，而《美国模范刑法典》针对该款的正式评注可引为旁证：

Thus ignorance or mistake is a defense when it negatives *the existence of a state of mind that is essential to the commission of an offense*, or when it establishes a state of mind that constitutes a defense under a rule of law relating to defenses.（Kadish & Schulhofer, 2003: 225）

显然，该评注后段针对的是（b）项，而前段则为（a）项。由此可见，（a）项所列"purpose, knowledge, belief, recklessness or negligence"均为"a state of mind that is essential to the commission of an offense"，因此依据语法规则理解画线部分的修饰范围是合理的。这也更加说明，修饰最后先行词的原则不可滥用，通常仅适用于依义义解释无法澄清原文表述歧义的情形。

11.1.9　手写条款效力高于打印或印刷条款原则与大写数额效力高于阿拉伯数字原则

手写条款效力高于打印或印刷条款（the rule that handwritten words prevail over typed or printed words）及**大写数额效力高于阿拉伯数字原则**（the rule that written amounts prevail over Arabic number）两项也不属语言推定，且只对合同文本的推定有效，但对于译者却另有作用。

尽管理论上合同各项条款的内容应当保持一致，然而实际上当事人却完全可能在签署合同的前一刻以手写的方式增加某些本应打印或者印刷的协议内容。法院确立手写条款效力高于打印或印刷条款原则的理由在于，手写条款往往反映了当事人的真实想法，其与打印或印刷条款的矛盾多数只是疏忽所致。此外，这也是对格式条款解释原则的扩展。所谓格式条款，是指"由当事人一方为与不特定多数人订约而预先拟定的，并且不允许相对人对其内容作变更的合同条款"（刘娜娜、耿淑芬, 2002: 78）。包含格式条款的标准合同通常都是由社会上具有一定垄断性质的当事人制定的，且多涉及普通消费者的生活。故各国法律通常都会对其采取严格解释，如《中华人民共和国民法典》（2020 年）第四百九十八条：

对格式条款的理解发生争议的，应当按照通常理解予以解释。对格式条款有两种以上解释的，应当作出不利于提供格式条款一方的解释。格式条款和非格式条款不一致的，应当采用非格式条款。

一般来说，格式条款的文本总是打印或者印刷的，而非格式条款多为手写。

综上所述，译者在处理合同文本时，应当特别注意对手写条款的理解，且必须在译文中注明此为手写，以便引起读者注意。同样需要在译文中注明的是，原文中大小写数字不一致处。尽管依据大写数额效力高于阿拉伯数字原则，大写数额通常具有更高的效力，然译者仍无权擅自更改阿拉伯数字，只能依据原文表述，不过应当另行注明二者之间的矛盾，以免读者误认为是译者的笔误。

11.2　翻译再现：译文的表述

法律文本的语言特色在本书第 1 章及其他相关章节中已有详细的论述。这些风格要素大都与撰写法律文本的语言自身的内在特征密不可分，因此它们在原文与译文中的表现方式迥然不同。而笔者以为，我们首要考虑的是如何在译文文本中以同样专业化的语体（professional tone）传递原文本的信息。而具体到细节处，则准确性（accuracy）与一致性（consistence）无疑应当成为我们检验的标准和关注的重心。

11.2.1　准确性

所谓准确性（accuracy），是指规定性法律文件应当尽可能避免语言表述含糊而导致理解上的歧义（ambiguity）。无论何种法律文本的翻译，准确性都是译者首先追求的目标，因为歧义往往是引发法律纠纷最主要的诉因（Haggard, 2004: 250）。下文将从语义与句法两方面展开分析。

1. 避免语义歧义（semantic ambiguity）

语义歧义源于特定词汇与短语的使用（Haggard, 2004: 256）。事实上，任何语言都包含大量多义词（homonym），但只要将之置于具体语境中进行理解，一般不会导致歧义。值得译者注意的反而是人们在日常生活中经常忽略的细节问题，其中时间的表述及其处理尤为重要，因为它不仅关乎规定性法律文件的效力，还涉及主体权利义务的存续。

（1）表述期间的单位

英汉规定性法律文件中表述期间的单位，最常见的莫过于"日/day""周/week""月/month""年/year"。

在普通法中，"day"通常有两种含义：一是指从午夜到午夜的连续 24 小时期间；二是指从任何时刻开始的连续 24 小时期间（陶博，2004: 163）。"week"也有两种解释：或为世俗周（secular week），即从任何日期开始的连续七日期间；或为圣经周（biblical week），即从星期日到星期六的连续七日期间（165）。而"month"一般是指日历月（calendar month），"year"则是指日历年（calendar year）。至于我国法律若无特别说明，"月"与"年"的解释与英美国家无甚差别，但"日"通常仅指从午夜到午夜的连续 24 小时，"周"亦仅指从任何日期开始的连续七日。故在英汉互译过程中，"日"与"周"的处理需要译者特别慎重［请参阅下文所引《中华人民共和国民法典》（2020 年）总则第十章规定］。

（2）表述期间的结构

英汉规定性法律文件中可用于表述期间的结构主要如下。

●英语结构

依据普通法判例，可对英语表述期间的结构分析如下（Haggard, 2004: 268-273）：

① "after"：不包括提到的日期；

② "before"：不包括提到的日期；

③ "within ... (after/from/of)"：排除第一天而包括最后一天；

④ "by*"：是否包括提到的日期尚有歧义；

⑤ "between ... and ...*"：是否包括提到的日期尚有歧义；

⑥ "from ... to/till/until ...*"：是否包括提到的日期尚有歧义。

●汉语结构

按照《中华人民共和国民法典》（2020 年）附则第一千二百五十九条的规定：

> 民法所称的"以上"、"以下"、"以内"、"届满"，包括本数；所称的"不满"、"超过"、"以外"，不包括本数。

及《中华人民共和国刑法》（2023 年修正）第九十九条的规定：

> 本法所称以上、以下、以内，包括本数。

结合我国司法实践，现对汉语表述期间的结构分析如下：

① "以上""以下"：包含本数；

② "届满"：包含本数；

③ "不满"：不包含本数

④ "以外"：不包含本数；

⑤ "（自）……（起）……内""以内"：包含本数，但不包括提到的日期；

⑥ "自……至……*"：是否包括提到的日期尚有歧义；

⑦ "前*""以前*""之前*"：是否包括提到的日期尚有歧义；

⑧ "后*""以后*""之后*"：是否包括提到的日期尚有歧义。

注意上文列举的英汉结构，凡加"*"号者皆可能存在歧义，应当尽量避免使用或者补充说明其含义，如在此类结构后补注（含/inclusive）或（不含/exclusive）：

by ... (inclusive/exclusive)

between ... (inclusive/exclusive) and ... (inclusive/exclusive)

from ... (inclusive/exclusive) to/till/until ... (inclusive/exclusive)

自（含/不含……）……至……（含/不含……）

……前、以前、之前（含/不含……）

……后、以后、之后（含/不含……）

（3）期间的计算

普通法中关于期间计算的规则主要有三条（陶博, 2004: 174-175）：

1）期间的计算通常排除第一天而包括最后一天，若最后一天是星期日或者其他法定休假日的，就以休假日的次日为期间的最后一天（世俗日或营业日）。

2）"month"通常是指从事件发生当日午夜开始至下个月对日午夜结束的期间。若下个月没有这一日期，就在下个月最后一日的午夜结束。

3）"day"则有两种不同表述：若表述中使用了"date"一词，如"... days from the date of ..."，即指从事件发生当日午夜开始计算期间；若表述中未使用"date"一词，如"... days from ..."，即指从事件发生之时开始计算期间。

比较下文所列我国现行法律的相关规定。

1）《中华人民共和国民法典》（2020 年）总则第十章"期间计算"：

> **第二百条**　民法所称的期间按照公历年、月、日、小时计算。
>
> **第二百零一条**　按照年、月、日计算期间的，开始的当日不计入，自下一日开始计算。按照小时计算期间的，自法律规定或者当事人约定的时间开始计算。

第二百零二条　按照年、月计算期间的，到期月的对应日为期间的最后一日；没有对应日的，月末日为期间最后一日。

第二百零三条　期间的最后一日是法定休假日的，以法定休假日结束的次日为期间的最后一日。

期间的最后一日的截止时间为二十四时；有业务时间的，停止业务活动的时间为截止时间。

2)《中华人民共和国票据法》（2004 年修正）第一百零七条：

本法规定的各项期限的计算，适用民法通则关于计算期间的规定。

按月计算期限的，按到期月的对日计算；无对日的，月末日为到期日。

3)《中华人民共和国民事诉讼法》（2023 年修正）第八十五条：

期间包括法定期间和人民法院指定的期间。

期间以时、日、月、年计算。期间开始的时和日，不计算在期间内。

期间届满的最后一日是法定休假日的，以法定休假日后的第一日为期间届满的日期。

期间不包括在途时间，诉讼文书在期满前交邮的，不算过期。

4)《中华人民共和国刑事诉讼法》（2018 年修正）第一百零五条：

期间以时、日、月计算。

期间开始的时和日不算在期间以内。

法定期间不包括路途上的时间。上诉状或者其他文件在期满前已经交邮的，不算过期。

期间的最后一日为节假日的，以节假日后的第一日为期满日期，……

可见二者并无实质区别，只是前者有关"day"的第二种计算方式是我国所没有的，而后者有关"时"的规定也是英美国家所没有的，在翻译过程中值得我们特别留意。

【例 9】

第八十八条　承运人根据本法第八十七条规定留置的货物，<u>自船舶抵达卸货港的次日起满六十日</u>无人提取的，承运人可以申请法院裁定拍卖；……

　　　　　　　　　　　　　　　　——《中华人民共和国海商法》（1992 年）

【对照译文】

Article 88　If the goods under lien in accordance with the provisions of Article 87 of this Code are not taken delivery of <u>within 60 days from the next day of the ship's arrival at the port of discharge</u>, the carrier may apply to the court for an order on selling the goods by auction; ...

基于前文的分析，我们不难发现上例中【对照译文】有关期间的翻译不妥：一则"within"用于表述期间，不包括"the next day"，与原文之"次日起"不符；再则"the next day of the ship's arrival at the port of discharge"用于表述期间的始点，指的是事件发生的时刻，而非从午夜起计算。故笔者以为，下面的译文更符合立法者的本意。

【推荐译文】

Section 88　If the goods under lien in accordance with Section 87 of this Act have not been taken delivery of <u>within 60 days from the date of the ship's arrival at the port of discharge</u>, the carrier may move the court for an order on selling such goods by auction; ...

下例节选自《施工合同条件》，其【对照译文】同样不尽如人意。

【例 10】

20.4 Obtaining Dispute Adjudication Board's Decision

If either Party is dissatisfied with the DAB's decision, then either Party may, within 28 days after receiving the decision, give notice to the other Party of its dissatisfaction. If the DAB fails to give its decision within the period of 84 days (or as otherwise approved) after receiving such reference, then either Party may, within 28 days after this period has expired, give notice to the other Party of its dissatisfaction.

—Conditions of Contract for Construction

【对照译文】

20.4 取得争端裁决委员会的决定

如果任一方对 DAB 的决定不满意，可在收到该决定通知后 28 天内，将其不满向另一方发出通知。如果 DAB 未能在收到此项委托后 84 天（或经认可的其他）期限内，提出其决定，则任一方可以在该期限期满后 28 天内，向另一方发出其不满的通知。

所引合同条款原文以介词结构"within ... after ..."表述期间，并未涉及"date"，故依据普通法的解释原则，该期间应当从事件发生的时刻开始计算，而非当日午夜。制定者的意图亦可以下面条款的行文作为旁证。

15.5 Employer's Entitlement to Termination

The Employer shall be entitled to terminate the Contract, at any time for the Employer's convenience, by giving notice of such termination to the Contractor. The termination shall take effect 28 days after the later of the dates on which the Contractor receives this notice or the Employer returns the Performance Security. ...

—Conditions of Contract for Construction

更何况汉语译文中的"后"是有歧义的，应当尽量避免。因此，笔者以为该款可译成：

【推荐译文】

20.4 取得争端裁决委员会的决定

任何一方当事人不满 DAB 的决定的，可以自收到该决定之时起 28 日内，将其不满通知另一方当事人。DAB 未能自收到上述委托之时起 84 日（或者经过认可的其他期间）内作出决定的，任何一方当事人可以自该期间届满之时起 28 日内，将其不满通知另一方当事人。

当然，我们在翻译实务中还应当注意所译之原文是否对所涉各种期间的表述做出了专门规定。如果相关规定性法律文件中确有此类条款，那么译者的理解必须与之相符。

2. 避免句法歧义（syntactic ambiguity）

（1）指称歧义（referential ambiguity）

代词通过照应上下文衔接语篇，是英汉规定性法律文件中不可或缺的，但英语代词出现的频率远较汉语为高，这主要是因为汉语法律文本中多见省略主语的连动句式（吴江水，2006: 202）。

现代英汉比较研究表明，汉语的语篇衔接依靠意合，故主语对谓语动词的形式不起决定作用，其句法地位并不显著，省略的情形极为普遍，但在依靠形合衔接语篇的英语中，此类隐含主语却必须由代词指示出来（何善芬，2002: 217）。请看下例。

【例 11】

第一百条 承租人应当提供约定的货物；经出租人同意，可以更换货物。……

——《中华人民共和国海商法》（1992 年）

【推荐译文】

Section 100 The charterer shall provide the intended goods, but <u>he</u> may replace the goods with the shipowner's consent. ...

该款前段采用主谓结构表述当事人的行为模式，这也是规定性法律文件中最为常见的；而后段则为无主句，承前省略的主语无疑就是"承租人"。由于英语的语篇衔接必须借助词汇手段，故【推荐译文】中后段增补了人称代词"he"，指代前段的主语。

尽管汉语中零指称才是常规（胡壮麟, 1994: 64-66），但代词的省略绝非随心所欲，必须以不致引起歧义为前提。这在汉译英语规定性法律文件的过程中，尤其应当引起我们的重视。

【例 12】

SECTION 212.1   KIDNAPPING

A person is guilty of kidnapping if <u>he</u>① unlawfully removes another from <u>his</u>② place of residence or business, or a substantial distance from the vicinity where <u>he</u>③ is found, or if <u>he</u>④ unlawfully confines another for a substantial period in a place of isolation, with any of the following purpose:

—Model Penal Code

【推荐译文】

第 212.1 条   绑架

行为人为下列目的，〈他〉①非法将他人带离该人/〈其〉②居所或者营业场所，或者带离该人/〈其〉③所处位置相当距离，或者〈他〉④非法将他人拘禁在隔离场所相当时间的，是绑架罪：

上例原文共使用了四个代词，其中第①、④处代词于并列条件状语从句中作主语，前指主句主语"a person"。由于汉语译文连动句式的语境足以使读者推断出行为的实施者，故可省略代词而不产生歧义。但第②、③处代词却有所不同，其作用在于分别指明"place"与"vicinity"之所属。

英语重形式结构，正式文体中代词的照应功能多遵循就近原则，若法典制定者意在指称行为人则必然以"the actor"替之，如该法典第 211.2 条（SECTION 211.2   RECKLESSLY ENDANGERING ANOTHER PERSON）：

... Recklessness and danger shall be presumed where a person knowingly points a firearm at or in the direction of another, whether or not the actor believed the firearm to be loaded.

因此，"his"与"he"用于指称"another"，不会引起读者歧义。相比之下，汉语重意思逻辑，仅用代词"其"可能导致歧义：究竟指称的是"他人"呢？还是"行为人"？所以，笔者认为，唯有译成"该人"方能避免照应不明。

（2）修饰歧义（ambiguity of modifiers）

英汉句式的修饰成分主要包括状语与定语两大类。笔者以为在法律互译过程中我们应当特别注意调整这些语言成分的位置，以避免模糊其修饰范围。如下例。

【例 13】

第四十条 船长在航行中死亡或者因故不能执行职务时，应当由驾驶员中职务最高的人代理船长职务；在下一个港口开航前，船舶所有人应当指派新船长接任。

——《中华人民共和国海商法》（1992 年）

【对照译文】

Section 40 Should death occur to the Master or the Master be unable to perform his duties for whatever reason, the deck officer with the highest rank shall act as the Master; before the ship sails from its next port of call, the shipowner shall appoint a new Master to take command.

该例原文中"因故"及"在下一个港口开航前"两处状语分别用于修饰紧接其后的"不能执行职务"和"船舶所有人应当指派新船长接任"。然而，我们却无法确定【对照译文】中与"因故"相应的状语"for whatever reason"，其修饰范围到底是仅限于"the Master be unable to perform his duties"，还是同样涵盖了"death occur to the Master"？从这个角度分析，将"before the ship sails from its next port of call"置于主句前无疑是极为明智之举。

【推荐译文】

Section 40 If the Master dies or is for cause unable to perform his duties, the deck officer of the highest rank shall act as the Master and the shipowner shall, before the ship sails from its next port of call, appoint a new Master to take command.

再者，中文特有的一类"动词＋名词＋名词"结构也极易引起歧义，笔者以为汉语译文中应当尽量消除其语义含糊之处。如下例所示。

【例 14】

7.4 Testing

The Contractor shall provide all apparatus, assistance, documents and other information, electricity, equipment, fuel, consumables, instruments, labour, materials, and suitably qualified and experienced staff, as are necessary to carry out the specified tests efficiently. ...

—Conditions of Contract for Construction

【对照译文】

7.4 试验

为有效进行规定的试验，**承包商**应提供所需的仪器、帮助、文件和其他资料、电力、装备、工具、劳力、材料，以及具有适当资质和经验的工作人员。……

上例中，【对照译文】画线部分由动词"具有"、名词短语"适当资质和经验"及名词短语"工作人员"组成，其结构可作两种分析：或理解为偏正短语，即由"具有适当资质和经验"构成的动宾短语作定语修饰"工作人员";或理解为动宾短语,即由"适当资质和经验的工作人员"构成的偏正短语作为"具有"的宾语。为避免不必要的意思含糊,笔者以为【推荐译文】显然更为合适。

【推荐译文】

7.4　试验

为有效进行规定的试验,**承包商**应当根据需要提供仪器、协助、文件及其他资料、电力、装备、工具、劳动力、材料,并提供具有适当资质和经验的工作人员。……

（3）否定歧义（negative ambiguity）

正如众多法律起草专家所言,规定性法律文件中应当尽可能避免使用否定句式,因为这会使内容的表述处于间接状态,并最终导致歧义（都南、福斯特, 2006: 124）。然而,有时为将条款表述得更为准确、简洁,偶尔使用否定句式也是必不可少的。对译者而言,必须注意的是此类文本中否定句式的处理,绝不可采用正反译法。原因在于原文中特殊事项的否定,亦可被推定为对未否定事项的承认（Haggard, 2004: 291）。若译文随意变更句式,很可能会不经意间篡改了制定者的本意。故笔者以为下例只应采用【推荐译文】。

【例 15】

　　第一百三十六条　承租人有权就船舶的营运向船长发出指示,但是不得违反定期租船合同的约定。

——《中华人民共和国海商法》（1992 年）

【推荐译文】

Section 136　The charterer shall be entitled to issue the Master with instructions concerning the operation of the ship, except that such instructions shall not be inconsistent with the time charter/subject to the time charter.

如将原文译成"such instructions shall be given in accordance with the time charter",则读者很可能误解为承租人仅可对定期租船合同明确约定的事项发出指示,而实际上立法者的本意较此宽泛得多,只要承租人指示的内容不违反合同约定即可。

同理,此原则也适用于英语规定性法律文件的汉译。

【例 16】

SECTION 213.6　PROVISIONS GENERALLY APPLICABLE TO ARTICLE 213

(5) Testimony of Complainants. No person shall be convicted of any felony under this Article upon the uncorroborated testimony of the alleged victim. ...

—Model Penal Code

【推荐译文】

第 213.6 条　适用于第 213 节的一般性规定

　　（5）控告人的证言。假定被害人提供的陈述未经证实的,不得据此认定行为人成立本节规定的重罪。……

该法条若依正反译法表述为"应当依据经过证实的由假定被害人提供的陈述认定行为人成立本节规定的重罪",显然与原文的本意相去甚远:因为基于法理,刑法条款的解释应当遵循限缩原则，所以正反译文只能理解为由假定被害人提供的陈述是认定行为人的罪行所不可或缺的。就此而言，笔者认为【推荐译文】更可取。

11.2.2　一致性

起草规定性法律文件必须遵循的黄金法则是："Never change your language unless you wish to change your meaning and always change your language when you wish to change your meaning."（陶博，2004: 55）此所谓一致性（consistency）。事实上，该原则对法律文本的译者同样适用：译文表述的不统一当然是我们应当尽可能避免的。诚如哈格德所言，一致性的文本风格主要体现在三个层面上：术语、语法结构与篇章结构（Haggard, 2004: 309-314）。

1. 一致的术语（consistent terminology）

术语层面的一致性可以从正反两个角度来理解：一方面，总是使用相同的术语来表述相同的人、物、实体或概念；另一方面，总是使用不同的术语来表述不同的人、物、实体或概念（310）。但值得译者注意的是，英汉语言的构词方式存在本质差别，故二者在术语一致性方面的表现也有所不同。

就语言的词汇形态特征而言，英语偏向于综合语，其词类转化通常必须借助加缀派生法（何善芬，2002: 111），所以，英语法律术语往往具有词缀各异的多种形态，以便发挥不同的语法功能，但其所指却是一致的。请看《施工合同条件》第 1 章第 1.2 条第 1 款（d）项：

(d) "written" or "in writing" means hand-written, type-written, printed or electronically made, and resulting in a permanent record.

笔者以为，上述条款的设定正是黄金法则的体现，因为英语规定性法律文件的表述必然涉及不同形态的术语，而使用不同的词汇表示相同的含义，又容易导致歧义的产生，制定者方才择其要者特别注明。不仅合同文本如此，立法文本也是如此。如《美国模范刑法典》第 1 编第 1.13 条（SECTION 1.13　GENERAL DEFINITIONS）第 13 款：

(13) "knowingly" has the meaning specified in Section 2.02 and equivalent terms such as "knowing" or "with knowledge" have the same meaning;

我们就按照上述条款的规定，以该法典第 2 编第 212 节第 4 条为例展开分析。

【例 17】

(1) CUSTODY OF CHILDREN. A person commits an offense if he **knowingly** or recklessly takes or entices any child under the age of 18 from the custody of its parent, guardian or other lawful custodian, when he has no privilege to do so. ...

(a) ...

(b) the child, being at the time not less than 14 years old, was taken away at its own instigation without enticement and without purpose to commit a criminal offense with or against the child.

... The offense is a misdemeanor unless the actor, not being a parent or person in equivalent relation to the child, acted **with knowledge** that his conduct would cause serious alarm for the child's safety, ..., in which case the offense is a felony of the third degree.

—Model Penal Code

该款原文先是出现了副词"knowingly"，然后则是介宾短语"with knowledge"，二者皆为状语修饰动词。按照该法典第 13 条第 13 款的规定，其所指显然是一致的，差别仅在于唯后者能引导同位语从句，以便明确描述构成该罪的主观要件。由此可见，使用不同形态的术语，完全是为了满足英语语言结构形式上的需要，与词汇自身的含义无关。此外，这类语言现象不限于规定性法律文件专门定义的术语，还包括一般法律术语，类似该条款中的"entice"与"enticement"。

比较而言，汉语则更接近于孤立语，其词汇的语法功能无须依赖词尾变化形式，故汉语词多是兼类的（111）。因此，汉语规定性法律文件中大都没有类似《施工合同条件》第 1.2 条第 1 款或《美国模范刑法典》第 13 条第 13 款的规定。笔者以为，我们在英汉互译的过程中也应当尽可能保持术语的统一。

【推荐译文】

（1）对未成年人的监护。无法定特权的行为人明知或者轻率地拐带或者诱骗不满 18 周岁的未成年人脱离其父母、监护人或者其他合法监管人监护的，构成犯罪。……

（a）……

（b）已满 14 周岁的未成年人，未受诱骗而是自己要求行为人带走，且行为人对儿童没有实施犯罪的意图。

……本罪属于轻罪，但既不是未成年人的父母又不是与未成年人之间的关系相当于其父母的行为人，明知其行为将对未成年人的安全造成重大危险，……，而实施该行为的，属于三级重罪。

当然，我们在法律翻译过程中贯彻术语一致性原则，不可流于机械化的形式，而是应当基于文本蕴含的法律文化背景知识，因地制宜地做出恰当的处理。如下例。

【例 18】

第一百二十六条 海上旅客运输合同中含有下列内容之一的条款无效：

（一）免除承运人对旅客应当承担的法定责任；

（二）降低本章规定的承运人责任限额；

（三）对本章规定的举证责任作出相反的约定；

——《中华人民共和国海商法》（1992 年）

【推荐译文】

Section 126 Any of the following clauses contained in a contract of carriage of passengers by sea shall be null and void:

(1) Any clause that exonerates the legal *duty* of the carrier in respect of the passenger;

(2) Any clause that reduces the limitation of *liability* of the carrier as contained in this Chapter;

(3) Any clause that contains provisions contrary to those of this Chapter concerning *burden of proof*;

尽管本款前三项均使用了"责任"一词，但在此三项规定中该词本身并不构成独立的法律术语，而是三个不同术语"法定责任""责任限额"及"举证责任"的组成部分，故译者无须受制于中文形式上一致性的束缚。事实上，笔者以为，这些术语的含义才是我们应当关注的重心，因此将之分别译成相应的英语法律术语"the legal duty""the limitation of liability""burden of proof"并不违背黄金法则。

2. 一致的语法结构（consistent grammatical structure）

规定性法律文件的条款往往包含数个短语，一致性原则要求所有这些短语都必须尽可能采用相同或者平行的语法结构进行表述。请比较【例19】的两种译文。

【例19】

SECTION 1.02 PURPOSE; PRINCIPLES OF CONSTRUCTION

(1) The general purpose of the provisions governing the definition of offenses are:

(a) to forbid and prevent conduct that unjustifiably and inexcusably inflicts or threatens substantial harm to individual or public interests;

(b) to subject to public control persons whose conduct indicates that they are disposed to commit crimes;

(c) to safeguard conduct that is without fault from condemnation as criminal;

(d) to give fair warning of the nature of the conduct declared to constitute an offense,

(e) to differentiate on reasonable grounds between serious and minor offense.

—Model Penal Code

【对照译文】

第1.02条 目的；解释原则

（1）本法典中定义犯罪的规定的一般目的如下：

（a）禁止并预防无正当事由或者无免责事由而对个人或者公共利益造成实质危害或者危险的行为；

（b）对于行为显示其有犯罪倾向的行为人，应当运用公共权利加以控制；

（c）应当保障无过错行为不受刑事谴责；

（d）对于性质上构成犯罪的行为，应当给予相应的警诫；

（e）基于合理根据，区分严重犯罪与轻微犯罪。

【推荐译文】

第1.02条 目的；解释原则

（1）本法典中界定犯罪的规定的总体目的如下：

（a）禁止并预防无正当理由或免责事由而对个人或公共利益造成实质危害或危险的行为；

（b）运用公共权利控制行为显示犯罪倾向的人；

（c）保障无过错行为不被认定为犯罪；

（d）恰当警示被宣告构成犯罪的行为性质；

（e）合理区分严重犯罪与轻微犯罪。

上例中，【对照译文】与【推荐译文】就意思而言，差别并不大，但原文的五项规定均采用不定式短语与该款的导言（introductory word）相衔接，而【对照译文】的结构却缺乏一致性，不如【推荐译文】统一采用动宾结构。【推荐译文】显然符合黄金法则的要求。

当然，语法结构的一致性不仅体现于条款内部，还体现在平行条款之间。就此而言，【例20】的【对照译文】似有欠缺。

【例20】

第一百一十九条　行李发生明显损坏的，旅客应当依照下列规定向承运人或者承运人的受雇人、代理人提交书面通知：

（一）自带行李，应当在旅客离船前或者离船时提交；

（二）其他行李，应当在行李交还前或者交还时提交。

行李的损坏不明显，旅客在离船时或者行李交还时难以发现的，以及行李发生灭失的，……

——《中华人民共和国海商法》（1992 年）

【对照译文】

Article 119　In case of apparent damage to the luggage, the passenger shall notify the carrier or his servant or agent in writing according to the following:

(1) Notice with respect to cabin luggage shall be made before or at the time of his embarkation;

(2) Notice regarding luggage other than cabin luggage shall be made before or at the time of redelivery thereof.

If the damage to the luggage is not apparent and it is difficult for the passenger to discover such damage at the time of his disembarkation or of the rediscovery of the luggage, or if the luggage has been lost, ...

上例原文表述的两个条款针对的是互补的两种情形，即行李损坏明显与不明显之分，故制定者采用相同的句式"……的"来分别规定适用此两款的条件，以实现此类文本所要求的严密逻辑，因而更易于读者理解其实质。反观【对照译文】，我们则不难发现，前后两款规定的句式变得大相径庭：前者以"In case of apparent damage to the luggage"表述条件，而后者则采用"If the damage to the luggage is not apparent and it is difficult for the passenger to discover such damage at the time of his disembarkation or of the rediscovery of the luggage, or if the luggage has been lost"；甚至连前款中的两项短语"Notice with respect to cabin luggage（自带行李）"与"Notice regarding luggage other than cabin luggage（其他行李）"，也使用了不同的介词结构来表示完全相同的意思。笔者以为，这是有悖于黄金法则的，译者应当将之统一起来。

【推荐译文】

Section 119　If the damage to the luggage is apparent, the passenger shall give written notice to the carrier or his employee or agent

(1) before or at the time of his embarkation in the case of cabin luggage; or

(2) before or at the time of redelivery thereof in the case of luggage other than cabin luggage.

If the damage to the luggage is not apparent enough for the passenger to discover at the time of his disembarkation or of the rediscovery of such luggage, or the luggage has been lost, ...

3. 一致的篇章结构（consistent document structure）

通过平行的篇章结构组织规定性法律文件的内容，有助于读者把握其内在逻辑。笔者将从文本名称与章节条款两方面来探讨这个问题。

（1）名　称

●法律文本的名称

法律文本的命名有其固定的规则，且与该成文法的效力保持一致。英语中表示法律的词汇主要有"law""statute""bill""constitution""code""act""regulation""rule""ordinance"。不过，它们并非全都可用于法律文本的名称，且可用于命名法律文本的也各有所指。根据《布莱克法律词典》的定义：

Law: The set of rules or principles dealing with a specific area of a legal system.（Garner, 2019: 1056）

Statute: A law enacted by a legislative body; specif., legislation enacted by any lawmaking body, such as a legislature, administrative board, or municipal court.（1703）

Bill: A legislative proposal offered for debate before its enactment.（202）

Constitution: The fundamental and organic law of a nation or state that establishes the institutions and apparatus of government, defines the scope of governmental sovereign powers, and guarantees individual civil rights and civil liberties; a set of basic laws and principles that a country, state, or organization is governed by.（388）

Code: A complete system of positive law, carefully arranged and officially promulgated; a systematic collection or revision of laws, rules, or regulations.（323）

Act: The formal product of a legislature or other deliberative body exercising its powers; esp., STATUTE.（32）

Regulation: An official rule or order, having legal force, usu. issued by an administrative agency.（1538）

Rule: A regulation governing a court's or an agency's internal procedures.（1595）

Ordinance: An authoritative law or decree; esp., a municipal regulation, esp. one that forbids or restricts an activity.（1325）

事实上，"law（法律）"是指某一领域多部法律法规的集合，"statute（成文法）"则是与判例法相对应的法律术语，而"bill（法案）"指的是供立法机关讨论的法律议案，这三个词通常都不用于表述具体法律的名称。至于其他术语，则分别近似汉语词汇"宪法（constitution）""法典（code）""法（act）""条例（regulation）""规则（rule）"与"办法（ordinance）"。

值得注意的是，我国法律中所谓条例实际上包括四类：国务院制定的行政法规、地方人大制定的地方性法规以及民族自治地方制定的自治条例和单行条例。显然，其中只有第一类规范才可译为"regulation"，而余下三类则是由立法机关制定的，更接近于英语词汇"act"。

●合同文本的名称

比较而言，合同名称的形式相对单一，多数采用"合同/contract"，也有使用"协议/agreement"及"备忘录/memo"的，其含义与用法并无本质差别。需要稍加留意的是，某些特殊的合同如"租约（lease）"等通常有专门术语与之对应。

（2）章节条款

规定性法律文件的内容编排大同小异。现以法律为例，《中华人民共和国立法法》第六十五条规定：

法律根据内容需要，可以分编、章、节、条、款、项、目。

编、章、节、条的序号用中文数字依次表述，款不编序号，项的序号用中文数字加括号依次表述，目的序号用阿拉伯数字依次表述。这些术语分别对应英美法律术语"part""chapter""article""section""paragraph""subparagraph""item"[①]。事实上，合同的结构也是如此。

下面节选《施工合同条件》与《中华人民共和国海商法》（1992 年）的目录，供读者了解文本结构的一致性在英汉法律互译中的表现。

【例 21】

Conditions of Contract for Construction
CONTENTS

1　GENERAL PROVISIONS
　　1.1　Definitions
　　1.2　Interpretation
　　1.3　Communications
　　1.4　Law and Language
　　...

2　THE EMPLOYER
　　2.1　Right of Access to the Site
　　2.2　Permits, Licences or Approvals
　　...

3　THE ENGINEER
　　3.1　Engineer's Duties and Authority
　　3.2　Delegation by the Engineer
　　...

—Conditions of Contract for Construction

---

① 目前，国内规定性法律文件的翻译，通常将"节"译成"section"，"条"译成"article"，这符合英文版国际公约通常的行文习惯；但在英美法系中，"article"多指"节"，"section"则用于指"条"，故而本书的【推荐译文】遵循了英美法系的习惯。

【推荐译文】

施工合同条件
目 录

1 一般规定

【例 22】

中华人民共和国海商法

——《中华人民共和国海商法》（1992 年）

【推荐译文】

Maritime Act of the People's Republic of China

Contents

Chapter I　General Provisions

Chapter II　Ships

    Article 1　Ownership of Ships

    Article 2　Mortgage of Ships

    Article 3　Maritime Liens

Chapter III　Crew

    Article 1　Basic Principles

    Article 2　The Master

Chapter IV　Contract of Carriage of Goods by Sea

    Article 1　Basic Principles

    Article 2　Carrier's Duties

    Article 3　Shipper's Duties

...

◎英译汉实践练习◎

1. **Agreement to Sell Personal Property**

Purchase and Sell Agreement made by and between _____ of _____(Seller), and _____ of _____(Buyer).

Whereas, for good consideration the parties mutually agree that:

1. Seller agrees to sell, and Buyer agrees to buy the following described property:

2. Buyer agrees to pay to Seller and Seller agrees to accept as total purchase price the sum of $_____, payable as follows:

$_____ deposit herewith paid

$_____ balance payable on delivery by cash

$_____ bank per certified check

3. Seller warrants it has good and legal title to said property, full authority to sell said property, and that said property shall be sold by warranty bill of sale free and clear of all liens, encumbrances, liabilities and adverse claims of every nature and description whatsoever.

4. Said property is sold in "AS IS" condition, Seller disclaiming any warranty of merchantability, fitness or working order or condition of the property except that it shall be sold in its present condition, reasonable wear and tear expected.

5. The parties agree to transfer title on _____, 20____, at the address of the Seller.

6. This agreement shall be binding upon and inure to the benefit of the parties, their successors, assigns and personal representatives.

Signed this _____ day of _____, 20____.

_____　　　_____

Witness　　　　　　　　　　　Buyer

_____　　　_____

Witness　　　　　　　　　　　Seller

2. Agreement to Sell Works of Art

The following constitutes the entire agreement with respect to the sale by _____

[Buyer's full name] ("Buyer") of sculptures, drawings and graphics created by _____

[Artist's full name] ("Artist"):

1. For a period of _____ years commencing on the date of this agreement, Buyer shall have the exclusive right, in any part of the world, to offer for sale and to authorize others to offer for sale, all items of art works created and owned by Artist. Artist shall initially deliver each such item of his work to Buyer at such location as may be designated by Buyer.

2. During the period of _____ years, Buyer shall have the exclusive right to arrange, and to authorize others to arrange, for the publication and/or sale, in any part of the world, of books and catalogues containing illustrated reproductions of the art work of Artist.

3. During the period of _____ years, Buyer shall arrange for exhibitions of Artist's works in the Cities of _____, _____ and such other places as the parties shall jointly determine. Buyer shall be responsible for all of the expenses of such exhibitions, including advertising and catalogue costs and insurance, and shall bear the entire cost of storing all items of Artist's work delivered to Buyer pursuant to this agreement.

4. The parties acknowledge that Artist has furnished to Buyer photographs of each item of Artist's works owned by Artist on the date of this agreement. The price at which Buyer shall offer each such item for sale shall not be less than the price set forth on the back of such photograph. The parties shall jointly determine the minimum sales price to be charged as to those art works to be created by Artist during the term of this agreement. Minimum prices may be changed from time to time in such manner as shall jointly be determined by the parties.

5. Upon the sale of any of the art works covered by this agreement, Buyer shall be reimbursed, from the actual net proceeds of sale, for any initial shipping cost advanced with respect to such item. In addition and as compensation for Buyer's services in effecting the sale of a particular work, Buyer shall be entitled to retain _____% of the balance of the net proceeds of the particular sale, as and for Buyer's commission for having effected such sale, with the remaining _____ percent of such balance, less any amounts otherwise due to Buyer under this agreement, to be paid to Artist on a quarterly basis.

6. This agreement shall be governed by and construed in accordance with the laws of the State of _____ and shall be binding upon and inure to the benefit of the respective executors, administrators, successors and assigns of the parties.

Dated _____.

Buyer:

_____

[Buyer's Signature]

_____

[Buyer's Printed Name]

Artist:

_____

[Artist's Signature]

_____

[Artist's Printed Name]

◎汉译英实践练习◎

国际销售合同

合同编号：

日期：

签约地点：

卖方：

地址：　　　　　　　　　　　　　　邮政编码：

电话：　　　　　　　　　　　　　　传真：

买方：

地址：　　　　　　　　　　　　　　邮政编码：

电话：　　　　　　　　　　　　　　传真：

　　买卖双方同意按下列条款由卖方出售，买方购进下列货物：

第一条　货号

第二条　品名及规格

第三条　数量

第四条　单价

第五条　总值

　　数量及总值均有_____%的增减，由卖方决定。

第六条　生产国和制造厂家

第七条　包装

第八条　唛头

第九条　装运期限

第十条　装运口岸

第十一条　目的口岸

第十二条　保险：由卖方按发票全额110%投保至_____为止的_____险。

第十三条　付款条件

买方须于_____年_____月_____日通过_____银行开出以卖方为受益人的保兑的、不可撤销的、可转让、可分割的即期信用证。信用证议付有效期延至上列装运期后15天在中国到期，该信用证中必须注明允许分运及转运。

第十四条　单据

第十五条　装运条件

第十六条　品质与数量、重量的异义与索赔

如经中国_____检验机构复检，发现货物有损失、残缺或品名、规格、数量及质量与本合同及质量保证书之规定不符，买方可于货到目的港_____天内凭上述检验机构出具的证明书向卖方要求索赔。如上述规定之索赔期与质量保证期不一致，在质量保证期限内买方仍可向卖方就质量保证条款之内容向卖方提出索赔。

第十七条　人力不可抗拒因素

由于水灾、火灾、地震、干旱、战争或协议一方无法预见、控制、避免和克服的其他事件导致不能或暂时不能全部或部分履行本协议，该方不负责任。但是，受不可抗力事件影响的一方须尽快将发生的事件通知另一方，并在不可抗力事件发生15天内将有关机构出具的不可抗力事件的证明寄交对方。

第十八条　仲裁

在履行协议过程中，如产生争议，双方应友好协商解决。若通过友好协商未能达成协议，则提交中国国际经济贸易仲裁委员会，根据该会的仲裁规则进行仲裁。仲裁地点在中国。仲裁裁决是终局的，对双方均有约束力。

第十九条　法律适用

本合同之签订地或发生争议时货物所在地在中华人民共和国境内或被诉人为中国法人的，适用中华人民共和国法律。除此规定外，适用《联合国国际货物销售合同公约》。

第二十条　效力

本合同中、英两种文字具有同等法律效力，如文字解释有异议，应以中文本为准。

第二十一条　生效日期

本合同共_____份，自双方代表签字（盖章）之日起生效。

买方代表人：　　　　　　　　　　　　卖方代表人：

签字：　　　　　　　　　　　　　　　签字：

第 12 章
非规定性法律文件

◎学习目标◎

1. 掌握非规定性法律文件的文本风格；

2. 掌握非规定性法律文件的书写规则；

3. 掌握非规定性法律文件的特殊语法；

4. 理解上述要素在法律翻译中的体现。

导　言

非规定性法律文件针对纷繁复杂的具体法律事务，适用领域广阔，种类繁多且功能各异，远不同于惯以条文汇集形式出现的成文法及合同等规定性法律文件。尽管如此，非规定性法律文件的文本风格却是鲜明而统一的，并深刻影响到其制作与翻译，这也是本章第 1 节关注的重心。

本章第 2 节则探讨英汉非规定性法律文件的不同书写规则。鉴于法律文件的翻译以信息为重，译文当然无须保留原文的书写规则，但译文应当适用目的语书写规则，方能更好地为目的语读者所接受。

12.1　文本风格及翻译技巧

我国著名的法律文书学与法律语言学专家宁致远（2006）将非规定性法律文件的特点概括为六个方面：1）主旨的鲜明性；2）材料的客观性；3）内容的法定性；4）形式的程式性；5）解释的单一性；6）使用的实效性。其中，除使用的实效性专属于原文而与译者无涉外（请参阅本书第 2 章），笔者将从文本风格的角度对余下五项展开概括研究。

12.1.1　主旨的鲜明性

非规定性法律文件是为解决一定的实际法律问题而制作的，故具有鲜明突出的主旨（宁致远，2006: 11）。法律文书的主旨不同于其实效。如起诉状、判决书等与诉讼相关的法律文书（litigation-related writing）的实效性在于实现诉讼上的效果，此效果不是语言文字本身所能达到的，而是必须同时借助其撰写人的特定身份方能实现，故译文不可能具有原文同样的实效性。而文本主旨则是指语言本身通过特定方式遣词造句、谋篇布局实现的写作目的。

英美法律语言学家以主旨为依据，将律师撰写的法律文书划分为两大类：预测性文书（predicative writing）与劝说性文书（persuasive writing）。前者旨在预测法院可能做出的决定；后者旨在劝说法院做出有利的决定。此外，笔者以为，还有另一类非规定性法律文件，即由法官撰写的裁判文书。此类文书旨在就当事人争议的法律问题做出结论性的决定，故可称之为结论性文书（conclusive writing）。

三类文书之差别最典型地体现于案情事实的陈述。尽管该部分语言要求客观真实（请参阅 12.1.2），但预测性文书为预测准确而力求平等地陈述有利与不利的材料；劝说性文书则为劝说得力而难免突出有利事实、弱化不利事实；至于结论性文书却通过依法采信的证据认定案情，虽然事实材料对于法院而言无所谓利与不利，但其裁判结果却是以事实为基础陈述理由后得出的结论，二者须辩证统一。故即使为同一案件撰写的各类文书，其事实陈述的角度也不完全一致，译者在处理时必须仔细斟酌原撰写人为实现其主旨而精心组织的词句，尽可能在译文中再现原文的语言效果。

12.1.2 材料的客观性

毫无疑问，非规定性法律文件主旨的实现，必须以事实材料为基础，而事实的陈述则应力求客观真实（宁致远，2006: 12）。为了实现材料的客观性，笔者以为首要的是必须在这部分陈述中尽量限制使用带有明显感情色彩的词汇。

此外，为避免扭曲事实，还要求文书语体既朴实又庄重。所谓朴实、庄重的语体，即直书其事，以致平实郑重（35）。朴实的语言使事实陈述通俗易懂，庄重的语言使事实陈述严肃正式。正因为如此，日常生活或文学作品中比比皆是的委婉语、俚俗语，却罕见于非规定性法律文件。

委婉语多是"迂回表达死亡、性、疾病和身体机能"（Garner, 2005: 330）的词汇，为倡导平铺直叙的法律语言所摒弃，如"死亡/die"便不可写成"去世/pass away"。请看下例。

【例 1】

The defendant claimed that he planned to undergo surgery to remove his <u>penis, testicles,</u> and <u>scrotum</u> and replace them with an artificially constructed <u>vagina</u> (R. at 197), but he and his doctors all admitted that such an operation had not yet occurred.

【例 1】节选自《法律推理与法律文书写作》（*Legal Reasoning and Legal Writing*）附录 G（Neumann, 2003: 485-501）中的上诉辩论意见书范例（Sample Appellant's Brief）。该文书指控被告人犯游荡罪。为说明被告人是男性而穿着女性服饰，案情陈述中提及了很多男性器官的名称。原文中的"penis""testicles""scrotum""vagina"都是解剖学上的正式术语，绝不致引发歧义，因此笔者以为译文也不应使用委婉语，如"阳物"等都是不妥的。

【推荐译文】

被告人声称他计划通过手术摘除<u>阴茎</u>、<u>睾丸</u>和<u>阴囊</u>，代之以人造<u>阴道</u>（《记录》第

197 页），但他和他的医生全都承认上述手术还未实施。

而俚俗语除非是直接引用他人证言，否则不宜使用，以免损害非规定性法律文件的正式性程度（Dworsky, 2006: 21）。请看下例。

【例 2】

She recalls "signing <u>a bunch of</u> papers," but she did not read them and does not know what they said.

【例 2】节选自《法律文书写作》（*Legal Writing—Process, Analysis, and Organization*）附录 A（Edwards, 2003: 395-400）中的对内法律意见书范例（Sample Office Memorandum）。该文书撰写人在陈述事实时直接引用了其客户的语言，其中就包括非正式美语口语 "a bunch of"（陆谷孙, 2007）。笔者以为译文也应保持此文体风格上的变异。

【推荐译文】

她回忆说"签署了<u>一堆</u>文件"，但她没有看这些文件，所以不知道文件内容。

12.1.3　内容的法定性

非规定性法律文件的内容具有明显的法定性（宁致远, 2006: 12-13）。这不仅表现在法律上要求提供的具体要素，如裁判文书中必须提供的诉讼参加人的基本情况，除姓名、性别外，还有年龄等；更表现为叙述事实、论述理由应当围绕解决争议适用的法律规定展开，如《法律推理与法律文书写作》附录 C（Neumann, 2003: 443-446）中对内法律意见书范例（Sample Office Memorandum）的讨论（Discussion）部分。请看【例 3】。

【例 3】

DISCUSSION

A constructive trust will be imposed where the record shows "(1) <u>a confidential or fiduciary relation</u>, (2) <u>a promise</u>, (3) <u>a transfer in reliance thereon</u>, and (4) <u>unjust enrichment</u>." *McGrath v. Hilding*, 363 N.E.2d 328, 330 (N.Y. 1977) (citations omitted)

本例是该文书讨论部分的首段，引用了解决所议法律问题的判例规则，从而为整个环节的展开提纲挈领。实际上，其下各小标题均以该规则列举的四项要素为基础："Confidential or Fiduciary Relationship""Implied Promise by the Transfer""Transfer in Reliance on the Promise""Unjust Enrichment"。由此可见内容的法定性对于法律文书撰写的重要性。笔者以为处理时应当谨慎斟酌，因为该处关键文字将在论述法律问题的过程中反复出现。下面仅为其中数例。

【例 4】

<u>A confidential or fiduciary relationship</u> exists where one person is willing to entrust important matters to a second person.

【例 5】

The courts are also likely to find here <u>a promise</u>—even if not stated in words—by the nephew to hold title in name only for Goslin's benefit while doing nothing that might prevent Goslin from continuing to live in his home.

【例 6】

The <u>transfer</u> itself is not in dispute here, and, for the reasons described above, Goslin should be able to prove that he granted the deed <u>in reliance on</u> his nephew's promise.

【例 7】

Goslin should also be able to establish the fourth element, which has been described variously as "<u>unjust enrichment</u> under cover of the relation of confidence," ...

故译者除准确理解原文含义外，还须保持译文表述的一致性。

【推荐译文】

讨　论

若记录表明存在"（1）<u>信任或委托关系</u>，（2）<u>承诺</u>，（3）<u>因信赖承诺而发生的所有权转移</u>，以及（4）<u>不当得利</u>"，即构成推定信托（《东北地区州法院判例汇编·第二辑》第 363 卷第 328 页 *McGrath* 诉 *Hilding* 案（纽约州 1977 年），引文摘自第 330 页）（引文经过删减）。

【推荐译文】

如果一个人愿意将重要事情托付另一人，那就存在<u>信任或委托关系</u>。

【推荐译文】

法院还可能因本案中 Goslin 的侄儿在名义上拥有所有权，仅是为 Goslin 的利益且未作任何可能妨碍 Goslin 继续居住在自己房屋的事，而认定存在<u>承诺</u>，即使没有语言上的陈述。

【推荐译文】

本案中<u>所有权转移</u>本身并没有争议，且基于上述理由，Goslin 能够证明他<u>因信赖侄儿的承诺</u>而同意该契约。

【推荐译文】

Goslin 也能够证明第四个要素，该要素有各种不同的表述，诸如"以信托关系为掩饰的<u>不当得利</u>"，……

以上几例全部出自英美国家法律文书，而我国非规定性法律文书的撰写也遵循同样的原则。另外还请注意，围绕适用法律规范展开陈述的除理由外还有事实。

12.1.4　形式的程式性

非规定性法律文件的形式呈现突出的程式性，这主要体现在结构的固定化与用语的成文化两个方面（宁致远, 2006: 13-14）。

1. 结构的固定化

该类文本结构的固定化是显而易见的，且此固定结构也具有法定性质。这是因为无论在英美国家还是在我国，法院对文本结构都有明确规定。

译者处理非规定性法律文件时，对原文固定化的结构，译文原则上应当予以保留。但这只是大致而言，并非绝对化的要求，有时亦当因地制宜。如我国的诉讼法律文书，大都在正文之后末尾处写明"此致……人民法院"。请看【例 8】所引民事起诉状格式（刘国涛、范海玉, 2005: 256）。

【例 8】

民事起诉状

原告：

被告：

诉讼请求

......

事实与理由

......

证据和证据来源，证人姓名和住址

......

　　　　此致
××人民法院

起诉人：

年　月　日

　　当然，我们可将之译成"To ... People's Court"置于文末相应处，但这完全不符合英美法律文书的行文习惯。请看【例 9】所引美国申请法院做出简易判决的通知书（李斐南等, 2005: 81）。

【例 9】

TO EACH PARTY AND THEIR ATTORNEY OF RECORD:

　　PLEASE TAKE NOTICE that on January 12, ××××, at 9 a.m., or as soon thereafter as the matter may be heard in the above-entitled court, located at 191 North First Street, San Jose, California, plaintiffs will move the court for the following order:

　　...

　　This motion will be based on this notice, on the complete record of this action, the statement of undisputed facts, the memorandum of points and authorities, the declaration of _____, and oral argument in support of this motion.

　　DATED: _____　　　_____

U. R. Aiken

Attorney for Plaintiffs

　　实际上，英语应用文包含抬头一项的，总是处于正文之前，故笔者以为，【例 8】画线部分的译文也应移至正文之前，否则可能难以为读者所接受。

【推荐译文】

CIVIL COMPLAINT

Plaintiff:

Defendant:

TO ... PEPOLE'S COURT:

Claims

....

Facts & Arguments

....

相反，汉语应用文中却有不少是将抬头置于正文之前的，故笔者以为，【例9】画线部分的译文无须移至正文之后，也可为读者所理解。

【推荐译文】

<u>致各方当事人及其登记在册的代表律师：</u>

请注意：××××年 1 月 12 日上午 9 时或之后本案在上述位于加利福尼亚州圣何塞市第一大街北 191 号的法院接受审理时，原告将向该院提出申请，要求作出如下决定：

......

2. 用语的成文化

用语的成文化也是该类文本的鲜明特色，无论中英文都是如此。若英语与汉语中同类法律文本具有类似的成文化用语的，该部分文字当然只需略做修改便可套译（陈建平，2007: 50），从而使译文不仅传递内容准确，且表现风格相似，语言效果趋于一致。但这只常见于规定性法律文件，至于非规定性法律文件则大多不相契合。

如传统美国民事起诉状的正文总是以"COMES NOW"起始，并以"WHEREFORE"于正文末尾引出原告的诉讼请求。请看下例（李斐南等，2005: 14-16）。

【例10】

<u>COMES NOW</u>, Plaintiff above named and hereby complaints of Defendant and for cause of action alleges:

...

<u>WHEREFORE</u>, Plaintiff prays judgment as follows:

...

试比较【例10】与【例8】，两者虽同为起诉状，其习惯用语却大相径庭，中英文非规定性法律文书成文化的不同方式由此可见一斑。再如【例11】所引我国律师代理词的前言部分（刘国涛、范海玉，2005: 350），显然也不同于英美国家辩论意见书（brief）的行文。

【例11】

<u>依照</u>法律规定，受原告/被告的<u>委托</u>和××律师事务所的<u>指派</u>，<u>我担任</u>原告/被告×× <u>的诉讼代理人</u>，<u>参与本案诉讼活动</u>。

笔者以为，处理该类成文化用语，尽管无法在段落句式的层面上完整套译习惯行文，但原文关键性的法律术语依然应当借鉴译入语的对等表述。唯有这样，方能使译文读之如同原文一般庄重正式。

【推荐译文】

<u>兹有</u>上述原告通过本状向法院起诉被告，并提出如下诉讼理由：

......

综上，原告请求法院做出如下判决：

……

【推荐译文】

Pursuant to provisions of law, I, underlined{authorized by} the Plaintiff/Defendant and underlined{assigned by} ... Law Firm, take part in this action as attorney on behalf of Plaintiff/Defendant ...

12.1.5　解释的单一性

精确性是法律文件的共同特征。非规定性法律文件也不例外，同样要求文字精练、准确，解释单一（宁致远，2006: 14）。所谓解释的单一性，并非是指法律文件中不得使用具有多重含义的词句，不过这些词句在文本所示语境中只能作单一解释。

1. 遣　词

词汇、短语的精确使用，没有放之四海而皆准的具体规则可供遵循，故译者唯有量体裁衣。因此，词语层面上的精确性不是三言两语可以说清楚的，本节仅就绝大多数非规定性法律文件在翻译过程中所面临的共同难题（即代词）深入研究。

非规定性法律文件中代词的使用与规定性法律文件有所不同，这最集中地体现于第一人称。规定性法律文件为了提高文本的正式性程度，总是尽量少用人称代词，尤其是第一人称更为罕见。相比之下，非规定性法律文件的正式程度较规定性法律文件有所不如，且除说明性文字外，尚有记叙性与议论性的段落，故无法避免人称代词的使用，这也可使文本与读者保持一定的联系（海埃，2007: 18）。但第一人称的使用，在非规定性法律文件中另有其规则。

无论如何，汉语法律文书中的法官总是自称"本院"；而律师则自称"本人"，或与其所代表的当事人合称"我方"。但在英语法律文书中，法官完全可以自称"I"，也可以用"we"指称其所在法院（Garner, 2005: 379），还可使用"this court"；而律师则应尽力避免使用第一人称代词，以突出文字的客观性，使之更具说服力（Dworsky, 2006: 19）。然而，这并不意味着律师也可以用"the present person""this writer"等指称自身，反而应当从准确、精练的角度出发，丢弃累赘的表述如"I feel/I believe/in my opinion/it seems to me, etc."及模糊自我的措辞如"It is suggested that ..."等（Garner, 2005: 378）。事实上，英美国家律师的惯例是将意见提供给其客户，不是"I contend"，而是"...（客户姓名）contend(s)"，或使用"we contend"合指律师自身及其所代表的客户。

另外，英语法律文书是以第三人称单数"it"指称私法人及包括法院在内的其他单位的（Dworsky, 2006: 116），而汉语法律文书却总使用其名称或简称。

译者在处理文本时应当时时留意此类微妙差别，对于这些不涉及文本信息传递的细节，可采用归化的译法，以便增进读者的理解。如下例。

【例 12】

申请人 DOC 公司诉称：……裁决我公司承担根本不存在的损失赔偿责任，严重侵犯了我公司的合法权益。

——（1999）二中经仲字第 61 号

【推荐译文】

Petitioner DOC Company claims as follows: ... it adjudged <u>us</u> to take the non-existent liability for the damages, which seriously violated <u>our</u> lawful interests.

—(1999) S.I.E.A NO 61

2. 造　句

（1）主动句与被动句

通常，以主动语态构建的句式较被动句式更为精练、准确，也更为有力（Dworsky，2006: 112）。相比之下，被动语态若提及施动者则嫌累赘，不提施动者则嫌模糊（Garner，2005: 46-47）。过多使用被动语态将会削弱文本的说服力，但被动语态也并非完全无用，它将行为隐藏在句子较为次要的部位，以达到减弱行为影响、引导读者注意力的效果，显得既抽象又间接，语气也更为正式（海埃，2007: 38）。

因而，非规定性法律文件的撰写人使用被动语态时大都是有意而为之，译文也应尽量保留此类句式安排，在不损害信息传递的前提下，最大限度地实现原文的语言效果。请看【例 13】。

【例 13】

DOC 公司认为仲裁的程序与仲裁规则不符，要求撤销裁决书的理由于法无据，不符合《中华人民共和国仲裁法》规定的法定撤销情形，<u>本院不予支持</u>。

—— （1999）二中经仲字第 61 号

【对照译文】

As such, this court finds that the DOC Company's claims that the arbitration procedure was inconsistent with the Arbitration Rules and that the arbitration award shall be revoked are not supported by law and fail to satisfy the legal requirements for revocation under the Arbitration Law of the People's Republic of China. <u>The claims are denied by this court</u>.

【推荐译文】

As DOC Company's request to revoke the Arbitration Award on the ground that the arbitration procedure was inconsistent with the Arbitration Rules fails to meet the legal requirements for revocation under the Arbitration Law of the People's Republic of China, <u>this court denies it</u>.

—(1999) S.I.E.A NO 61

本例原文画线部分以主动句式直接表明法院的决定，而【对照译文】却将之译成被动语态。较之【推荐译文】，显然后者的主动语态更为简洁明了。

（2）肯定句与双重否定

通常，以肯定形式构建的句式较双重否定句式表达意思更为精确（海埃，2007: 39）。但在下列几种情形时应当使用否定形式。

1）为不改变句子意思（... may/shall not ... if not ...）

该情形主要出现在规定性法律文件，而非规定性法律文件通常只在引用法律或合同条款时才会有此遭遇。特别注意，"if not" 与 "unless" 不可等而视之。

2）为强调关键事实理由

该情形下双重否定句式的运用，旨在强调支持撰写人观点的关键性事实与理由。请看【例 14】。

【例 14】

Goslin owned nothing of substance other than his home.

本例节选自《法律推理与法律文书写作》附录 C（Neumann, 2003: 443-446）中对内法律意见书范例（Sample Office Memorandum）的讨论（Discussion）部分。该文书的撰写人为论证其客户 Goslin 与侄儿 Skeffington 之间存在推定信托关系，故再三强调争议房屋为 Goslin 仅有的资产。尽管原文可采用肯定句式 "Goslin owned only his home"，但为了引起读者的关注，还是以双重否定进行表述。笔者认为，译文也应尽量保留该句式。

【推荐译文】

Goslin 除自己的房屋外不再拥有其他实质性财产。

即使某些情况下因源语与译入语的本质差别而无法保留原文句式的，也应借助其他方式实现译文的强调意图。

3）否定词之一为法律术语

该情形下双重否定句式的运用完全是因为专门法律术语的特殊需要，故而无法避免。请看【例 15】[亦节选自《法律推理与法律文书写作》附录 C（Neumann, 2003: 443-446）中对内法律意见书范例]。

【例 15】

And without a constructive trust, Skeffington would be unjustly enriched because he would have clear title to a $95,000 asset in exchange for $11,500 in mortgage payments.

【推荐译文】

再者，如果不存在推定信托，那么 Skeffington 支付 11 500 美元的按揭款，换取价值 95 000 美元资产的无负担所有权，将构成不当得利。

（3）修饰语与被修饰语

非规定性法律文件的文本风格之一就是应尽可能使修饰语紧密联系被修饰语，以免理解时产生不必要的歧义（Garner, 2005: 342）。请看【例 16】。

【例 16】

……同时 2530A、2530B 两份合同仅系该案争议的 "佐证" 材料，仅供仲裁庭参考使用，……

——（1999）二中经仲字第 61 号

【对照译文】

... Further, contract 2530A and contract 2530B merely are "circumstantial evidence" for the dispute in question and for the tribunal's reference, ...

【推荐译文】

... Furthermore, Contract 2530A and Contract 2530B are merely "circumstantial evidence" in the dispute, offered only to the arbitration board for reference, ...

本例原文之所以使用了两个"仅"字,其意无非在于明确揭示"仅"与"供仲裁庭参考使用"间的修饰关系,先行排除多重解释的可能性。而【对照译文】将之合并处理为"merely",置于系动词前,显然其修饰范围只限于"circumstantial evidence",不若【推荐译文】更贴近原文撰写人的意图。

12.2　书写规则及特殊语法

作为特殊的应用文,英汉非规定性法律文件各有其不同的书写规则,译者应当熟知二者之间的差异,从而依据译入语的需要,做出恰如其分的处理。此外,英语非规定性法律文件中还有异于普通文体的特殊语法,这也是英译汉语法律文书所需借鉴的。

12.2.1　书写规则

1. 数　字

（1）英语非规定性法律文件的规则（Garner, 2005: 92-93）

1）通常,不涉及科学的数字小于 11 的,无论基数词还是序数词,都应当拼写出来。但若数字在文本中不断出现或用于计算,则所有数字都应当采用阿拉伯数字。

2）表示"大概的"数字应当拼写出来。

3）在计量单位中,尽可能使用词汇来代替一连串零（如"trillion""billion""million"等）。

4）句首的数字必须拼写出来。

5）百分数既可以采用阿拉伯数字也可以拼写出来。

6）若所指事物为同一类型的数字,有的小于 11,有的不小于 11,则可全部采用阿拉伯数字。

（2）汉语非规定性法律文件的规则（刘国涛、范海玉, 2005: 43）

1）必须由汉字表示的数字:

①法院诉讼文书引用的法律条款项和判处的刑罚。

②邻近的两个数字并列连用表示概数的词语,连用的两个数字之间不用顿号隔开。

③数字作为词素构成定型的词、词组、惯用语、缩略语的语句（如三心二意等）。

2）必须由阿拉伯数字表示的数字:

①文书编号涉及的数字,即年度号和发文顺序号。

②表示记数与计量的正负整数、分数、小数、百分比。

3）关于数字的写法尚未达成共识的,至少在同一份文书中必须保持前后一致,不能汉字与阿拉伯数字混用。

2. 日期与时间

（1）英语非规定性法律文件的规则（Dworsky, 2006: 37）

1）日期不可以缩写表示,也不应加入多余的字,必须表示为如"November 9, 1998"的形式。

2）陈述事实时，除第一个事件需提供完整日期外，其他事件发生的年份可省略不提，但前提是读者能从正文中了解这些事件与第一个事件发生在同一年。

（2）汉语非规定性法律文件的规则（刘国涛、范海玉, 2005: 43）

1）汉字表示法律文书尾部的签发日期，但以"〇"代替"零"。

2）汉字表示"星期几"。

3）阿拉伯数字表示除此以外的公历日期及时刻。

3. 大　写

适用于非规定性法律文件的英语大写规则如下（Dworsky, 2006: 32-34）：

1）法院及政府部门名称大写，包括本法院（this Court）；

2）本案诉讼参加人（litigation role）名称大写，如"Plaintiff（原告）""Defendant（被告）""Appellant（上诉人）""Appellee（被上诉人）""Applicant（申请人）"等；

3）诉讼文件（litigation document）名称大写。

汉语文字并无大写形式，而译文对上述三类专有名词也无须特别标注。只是另有一类专有名词即法律法规的名称，其英语大写形式则对应于汉语中的书名号，这是译者所要注意的。

综合前三项（数字、日期与时间、大写）书写规则，请看【例17】。

【例17】

On August 3, 1991, the Plaintiff filed this diversity action alleging medical malpractice against Dr. June Temple and the Northpark Family Clinic. (R. 1.) On January 17, 1992, after extensive discovery, the Defendants moved for summary judgment. (R. 11.) The District Court took the motion under advisement.

On June 1, 1992, while the motion was pending, the Defendants made an Offer of Judgment in the amount of $100,000, pursuant to Fed. R. Civ. P. 68. (R. 24.) The Plaintiff did not accept the offer but rather, on June 4, he served a document entitled "Plaintiff's Offer of Judgment." (R. 27.) The document purported to be a Rule 68 offer to accept the entry of judgment in the amount of $225,000. The Plaintiff never specified that he was still considering the Defendants' initial Offer. (R. 27.)

On June 7, the District Court granted the Defendants' Motion for Summary Judgment. (R. 18-23.) After learning of the Order granting summary judgment against him, the Plaintiff attempted to accept the Defendants' initial Offer of Judgment by serving an Acceptance of Offer of Judgment on June 8, 1992. (R. 25.) ...

本例节选自《法律文书写作》附录C（Edwards, 2003: 395-400）中的上诉辩论意见书范例（Sample Appellate Brief）。注意原文中的日期有的注明年份，有的则没有，却未导致歧义，这是符合英语非规定性法律文件的书写规则的。但译文却应将年份一律补全，才符合汉语文书的要求。此外，"R."与"Fed. R. Civ."并非诉讼文书，故其译文皆加书名号标注。

【推荐译文】

原告于 <u>1991 年 8 月 3 日</u>提起跨州诉讼，诉 June Temple 医生与 Northpark 家庭诊所医疗事故纠纷（《记录》第 1 页）。在全面开示证据后，<u>被告于 1992 年 1 月 17 日</u>提议简易程序审理（《记录》第 11 页）。<u>地区法院仔细审议了该动议。</u>

在案件审理过程中，<u>被告于 1992 年 6 月 1 日依照《联邦民事诉讼程序规则》第 68 条规定，提出赔偿 100 000 美元的判决提议书</u>（《记录》第 24 页）。原告没有接受该提议，反而于 <u>1992 年 6 月 4 日送达名为《原告判决提议书》的文件</u>（《记录》第 27 页）。该文件主张基于<u>第六十八条规则</u>，接受赔偿 <u>225 000 美元的判决。原告未表示他仍在考虑被告最初的提议</u>（《记录》第 27 页）。

<u>地区法院于 1992 年 6 月 7 日核准了被告的简易判决动议书</u>（《记录》第 18-23 页）。原告获悉法院裁定准许不利于他的简易判决后，于 <u>1992 年 6 月 8 日送达接受判决提议书，欲接受被告最初的判决提议书</u>（《记录》第 25 页）。……

4. 斜　体

英语非规定性法律文件通常以斜体表示强调，但斜体的功能就等于下画线，且同一份文书中斜体与下画线只能取其一（Garner, 2005: 374）。考虑到汉语文字并无斜体形式，笔者以为，译文可借下画线发挥与原文斜体相同的强调功能。请看节选自《法律文书写作》附录 A（Edwards, 2003: 395-400）中的对内法律意见书范例（Sample Office Memorandum）。

【例 18】

However, the appellate court affirmed the trial court's jury instruction, stating that a minor's false representation of age "will not affect his power to disaffirm a contract unless [the representation] was made *fraudulently*." *Id.* at 910 (emphasis supplied).

【推荐译文】

但上诉法院肯定了初审法院给陪审团的指示，并阐明未成年人虚假陈述年龄"不影响他撤销合同的权利，但[该陈述]具有<u>欺诈性</u>的除外"。（同前第 910 页，下画线由撰写人添加。）

12.2.2　特殊语法

英语非规定性法律文件中有两项关键性的特殊语法尤其值得译者注意。下文将通过具体实例详细说明，且三个实例皆节选自《法律推理与法律文书写作》附录 D（Neumann, 2003: 447-450）中的客户信件范例（Sample Client Letter）。

1. "and""but""because"起始

英语非规定性法律文件中即便是最正式的文体，也可在句首使用"and""but""because"（海埃, 2007: 18）。请看【例 19】。

【例 19】

His medical condition did not deteriorate before rescuers broke down the door. <u>But</u> after he regained consciousness and learned what had happened, he experienced nightmare.

【推荐译文】

在救援人员破门而入前，他的病情没有恶化。但在他恢复知觉并了解事实情况后，却噩梦连连。

2. 介词结尾

英语非规定性法律文件中即便是最正式的文体，也可以介词结尾（海埃，2007: 18）。请比较【例20】【例21】。

【例20】

He locked every outer door and hatch—including the door separating the main deck from the passageway <u>on</u> which the passengers' cabins were situated—removed the gangway, locked it in a shed, and went home.

【例21】

It might be possible to reduce the expense of suing if other passengers join with you and sue to get the refunds they are entitled <u>to</u>.

【例20】将本位于定语从句末尾的介词"on"置于关系代词"which"前，这是符合英语习惯用法的，但在法律文书中也可将之简化为"... from the passageway the passengers' cabins were situated on ..."。不过，此处简化的表述不若习惯用法更为自然，故撰写人没有采纳。

而【例21】则采用了简化的表述，将介词"to"置于句尾。比较习惯用法"... the refunds to which they are entitled"，简化的表述显然更为精练。

【推荐译文】

他锁上了每道外门和舱口，包括分隔主甲板与客舱所在过道的大门，并移走舷梯锁入工具间，然后回房。

【推荐译文】

如果其他乘客与你共同起诉主张他们有权得到的退款，便可能减少诉讼费用。

◎英译汉实践练习◎

1. **Bad Check Notice Form**

Date: _____

To:

Dear _____:

Payment on your Check No. _____ in the amount of \$_____, tendered to us

on _____, 20_____, has been dishonored by your bank. We have verified with your bank

that there are still insufficient funds to pay the check.

Accordingly, we request that you replace this check with a cash (or certified check) payment.

Unless we receive good funds for said amount within _____ days, we shall immediately commence appropriate legal action to protect our interest. Upon receipt of replacement funds we shall return to you the dishonored check.

Sincerely,

Certified Mail, Return Receipt Requested.

2. Demand Note

Date: _____

On demand, the undersigned, for value received, jointly and severally promises to pay to the order of _____ [insert name of lender] the sum of _____ dollars ($_____.00) together with interest thereon from the date hereof until paid at the rate of _____% per annum.

In the event this note is not paid when due, the undersigned shall pay all attorney's fees and reasonable costs of collection.

NOTICE TO BORROWER: THIS IS A DEMAND NOTE AND SO MAY BE COLLECTED BY THE LENDER AT ANY TIME. A NEW NOTE MUTUALLY AGREED UPON AND SUBSEQUENTLY ISSUED MAY CARRY A HIGHER OR LOWER RATE OF INTEREST.

_____

[Maker's signature]

_____

[Maker's typed or printed name]

NOTICE TO CO-SIGNER: YOUR SIGNATURE ON THIS NOTE MEANS THAT YOU ARE EQUALLY LIABLE FOR REPAYMENT OF THIS LOAN. IF THE BORROWER DOES NOT PAY, THE LENDER HAS A LEGAL RIGHT TO COLLECT FROM YOU.

_____

[Co-signer's signature]

_____

[Co-signer's typed or printed name]

Witnessed:

_____

[Witness's signature]

_____

[Witness's typed or printed name]

3. Notice of Default in Payment

Date: _____

To: _____

You are hereby notified that your payment of _____ Dollars ($_____), due on or before _____, has not been received by the undersigned. If said payment is not paid by _____ [date], the undersigned shall invoke the remedies under the agreement between us dated _____, together with such other remedies that the undersigned may have.

_____

4. **Notice of Dismissal**

Date: _____

To: _____

We regret to notify you that your employment with the firm shall be terminated on _____,

20_____, because of the following reasons:

_____

_____

_____

_____

Severance pay shall be in accordance with company policy. Within 30 days of termination we shall issue you a statement of accrued benefits. Any insurance benefits shall continue in accordance with applicable law and/or provisions of our personnel policy. Please contact _____, at your earliest convenience, who will explain each of these items and arrange with you for the return of any company property.

We sincerely regret this action is necessary.

Very truly,

_____

Copies to:

5. **Product Defect Notice to Manufacturer, Distributor, or Seller**

VIA EMAIL

VIA CERTIFIED MAIL, RETURN RECEIPT REQUESTED

Date: _____

To: _____

Dear _____:

Notice is hereby provided that we have purchased a product manufactured, distributed, or sold by you and described as:

_____

_____

_____

You are advised of a product defect or warranty claim. In support of same we provide the following information:

1. Date of Purchase: _____

2. Nature of Defect: _____

3. Injuries or Damage: _____

4. Item Purchased From: _____

This is provided to give you earliest notice of said claim. I request that you or your representative contact me as soon as possible.

Sincerely,

_____

Name

_____

Address

_____

City, State, Zip

_____

Telephone Number

6. **Receipt**

BE IT KNOWN, that the undersigned hereby acknowledges receipt of the sum of $_____ paid by _____, which payment constitutes _____ [indicate full or partial] payment of the below described obligation:

_____

_____

_____

If this is in partial payment of said obligation, the remaining unpaid balance on this date is $_____.

Signed this _____ day of _____, 20_____.

Witnessed:

_____

Obligor Signature

_____

Obligor Printed or Typed Name

_____

Witness Signature

_____

Witness Printed or Typed Name

◎汉译英实践练习◎

1. 初审民事判决书（样本）

××××人民法院

民事判决书

（××××）……民初……号

原告：×××，……

被告：×××，……

原告×××与被告×××（写明案由）纠纷一案，本院于××××年××月××日立案后，根据《全国人民代表大会常务委员会关于授权最高人民法院在部分地区开展民事诉讼程序繁简分流改革试点工作的决定》，依法适用普通程序，由审判员独任审理，于××××年××月××日公开开庭进行了审理。原告×××、被告×××、第三人×××到庭参加诉讼。本案现已审理终结。

原告×××向本院提出诉讼请求：……（明确原告的诉讼请求）。事实和理由：……（概述原告主张的事实和理由）。

被告×××辩称，……（概述被告答辩意见）。

第三人×××诉/述称，（概述第三人陈述意见）。

原告×××在庭审期间，向法院提交了以下证据材料：……。

被告×××对原告×××提交的证据……没有异议；对证据……提出异议。被告×××认为……。

通过庭审质证，本院认为……。

根据上述有效证据，本院认定以下事实：……。

本院认为，……（写明争议焦点，根据认定的事实和相关法律，对当事人的诉讼请求作出分析评判，说明理由）。

综上所述，……（对当事人的诉讼请求是否支持进行总结评述）。依照《中华人民共和国……法》第 X 条、……（写明法律文件名称及其条款项序号）规定，判决如下：

…………、…………

（以上分项写明判决结果）

案件受理费××元，由×××负担。

如不服本判决，可在判决书送达之日起十五日内，向本院递交上诉状，并按照对方当事人人数提出副本，上诉于××××人民法院。

审判员×××

××××年××月××日

（院印）

法官助理×××

书记员×××

◆第五编翻译实践练习

● 宪法翻译的启示 5：文本结构篇

● 宪法翻译的启示 6：宪法序言

● 附录　《中华人民共和国宪法》（2018 年修正）的序言原文及英语译文

参考答案

参考文献

Baker, Mona. *Routledge Encyclopedia of Translation Studies* [C]. Shanghai: Shanghai Foreign Language Education Press, 2004.

Bussmann, Hadumod. *Routledge Dictionary of Language and Linguistics* [Z]. Trauth, Gregory P. & Kazzazi, Kerstin (trans. & eds.). Beijing: Foreign Language Teaching and Research Press, 2000.

Chafee, Zachariah. The disorderly conduct of words [J]. *The Canadian Bar Review*, 1942, 20(9): 752-776.

Cohen, Morris L. & Olson, Kent C. *Legal Research* [M]. Beijing: Legal Press, 2004.

Davies, Jack. *Legislative Law and Process* [M]. 2nd ed. Beijing: Law Press, 2005.

Dworsky, Alan L. *The Little Book on Legal Writing* [M]. Beijing: Beijing University Press, 2006.

Edwards, Linda Holdeman. *Legal Writing—Process, Analysis, and Organization* [M]. Beijing: CITIC Publishing House, 2003.

Garner, Bryan A. *A Dictionary of Modern Legal Usage* [Z]. 2nd ed. Beijing: Law Press, 2003.

Garner, Bryan A. *The Elements of Legal Style* [M]. Beijing: Intellectual Property Press, 2005.

Garner, Bryan A. *Black's Law Dictionary* [Z]. 11th ed. New York: Thomson Reuters, 2019.

Glendon, Mary A., Gordon, Michael W. & Carozza, Paolo G. *Comparative Legal Traditions* [M]. Beijing: Legal Press, 2004.

Gutt, Ernst-August. *Translation and Relevance: Cognition and Context* [M]. Shanghai: Shanghai Foreign Language Education Press, 2004.

Haggard, Thomas R. *Legal Drafting* [M]. Beijing: Law Press, 2004.

Hatim, Basil & Mason, Ian. *Discourse and the Translator* [M]. Shanghai: Shanghai Foreign Language Education Press, 2001.

Hynes, J. Dennis. *Agency, Partnership, and the LLC.* 2nd ed. St. Paul, MN.: West Information Publishing Group, 2004.

Kadish, Sanford H. & Schulhofer, Stephen J. *Criminal Law and Its Processes* [M]. Beijing: CITIC Publishing House, 2003.

Kane, Mary Kay. *Civil Procedure* [M]. Beijing: Law Press, 2001.

Katan, David D. *Translating Cultures: An Introduction for Translators, Interpreters and Mediators* [M]. Shanghai: Shanghai Foreign Language Education Press, 2004.

Lyons, John. *Linguistic Semantics: An Introduction* [M]. Beijing: Foreign Language Teaching and Research Press, 2000.

Neumann, Richard K. *Legal Reasoning and Legal Writing* [M]. Beijing: CITIC Publishing House, 2003.

Nord, Christiane. *Translating as a Purposeful Activity* [M]. Shanghai: Shanghai Foreign Language Education

Press, 2001.

O'Barr, William. *Linguistic Evidence —Language, Power, and Strategy in the Courtroom* [M]. San Diego: Academic Press, 1982.

Reiss, Katharina. *Translation Criticism* [M]. Rhodes, Erroll F. (trans.). Shanghai: Shanghai Foreign Language Education Press, 2004.

Richards, Jack C., Platt, John & Platt, Heidi. *Longman Dictionary of Language Teaching & Applied Linguistics* [Z]. Beijing: Foreign Language Teaching and Research Press, 2000.

Snell-Hornby, Mary. *Translation Studies* [M]. Shanghai: Shanghai Foreign Language Education Press, 2001.

Taylor, John B. *Linguistic Categorization: Prototypes in Linguistic Theory* [M]. Beijing: Foreign Language Teaching and Research Press, 2001.

Walker, David M. *The Oxford Companion to Law* [Z]. London: Oxford University Press, 1980.

理查德·A. 波斯纳. 法理学问题[M]. 苏力，译. 北京：中国政法大学出版社，2002.

博登海默. 法理学：法律哲学与法律方法[M]. 邓正来，译. 北京：中国政法大学出版社，1999.

陈刚（总主编）. 滕超，孔飞燕. 英汉法律互译：理论与实践[M]. 杭州：浙江大学出版社，2008.

陈建平. 法律文体翻译探索[M]. 杭州：浙江大学出版社，2007.

陈兴良. 本体刑法学[M]. 北京：商务印书馆，2001.

大谷实. 刑法总论[M]. 黎宏，译. 北京：法律出版社，2003.

埃尔默·都南，查尔斯·福斯特. 法律文件起草之道[M]. 陈晓昀，译. 北京：法律出版社，2006.

杜金榜. 法律语言学[M]. 上海：上海外语教育出版社，2004.

甘世安. 析英汉语言表层结构的逆向性——汉语向心性与英语外展性特征[J]. 西北大学学报（哲学社会科学版），2002(4): 187-191.

鲁伯特·海埃. 法律英语[M]. 李玉木，译. 武汉：武汉大学出版社，2007.

何善芬. 英汉语言对比研究[M]. 上海：上海外语教育出版社，2002.

胡壮麟. 语篇的衔接与连贯[M]. 上海：上海外语教育出版社，1994.

马戈特·科斯坦佐. 法律文书写作之道[M]. 王明昕，刘波，译. 北京：法律出版社，2006.

伦道夫·夸克，等. 朗文英语语法大全[M]. 上海：华东师范大学出版社，1998.

李克兴，张新红. 法律文本与法律翻译[M]. 北京：中国对外翻译出版公司，2006.

李明. 中国语境下的现代法律语言[EB/OL]. (2002-05)[2024-07-20]. http://www.flrchina.com/research/ch/001/ch007.htm; http://flrchina.com/research/ch/001/ch008.htm.

李振宇. 中国法律语言学研究的思考[C]//王杰，苏金智，约瑟夫-G. 图里. 法律·语言·语言的多样性——第九届国际法律与语言学术研讨会论文集. 北京：法律出版社，2006: 182-193.

刘国涛，范海玉. 法律文书学[M]. 重庆：重庆大学出版社，2005.

刘红婴. 法律语言学[M]. 2 版. 北京：北京大学出版社，2007.

刘家琛. 新刑法条文释义[M]. 北京：人民法院出版社，2002.

刘家兴. 民事诉讼法学教程[M]. 北京：北京大学出版社，2001.

刘娜娜，耿淑芬. 合同法[M]. 北京：中国工商出版社，2002.

刘晴，路泽君. 民事诉讼法实务与案例评析（上）[C]. 北京：中国工商出版社，2002.

刘志远. 二重性视角下的刑法规范[M]. 北京：中国方正出版社，2003.

刘作翔. 法理学[M]. 北京：社会科学文献出版社，2005.

陆谷孙. 英汉大词典[Z]. 2 版. 上海：上海译文出版社，2007.

美国法学会，美国统一州法委员会. 美国《统一商法典》及其正式评述[M]. 孙新强，译. 北京：中国人民大学出版社，2004.

宁致远. 法律文书学[M]. 北京：中国政法大学出版社，2006.

潘庆云. 中国法律语言鉴衡[M]. 上海：汉语大词典出版社，2004.

齐树洁，王振志. 证据法案例精解[M]. 厦门：厦门大学出版社，2004.

沈宗灵. 法理学[M]. 北京：北京大学出版社，2001.

时延安. 论刑法规范的文义解释. 法学家，2002(6): 75-80+58.

孙懿华. 法律语言学[M]. 长沙：湖南人民出版社，2006.

孙懿华，周广然. 法律语言学[M]. 北京：中国政法大学出版社，1997.

陶博. 法律英语：中英双语法律文书制作[M]. 上海：复旦大学出版社，2004.

汪榕培. 英语词汇学高级教程[M]. 上海：上海外语教育出版社，2002.

王利明. 民法疑难案例研究[M]. 北京：中国法制出版社，2002.

王利明，杨立新. 侵权行为法[M]. 北京：法律出版社，1996.

戴维·M. 沃克. 牛津法律大辞典[Z]. 李双元，译. 北京：法律出版社，2003.

吴江水. 完美的合同[M]. 北京：中国民主法制出版社，2006.

吴伟平. 语言与法律——司法领域的语言学研究[M]. 上海：上海外语教育出版社，2002.

习近平. *Xi Jinping: The Governance of China I* [M]. 2 版. 英文翻译组，译. 北京：外文出版社有限责任公司，2018.

习近平. *Xi Jinping: The Governance of China II* [M]. 英文翻译组，译. 北京：外文出版社有限责任公司，2017.

习近平. *Xi Jinping: The Governance of China III* [M]. 英文翻译组，译. 北京：外文出版社有限责任公司，2020.

习近平. *Xi Jinping: The Governance of China IV* [M]. 英文翻译组，译. 北京：外文出版社有限责任公司，2022.

习近平. 习近平谈治国理政（第一卷）[M]. 2 版. 北京：外文出版社有限责任公司，2018.

习近平. 习近平谈治国理政（第二卷）[M]. 北京：外文出版社有限责任公司，2017.

习近平. 习近平谈治国理政（第三卷）[M]. 北京：外文出版社有限责任公司，2020.

习近平. 习近平谈治国理政（第四卷）[M]. 北京：外文出版社有限责任公司，2022.

信春鹰. 法律辞典[Z]. 北京：法律出版社，2004.

熊学亮. 含义分类标准评析[J]. 外语教学与研究，1997(2): 1-7.

薛波. 元照英美法词典[Z]. 北京：法律出版社，2003.

应松年，刘莘. 中华人民共和国行政复议法讲话[Z]. 北京：中国方正出版社，1999.

余叔通，文嘉. 新汉英法学词典[Z]. 北京：法律出版社，1998.

张恒山. 法理要论[M]. 2 版. 北京：北京大学出版社，2006.

张水波，何伯森. FIDIC 新版合同条件导读与解析[M]. 北京：中国建筑工业出版社，2003.

张文. 现代法律文本中的文言成分及其应用[J]. 北华大学学报（社会科学版），2020(5): 16-29.

张新红. 汉语立法语篇的言语行为分析[J]. 现代外语，2000(3): 283-295.

赵秉志. 中国刑法案例与学理研究（第一卷）[M]. 北京：法律出版社，2004.

郑竞毅. 法律大辞书[Z]. 北京：商务印书馆，2012.

周旺生. 立法质量与质量立法[EB/OL]. (2005-02)[2024-07-20]. http://iolaw.cssn.cn/flfg_99/201008/t20100825_4607708.shtml.